W9-CIN-294

What do you believe about beer . . .

- that it's better in a bottle than in a can?
- that it should be refrigerated at all times?
- that imported beer is better than domestic?
- that you could recognize your favorite beer even without its label?

Discover the facts as all these subjects are discussed and examined in THE GREAT AMERICAN BEER BOOK and the beers themselves are tasted and tested by a panel of everyday people who enjoy the pleasures of the brew.

You'll find your favorite brand here—from Guiness Stout to Old Frothingslosh, from Champale to Coors—described and rated, and 549 others you may someday want to try. Here's a marvelous opportunity to satisfy your curiosity as well as your taste, to broaden your beer horizons and become an expert on your beverage of choice.

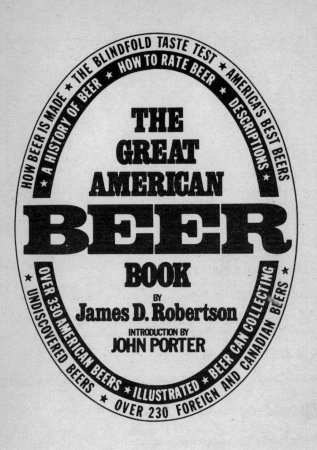

THE GREAT AMERICAN **BEER** BOOK

BY
James D. Robertson

INTRODUCTION BY
JOHN PORTER

HOW BEER IS MADE ★ THE BLINDFOLD TASTE TEST ★ HOW TO RATE BEER ★ AMERICA'S BEST BEERS ★ DESCRIPTIONS ★ OVER 330 AMERICAN BEERS ★ UNDISCOVERED BEERS ★ ILLUSTRATED ★ OVER 230 FOREIGN AND CANADIAN BEERS ★ BEER CAN COLLECTING ★ A HISTORY OF BEER ★

WARNER BOOKS

A Warner Communications Company

Acknowledgments

This book could never have been written without the assistance of a great many people.

First I want to thank Sheldon and Pauline Wasserman for encouraging me and for all their assistance in guiding me in the writing and preparation of the manuscript. Their help in locating and in dealing with the publisher was of even greater significance. In this regard I also wish to thank Art Ballant for his generous assistance.

The one person who did the most for me in writing the book, outside my immediate family, was Bill Geiger of Middletown, New Jersey. Bill and his wife Madeline served as regular members on the taste panel, wandered far and wide seeking out elusive brands of beer, and searched libraries all over the area looking for reference material. Together they saved me months of time.

The taste panel regulars, Col. Don Lambrecht (USAF), Vivian Robb, and Stan Freeny, deserve special mention for their dedication to the task. I also wish to thank the other panel members—Ken Nelson, Major Cory Adams (USAF), and Lt. Col. Tom Weathers (USAF) —all of whom aided immensely in obtaining obscure brands of beer. A number of visitors to our shores during the progress of the tastings also contributed significantly, by donating their time to test beers and by providing samples of their nation's brews. They are Lt. Col. Trevor Richards of Australia, Lt. Col. and Mrs. Brian Simons of Canada, and Lt. Col. Bob Farrell of Canada. The other panel members, who did spartan duty in beer tasting, were Richard and Jean Ackermann, Robert and Barbara Scott, Thom and Anne Leidner, Lt. Col. Jere Hetherington (USAF), Maj. Hollis Morris (US Army), Maj. Bill Kelly (USAF), Lt. Cmdr. Ray Belanger (USN), Major Ellis Grace (USAF), Jo Grace, Major Bob Kent (USAF), and Barbara and Larry Carton.

To Larry Carton, super thanks; he took all the extra cans and bottles that were left over from the tastings. Since many of the brands tried could be found only in case lots, this amounted to hundreds of packages. Larry was having his house remodeled throughout the tasting period and used tasting leftovers to slake the thirst of his carpenters, plumbers, and electricians. I wish to thank lead carpenter Russell Mount for his effort in behalf of the venture. Russell tasted as many beers as most panel members.

Others who went out of their way to find obscure or distant labels for the tastings were Fred Dieter, Margot Smith, George Hessel, Shirley and Andrew Gabriel, and Don Jameson. They lived too far away to take part in the tastings, but I felt their moral support, as evidenced by the regular arrival of small "care packages."

I also wish to thank Mr. Ross Heuer, editor of *Brewers Digest*, for his assistance in obtaining background information on some of America's smaller breweries, and Harry Foulds, of *New Jersey Epicure*, for his copies of various newspaper articles concerned with Pennsylvania brewers.

The assistance of the many brewers in the United States, Canada, and abroad who responded to my requests for information and illustration material is gratefully acknowledged. (Would other industries have been so cooperative?) Labels used as illustrations (and other photographic material) in this book were provided by the brewers and various brewers associations. Their use is by permission of the brewing companies and associations; the reader is advised that the labels are registered trademarks of the companies and permission for their reproduction must be secured in advance.

Finally, I want to thank the members of my family, especially my wife, Maryana, who had to put up with a sometimes tense, and frequently grumpy, author, who had little time for anything else; who had to act as hostess for almost forty beer tastings (as well as serve as a panel member); and who had to live in a house that was beer from wall to wall. I also give special thanks to Suzanne, the oldest of my four beautiful daughters, who contributed her pen and ink sketches to fill the empty nooks and crannies of the book.

As a postscript, I would like to say a brief word about John Porter, who graciously agreed to write the foreword to this work. Mr. Porter was educated as a brewer and spent many years in that profession. His great love, however, was in writing and he has since removed to that career. Meanwhile, he tied the two talents together in a most delightful book, *All About Beer*. Reading that volume was the most enjoyable part of all the time I spent researching my work. I recommend it for sheer pleasure.

Contents

5. The Beers

11

Introduction

A few years ago I proposed to a prestigious New York publishing firm that the time was ripe to publish a pleasant, informative primer on the subject of beer. I pointed to the obvious fact that bookstores were awash with volumes for winebibbers, while beer drinkers had trouble finding so much as a pamphlet devoted to man's oldest friend. Many, many weeks later the editors announced their considered opinions which added up to this: since beer drinkers weren't readers, there was little point in writing a book for them; and, what's more, you couldn't tell them anything about beer that they did not *think* they already knew.

This attitude struck me as both doctrinaire and fatuous, but perhaps not uncommon. Fortunately, the third publisher took a very different view, which is not the point. What is, it seems, is that beer and its drinkers are seen as rather low on the social scale (relative to wine, spirits, and coke drinkers) by a certain sector of the American public. For lack of a better explanation, we might hastily assume that this undemocratic variety of snobbism originated in the Old World. But in fact the superb beers, handsome beer books, and happy drinkers of the Old World are all accorded the highest esteem.

If indeed things beery bear a slight stigma (the man in his undershirt surrounded by empty cans while viewing TV), there are new forces at work to elevate the social status of the venerable "wine of the grain." One such is this comprehensive book, which the author tells us is a "labor of love." Surely it will do much toward putting beer in its rightful niche as entirely fit for the delectation of connoisseurs, and not less so than a good wine. I am very pleased to recommend this book to all who would enhance their enjoyment of beer by learning more about it.

John H. Porter

Underground Cellar.

Filling Beer Casks—Seventeenth Century

Preface

In 1903 the definitive work on beer made its appearance in America. This work, *One Hundred Years of Brewing*, has stood the test of time quite well, for all major literary efforts concerning beer written since then have relied heavily upon it.

Since that work was published, many changes have occurred on the brewing scene, not the least of which was Prohibition. During Prohibition, almost a full generation of "temperance", brewers were forced to eke out survival making soda pop, near-beer, ice, cheese, ham and bacon, ice cream, or whatever they could. Of the 1,500 pre-Prohibition breweries, less than 800 survived to take out a license upon repeal. By 1952 the number was less than 400, and this had halved again by 1963.

Today even fewer remain, and slowly but surely the small independents are being absorbed by the industry giants. Many of the old brands continue to be marketed as consolidation goes on, but this practice will pass if not economically sound.

While they still exist, I thought it important that the

April 7, 1933—Left to right, Adolphus Busch III, August A. Busch, Sr. and August A. Busch, Jr. celebrate repeal of prohibition by preparing the first case of relegalized Budweiser for shipment to President Franklin D. Roosevelt.

vast fraternity of beer lovers be made aware of the wide variety of beers out there waiting to be sampled and enjoyed. While wine-tasting reports, and even reports of Scots whiskey and bourbon tastings, have been seen frequently, similar reports on beer are nearly absent from the scene. Even books on the subject report on only a small portion of the total number of items available.

This work is the outgrowth of a labor of love—the task of locating and tasting all the beers available in America today. Although a few brands may have eluded me, my search embraces the most extensive sampling of beer ever attempted, a feat which may never be equaled, since the number of brewing companies and marketed brands are shrinking continually.

My earliest recollection of beer was in eastern Canada sometime in 1942. Up there the war was in full swing and there were soldiers everywhere. I remember watching a "zombie" (a soldier who had volunteered, but for home service only; he wore a blue diamond-shaped patch on his shoulder instead of a dark red rectangular patch) open an imperial pint bottle of Dow's by cracking off the neck on a gatepost. I was impressed when he then drank from it.

Alcoholic beverages were rare around our house. Occasionally a bottle of Carstairs White Seal appeared whenever my father hosted a poker game. I got the little plastic white seal that came from the neck of the bottle. Beer never entered the house—not even once. If the Boston Red Sox had not been sponsored by Narragansett, beer might have been unknown to me. In high school friends occasionally got drunk, but it was on wine—a fact very likely reflecting the heavy influence of the local Italian majority.

Beer first worked its way into my personal life in college, but the connection was loose and I would have preferred root beer at the time (I killed most of my passion for soft drinks by a surfeit of the stuff while working for a bottling company one summer). Not until 1961, when working in Germany for an extended period, did I begin to appreciate beer.

The Germans used beer as a table beverage, and eager to be assimilated, I too ordered beer with my meals. The status of beer in Germany was so different from what I had found it to be in America. I actually enjoyed beer for the first time. Of course, in Germany one can enjoy beer more regularly because most of it is so well made.

On my return to America, I did not find the domestic beers a suitable substitute on my table. Imported wines, however, which I had also discovered in Europe, were much closer to what I had found on the Continent than were imported suds. In the ensuing fourteen years beer was relegated to the back burner—as a drink in a bowling alley, after mowing the lawn, or in a restaurant where the wine was too high-priced.

Interest in wine and involvement in a wine-tasters soci-

21

ety led me back to the world of beer, this time to the extreme of making a detailed study of the subject. Having gone that deeply into the subject of beer—an everyday item that most people take for granted—I think it worth mentioning that beer is a commodity not really easy to appreciate to the full; it in fact approaches the study of wine in its complexity.

There are many that will chuckle at the thought of "serious" beer tasting, but all it takes is one such experience to make believers of most of them. Most of the first-timers who attended the tastings that resulted in this book came with an expectation of attending a ludicrous ceremony. They left more than half convinced that there was something to it after all. Almost everybody left the tasting with some degree of enlightenment, and all left entertained.

After you read this book, try it yourself. It will cost you little, and the reward of finding only one beer that you like above all others will be worth it. Not only that, within a short time you may qualify as a sort of expert on beer, and real experts on the subject (even amateur experts) are harder to find than expertly made beer.

1. The History of Beer

All vegetable material, given sufficient moisture, appropriate temperature range, and the proper yeasts (of which our atmosphere abounds) will undergo some kind of decomposition or fermentation. It is therefore no amazement that prehistoric man should have known foods and beverages that tasted pleasant, provided nourishment, and, if taken in sufficient quantities, brought on an exhilarated condition of mind.

These beverages differed widely according to climate and available flora. Tree sap, berries, fruit juices, tree bark, plant stems, and leaves were all used to make intoxicating beverages. Beers made from cereal grains were known long before history recorded the fact, but these were vastly different brews from today's product.

The oldest document known to man, a clay tablet inscribed in Babylonia around 6000 B.C., depicts a scene of the preparation of beer for sacrificial purposes. By 4000, the Babylonians had made sixteen different types of beer from barley, wheat, and honey. Bittering agents (to add character to the taste and a degree of shelf life) have been used in beer

Ancient Municipal Brewery of Nürnberg, Bavaria, Germany.

making since 3000. For almost three thousand years beer was important to daily life and religion in ancient Egypt. It was in common use in China about 2300 B.C., and the ancient Incas had used a corn-based beer for centuries before that continent was discovered.

The *Rig-Veda* of India (ca. 1000 B.C.) contains a prayer to Indra, offering an intoxicating beverage, *soma*, made from the juice of a creeping plant, *asclepas*. The common people of that time in India drank *sura*, a much more intoxicating brew made from *panicum*—an Indian grass—honey, water, curds, melted butter, and barley. According to the sacred book *Zend-Avesta*, the Persians had similar beverages in 1000 B.C. Though drunkenness was a violation of the religious tenets of Zoroaster, intoxicating beverages were included by him among the offerings to be made at religious rites. According to ancient Egyptian fables, beer had been present at the Creation.

In premedieval Europe, wherever there was no significant viticulture, beer or beer-like beverages (like barley wine) became deeply ingrained into the culture, both in religion and in everyday life. Even in Spain, where viticulture was widespread, the districts without wine made a beer from barley called *celia* and one from wheat named *ceria*. The Celts brewed something called *Kurmi*, which Doiscorides (about 25 B.C.) said brought on headaches, tired blood, and weak knees. History does not record how much *Kurmi* was required to bring on these effects. The Gauls, who were also not without wine grapes, brewed a beer, *cervisia*, and the Romans, who spread viticulture throughout Europe, had their *cerevisia* (in Latin: *Ceres*, the goddess of agriculture, and *vis*, strength).

The Romans introduced wine to the Saxons, who quickly adopted its use and it was drunk thereafter on all great occasions and at festivals, but the ancient national beverages of ale and meth remained the beverages of the people at all times. In the oldest epic of modern languages, *Beowulf* tells us of the mead hall, ale carvuse, and the beer hall. *Meth*, or mead, made from honey and water, originated in the remotest days and may have preceded any wines or beer used by man. Its popularity spans thousands of years. The ales of that time were cereal beverages and seem to have been of fairly high quality by modern standards, since clarity and mildness were deemed desirable features. Other beverages of that time were cider and *piment*, a mixture of wine, honey, and spices.

In his work *Germania* (A.D. 99), the Roman historian Tacitus reports that the ancient Teutons' daily activity was as likely to be a drinking bout as anything else. The drinking of a barley and wheat brew was an important part of all marriages, meetings, elections, decisions, and day-to-day living.

The great book of Northern mythology, the *Edda*, describes at length the part played by beer among the gods. The *Edda* also reported on the German beer conventionals, describing violations and the penalties, which were mainly drinking large quantities of beer in one draught. Some of these conventionals have carried into the twentieth century in such tradition-steeped establishments as Heidelberg University and in modern U.S. college fraternities.

Until the Middle Ages, the brewing of beer was left to

25

the women, as was everything except drinking, warring and carousing (where did we go astray?). In medieval times the brewing of beer shifted from the family to the brewhouses of the monasteries, convents, and villages. Brewing was believed to be a very important branch of monastery life and the staples of diet were bread and beer. Large monasteries often had a number of functioning breweries since the daily ration for a monk could be as high as a gallon.

The nobility had an interest in maintaining a ready supply of brew for their community and guests and all the larger courts and castles had their own brewhouses. Charlemagne took great interest in brewing and in 812 listed, in his *Capitulare de Villis Imperialibus*, beer brewers among the artisans and laborers to be employed by district public administrators.

Although bittering agents had been used in very early times, the first clear indication of the use of hops (and with it the early beginnings of modern beer) occurs in 768, when, in the record of a gift by Pepin, a hop garden is mentioned. A public document from the year 822 certifies that hops were used in the production of beer, but the "official" creditation usually goes to the Abbess Hildegard (1079) of Rupertsberg, who wrote in her *Physica Sacia*, "If one intends to make beer from oats, it is prepared with hops, but is boiled with *grug* [herbs, most likely], and mostly with ash leaves."

By this time a beer trade was well established—and firmly in the hands of the clergy. Of course, since there were no "states" at this time, most all cultural and economic activities were conducted by the clergy, as this class was the only tangible representation of society at that time. Christian clergymen were the wholesalers of beer and the Jews were the retailers, because the Christian clergymen were forbidden to make a profit. Beer was used in medieval Europe for tithing, trading, payment, and taxing; indeed, it participated fully in the economics of the time.

As early as the eleventh century the larger cities began to press for freedom of action for themselves by acquiring privileges from their territorial and spiritual lords. Over the next two hundred years this became more of a reality with the formation of the trade guilds, each forming a corporation for itself. The guilds were represented on the councils,

Medieval Tavern Sign   Medieval Cellarer

and commerce between the large cities flourished. In the fourteenth century great brewing houses were formed, especially in Germany. There was even a substantial export of German beer, since it had a wide reputation. In 1376, the great brewing center of the Middle Ages, Hamburg, had over a thousand brewmasters.

Aside from the great beers of Hamburg, the most famous beer of the Middle Ages was that from the city of Einbeck, whose inhabitants were principally occupied with the making of beer and linen. It was on draught everywhere and exported as far as Jerusalem. Brewed only in winter, it was top-fermented, heavily malted, and strongly hopped, enabling it to keep its quality a very long time.

For almost two hundred years the growth of beer popularity and brewing continued unabated. Then suddenly the situation reversed. Brewing had long been a favorite object of taxation, and more and heavier levies were laid on beer and grain as funds were required. Restrictions on trade appeared with the subsequent appearanc of the usual counter-restrictions. Brewers lowered the quality of the product to offset economic pressures, and consumers reacted by switching to the newly available coffees, teas, and spirituous liquors. Although these effects caused a great contraction in the industry, it was a temporary situation. The major victim was the industry. Man's preference for and use of malt bev-

Brew-House Cellar—Sixteenth Century.

erages continued; he could still make a palatable brew at home.

In 1614 the brewers at Munich discovered that they could successfully imitate the great beers of Einbeck and began a segment of the brewing trade that remains famous to this time. Many beer lovers today are grateful for the efforts of those Munich brewers. In 1602 Weiss (white) beer, which had been made locally and occasionally for several hundred years, attained renewed favor, and that favor was to grow and spread for over two hundred years. Today, Weiss Bier is still made by a few Munich brewers, but it is usually referred to as Berliner Weiss.

As for early Celtic brews, the beer of the Britons was alelike in nature; the British preference for ale continues to the present, with pale lager-style beers making serious inroads into the British markets only in the large cosmopolitan areas. The ale of Britain's past and the presently available brews are not the same, however. Hops were not introduced there until about 1500. Even then, there is evidence that the hops were not used in the ale for some time. Ale was made of malt and water and drunk new, with great pride taken in avoiding "unnatural" ingredients. The hops were used only for beer, in place of preserving it with various leaves and barks. Before the introduction of hops into Britain, the word *ale* was meant to indicate pure malted liquor, and the word *beer* meant imported German brew. When hops were finally added to the venerable ale (late in the sixteenth century), *ale* came to mean a stronger malted drink, which contained a greater quantity of unfermented extract than beer.

Although the end of the sixteenth century saw a softening of the brewing trades in Germany, it was the beginning of the heyday of Britain's fledgling industry. London was the center of this rapidly growing industry and considerable amounts of beer were being exported to France. The product of the British brewers was as lusty a brew as had ever been placed on the market. It was very strong and could be stored for several years without spoiling.

The prosperity and growth continued through the seventeenth and into the eighteenth century when porter was introduced (by Harwood in 1722). It had become popular in public houses to drink half-and-half (half ale and half "twopenny") or "three shreads" (ale, beer, and twopenny). Porter combined the taste of the various beers and removed the need to draw from different casks. By this time the growth of brewing was so great that the country had a general prob-

Ancient Brewers tools—A: Laddle for thick mash. Z: Dipper for wort. M: Stirrer for thick mash.

Brew-House Interior—Sixteenth Century.

lem with drunkenness and the attendant pauperism and rowdyism. Steps were taken to stem the tide of drunkenness, but no effective measures were devised until the tax man, who regarded the brewing industry as just another source of income, took an interest in matters.

The colonies in American never suffered a problem of

widespread drunkenness. Even though the Pilgrims may have made landfall at Plymouth because they had run out of beer, alcoholic beverages in the colonies had been regulated from the start. Breweries were born in America almost with the communities. The first brewery was built in New Amsterdam in 1612. Twenty years later Peter Minuit estab-

Sixteenth Century Cooperage.

lished the first public brewery in America. Taxes on malt liquors appeared in 1644. Governor general Peter Stuyvesant, a crusader in regulating public morals, leaned heavily on brewers and tavernkeepers. William Penn built the first brewhouse in Philadelphia in 1685. Most of the famous figures of colonial New England began or participated in brewing ventures beginning early in the seventeenth century, but the industry did not flourish there as barley could not advantageously be raised in that climate. A perhaps more important reason for the failure of a brewing industry to catch on in early New England was that a brewhouse was regarded as an essential part of a homestead. The few cities were seaports with ready access to imports from England and thus did not offer much of a market for a local brewing industry. This was to change with the taxation that was to lead to the Revolution, and after independence was achieved, the brewing industry was to thrive there for over a century.

The founding fathers of the new republic were kindly disposed toward beer and cider (but not to distilled spirits) and the popular bodies of the States viewed the subject similarly; in doing so, they believed they were upholding the cause of temperance. They even encouraged the brewing industry to a degree by withholding taxes on brewery property. Such leading citizens as Adams, Jefferson, and Madison either owned or promoted breweries and George Washington himself maintained a small brewery at Mt. Vernon.

About 1820, German immigrants began to arrive in large numbers. Since immigrants tended to settle in ethnic "colonies," wherever Germans settled they created an instant market for beer. With them came young men already educated and experienced in the field of brewing. Breweries sprang up by the hundreds and many flourished in the benign atmosphere of the new country. At this time, the beers made were mostly ales and porter. There were also a considerable number of breweries, especially in the New York City area, devoted to making Weiss beer.

The new chill-brewed lager first appeared in the United States in Philadelphia in 1840, manufactured by a man named John Wagner. Shortly thereafter, most of the German brewers began to produce malt beverages made in ac-

Fraunce's Tavern, New York City (Built in 1730).

Fraunces Tavern, New York. (Interior.)

The above is the famous Long Room of Fraunce's Tavern, in which the merchants and brewers of New York often met for consultation and action. Here, in 1768, was organized the New York Chamber of Commerce and it was in this historic room that Washington, in 1783, delivered his farewell address to his officers.

cordance with the new recipe fresh in from the old country. The lager enjoyed immediate public acceptance. And although it caused difficulties for brewers because it required the use of refrigeration facilities for brewing and storage, more and more brewers built plants to handle the rapidly growing market for the new lager beer.

The conquest of the American market by this pale lager (more appropriately called Dortmunder or Pilsener) beer is so complete that the number of true ales still brewed in America is quite small; there are no Weiss beers, few dark beers, and even less porter. One truly American phenomenon in brewing was the steam beer of the Pacific Coast. Because ice was prohibitive in San Francisco in the mid-nineteenth century and there was great demand for malt liquor that could not be satisifed by imports, a technique of beer making developed that employed bottom-fermentation in the 60°–68°F. range and cellaring at 60°–70°F. This beer too disappeared for a time, and only one brewery producing this uniquely American product remains in operation today.

2. The Art of Making Beer

The making of beer, or any fermented beverage, simply involves the conversion of sugar to alcohol by the action of yeast. The prime ingredient, and the oldest used in malt beverages, is barley. Barley was originally used in beer making because, of all the available grains, it was the least suitable for making bread. Fortunately for us beer lovers, it proved to be the best suited for the making of beer. The Chevalier, or two-rowed barley, is preferred by European brewers, particularly in Germany where it has been used since the earliest times. Much of it is grown in America, but is largely exported since it has a thin husk and a high percentage of albuminoids, a disadvantage in the American method of mashing. The common four-rowed barley is also used predominantly in Europe. The most popular strain of barley in the United States is the six-rowed barley, considered unsuitable by most of the big European brewers. The *row* refers to the number of rows of fertile flowers, and therefore the number of rows of barleycorn that are produced. Six-rowed barley is that in which all the flowers are fertile and produce three barleycorns, which result in six rows. Two-rowed bar-

Brew Kettle at the Olympia Brewery, Olympia, Washington

ley is generated from the type wherein only one of each of the three flowers is fertile. The six-rowed variety gathers more sunlight and has a higher protein content, which makes it less suitable for brewing, although it is more productive, which makes it less expensive to use. Understand? Well, if you find this barley double-talk confusing, you are in good company.

The barley gives the beer its flavor, its head, its body (in the form of maltodextrins and protein), and its color, but in modern brewing, barley is not the only cereal grain used. Properly malted barley, once the only grain used, is not suitable for making the pale beers preferred by most beer drinkers today—and is very expensive, compared to other grains. To make pale, light lager beer, the percentage of barley used is reduced and high-starch malt adjuncts are substituted. The list of adjuncts normally used includes corn, rice, unmalted barley, malt syrups, and tapioca starch. Corn is the most commonly used adjunct for pilseners; it makes a pale, brilliant, light-bodied beer. Rice is a close second as it produces the palest of possible brews, a big selling point with American beer drinkers today.

All have the important advantage to the brewer competing in the U.S. today of being cheaper than barley. They do, however, produce an inferior beer to one made only with finest barley malt. Many of the lower-priced beers, and most home-brewed beer, use malt extract. It is usually carried by grocery stores in rural areas. Another advantage of these adjuncts is that they are all high in starch, and fewer are required to provide the malt sugar required during fermentation. Beers made with heavy use of adjuncts may be higher in alcoholic content and less costly to make than barley beers, but suffer in comparison because they lack greatly in flavor. Wheat malt is often used to stimulate yeast growth, improve stability, and promote body and flavor, but it is expensive to use and is mostly used today in making Berliner Weiss. Oat and rye malt is used in making certain stouts.

The starches in the cereal grains are not readily fermentable without special preparation. The yeast (and in beer making it is always Brewer's yeast, *Saccharomyces cerevisiae*) cells need something good to "eat" and to metabolize, so that as they feed and reproduce themselves they will manufacture alcohols and tiny bubbles of carbonation. This process of preparing the barley (and other grains) for fermentation is called malting.

The first step in the malting process is to sort the grains of barley so that they are nearly the same size and weight to secure equal and uniform growth for the same batch of malt. Sorted, the barley is steeped, or soaked, in water to receive the necessary moisture to start germination. At this time, the dead grains can be removed and certain coloring and extractive matter eliminated. The barley is allowed to grow to a limited amount during which time the natural enzyme systems of the barley are released to break down the membranes of the starch cells. This is the process that requires the maltster's great skill, and timing is crucial. When germination has proceeded sufficiently, the grains are kiln-dried to stop the growth and for partial caramelization. The dried, sprouted barley resulting from this process is called malt.

The first main stage of the actual brewing process is called mashing. In mashing, heated water is added to the prepared malt and the starches in the grains are converted into soluble, fermentable sugars—maltose and dextrins. The temperature and chemical composition of the water are both strictly controlled and are what activate the amylolytic enzymes that convert the starches. The proteins are also partly modified during mashing. It is here that some brewers have to use additives (like salts, softeners, or dealkalinizers) to adjust or "condition" their water, or to add amylolytic enzymes to produce fermentable sugars if they are not supplied by their excuse for malt. If adjuncts, like corn or rice, are to be employed, they are milled and then boiled in a "cooker" before being added to the malt in the "mash kettle." The temperature and acidity of the mash are strictly controlled, for the outcome of the final product is highly dependent on the success of this stage. A high temperature, for example, will produce a beer with less alcohol, but with a greater flavor. In America, a quick-mashing method is used, where two mashes are employed, one at 145° and one at 172°F. The European method involves four temperature stages, ranging from 100° to 170°F., which gives the proteolytic enzymes a chance to convert the proteins into more soluble states. From the mash kettle, the mash is filtered and the resulting malt extract is sent to the brew kettle. The filter is called a Lauter tub, and the spent grains are removed for use as livestock feed. The remaining highly fermentable liquid is called the wort.

It is in the brew kettle that the hops are added to the wort, where they are boiled together. The finest hops are grown in central European countries, with the finest of all attributed to Czechoslovakia. This may be because the Czech hops (Saaz variety) are ideally suited to the now very popular pilsener-type brews. Most of the Munich beers use the German-grown Hallertau variety, and the popular strains in England are Golding for light ales and Fuggle for brown ales. Until recently, Bullion, the American-grown variety of hop, was our only commercially useful hop produced. It is a hop noted for its marked bitterness, and was favored only by foreign brewers for making stouts and long-aged beers, few of which are made in America today. For the usual American brews, domestic hops had to be blended with milder, imported varieties. In the past year, however, experiments with milder varieties of hops in the Yakima valley of Washington have yielded some successes, and there is some hope that American produced hops may, in the near future, yield the same quality of brews as the finest of European hops, all other things being equal. The use of hop extract by domestic brewers is becoming more prevalent, but most of the world's finest and proudest breweries still use only whole, unrefined hops; to do less, they believe, is to compromise the quality of their product.

As the wort and hops boil together, the hop resins add flavor, aroma, and bitterness to the brew. The hops also act as a preservative and hop tannin aids in precipitating protein. During this boil, which lasts about two hours, the wort is concentrated to the desired specific gravity, sterilized, and rid of protein substances.

Next, the hops are removed in a hop separator or jack. Also removed is the protein precipitate (called trub) result-

Beer Bottling at the Olympia Brewery, Olympia, Washington

ing from the boiling. The wort now proceeds to the wort-collecting tank, or hot-wort tank, where the remaining trub is removed. The next step in the process is cooling the wort from a temperature just under boiling to about 50°F., which takes only a few seconds in the wort cooler.

Fermentation follows, and is done in special tanks for the purpose. Jealously guarded "secret strains" of yeast are used. In all modern breweries, pure and unchanged yeast cultures are maintained so that a particular beer flavor is assured year after year. Throughout the fermentation period, which usually lasts about seven days in modern domestic brewing, strict temperature control is maintained, for if the fermenting wort were to become excessively warm, fermentation would cease.

With the fermentable material converted to alcohol, the "green" beer is transferred to the aging tanks in the storage cellars for the slow secondary fermentation. Protein and the yeast settle out and more carbon dioxide is generated. As long as the beer is not exposed to oxygen, the flavor slowly improves and after several weeks to several months, depending on the sort of beer being produced, it is ready for final processing and packaging. Some brewers add enzymes in the storage phase to break down the complex proteins and to speed up clarification of the beer. This action also tends to remove much of the distinction among individual brews, and a recipe so treated will essentially taste the same brew after brew.

The beer is filtered one more time, and a few more adjustments may be made, including the final carbonation. Some of the cheaper brews are simply charged with CO_2 just as are soft drinks. An older method, krausening, calls for the addition of a younger beer still in lively fermentation to the beer that has been aged and is ready for packaging. This method has a slight disadvantage in that it is difficult to prevent changing the character of the aged brew in adding the young beer. More recently, in 1798, the method of saving the natural carbonation from the fermenting brew and reinjecting it into the aged beer was developed. This is the method used today by most of America's leading brewers, though some, like Schaefer, still proudly assert that their beer is naturally carbonated through krausening. Natural carbonation results in smaller bubbles and is less likely to be overdone and offensive. Truly natural carbonation results from a very slow secondary fermentation where the carbonic gas is bound to the beer in very tiny bubbles. The result may be less "apparent" carbonation, but a smoother nongassy product.

Some brewers will add a solution of invert sugar (or lactose), caramel, or licorice to the brew after aging, when the beer is passed to final storage. This encourages some additional fermentation with resultant increased carbonation and some additional sweetness. Other brewers may use fining agents (such as asbestos or gelatin, which aids in precipitating out suspended matter in a solution) in an effort to increase the clarity of the product, a brilliantly clear brew being the most desired achievement. This sometimes results in a loss of natural head and foaming agents are used to compensate for the loss. A common example of such a foaming agent is propylene glycol alginate, a modified seaweed extract.

Beer that is to be packaged in bottles or cans is usually first pasteurized at a temperature of 140°F. for fifteen minutes (Coors is one very notable exception; it uses sterile technique and end-to-end refrigeration in its distribution). Beer that is to be kegged for draught service is not pasteurized but placed in aluminum or stainless steel barrels which must be kept refrigerated until used.

3. The Types of Beer

Up to the middle of the nineteenth century, the form of fermentation applied most generally was top-fermentation, so called because the yeast rose to the top of the fermenting vat during the process. The yeast of the previous brew was added to the cooled beer wort, which was then pitched and put up for fermentation in open tubs placed in a cellar with as low a temperature as possible. The chief object of the brewmaster at this time was to protect the beer against acidification, a condition highly likely in view of the high temperatures that might be reached within the fermenting mixture. This method was in general use in the United States up to 1850 and its use continued in England well into the twentieth century.

It was in Germany where brewers first began to pay more careful attention to the temperature of fermentation and to the length of fermentation. The thermometer and the saccharometer were to become the brewmasters' most important tools, as it was found that acidification could be best prevented by allowing the wort temperature not to exceed 75°F. Further, it was found that the best temperature range

Open Ale Fermentation at Labatt's, London, Ontario

for producing the desired taste of the beer was 55° to 60°F. in winter and 60° to 65°F. in summer. Actually, it was difficult in those times to maintain a temperature that low at all ambient temperatures, since a fermenting mass generates large amounts of heat.

The principal fermentation of ales usually lasted about forty-eight hours, that of porter somewhat less, and the Scots beer required fermentation of eleven to eighteen days or more.

Around 1850 bottom-fermentation began to gain favor in the United States and has since been almost universally adopted. This method originated in Bavaria about 1830 and its introduction has been credited to Gabriel Sedlmayr of Munich and Anton Dreher of Vienna. Bottom-fermentation takes place at a lower temperature (about 40°–50°F.) and the yeast settles to the bottom, instead of rising to the top. This method is now used exclusively for so-called lager beers.

While Sedlmayr took Munich to the heights in bottom-fermenting luscious dark brews, Dreher brought Vienna to the forefront of brewing with his magnificent light bottom-fermented beverages. When in 1843 Liebig published his theory of fermentation, with a carefully developed list of the disadvantages of top-fermentation, bottom-fermentation was greatly promoted throughout the world.

Two principal forms of beer were produced by the new method. Winter beer was brewed in October, November, March, April, and the summer months. Lager beer was brewed only during the months of December, January and February. In Bavaria the seasons for brewing were fixed by law; lager beer could be brewed only from Michaelmas (29 September) to St. George's Day (23 April). For the rest of the year only top-fermentation brews were allowed.

This situation changed in America about 1870 as a result of improved techniques of refrigeration. Brewers were able to operate during the entire year without regard to the outside temperature and the distinction between summer and winter beer disappeared.

Principal fermentation of lager beer is conducted somewhat more slowly, mainly because it allows the beer to retain a sufficient amount of unfermented substances for the long secondary fermentation in the aging cellars.

Lager Types

The term *lager* derives from a German word that means to store or stock. It refers to the long period of lagering, wherein the beer is stored in cellars to undergo the slow second fermentation. It is bottom-fermented and "long" aged. The aging of a better lager will last for several months, but all too many of our domestic products see little more than a week of cellar time, so great is the rush to the marketplace.

In America fermentation takes place at temperatures of 45° to 55°F. (and sometimes higher), and proceeds slowly, over a period of five to eight days. European lager brewers usually ferment at a slightly lower temperature, and less vigorous fermentation occurs over a longer period of time, often up to ten to fourteen days. Better domestic brews may also be done according to European practice. The aging is done very near to the freezing temperature for water, and proceeds very slowly. The longer the beer is aged, the more "complete" will be the flavor and the resultant brew will have more body and a longer shelf life.

Alcoholic content of lager is usually 3.0 to 3.8 percent by weight (3.4 to 4.2 percent by volume) as opposed to ales which are usually four to five percent. In the United States malt beverages with an alcohol content higher than five percent must be called malt liquor, stout, porter, or ale. They cannot be labeled beer.

Light lagers are pale gold in color, light in body, flavored with a medium to light hop taste, and are fairly high in carbonation. They generally have a soft, mellow, dry taste. They are best served cold, at around 40° to 45°F. The two most popular types, pilsener and Dortmunder, make up the major volume of U.S. beer production. These two styles, which differ only slightly best match the definition of light lager given above, with the malt having more influence in aroma and taste than the hops. The term *pilsener* is used interchangeably with the word *lager* in most of the world today, whereas use of *Dortmunder* has almost disappeared as a beer adjective in the U.S. With the utilization of corn or rice as an adjunct to the barley malt, the appearance of many domestic beers is tending to become paler and paler, with some already near to being as pale as water.

The Vienna type is characterized by an amber color and a very mild hop taste. It is usually brewed with less hops than the Dortmunder or pilsener type, but is not any less flavorful for the malt contribution is increased by the particular brewing method.

The Munich type, or dark lager, has a dark brown color, is full-bodied with a sweet malt flavor and slight hop taste. It is more aromatic and "creamy" than a light lager. The color of a true dark lager comes from the addition of roasted barley. Imitation dark lagers are made with caramel or with a roasted barley malt extract, a much less expensive process. The alcohol content in these dark lagers approaches five percent by weight. Light Munich beers are Dortmunder types and, like many of the current Dortmunder brews, have more of a hop flavor. The color of these German light lagers is darker than the corresponding American brews because of the slower fermentation. They can be likened to the Bohemian beers with their fine and strongly noticeable hop flavor, pronounced bitter taste, and vinous character.

Oktoberfest beer was once brewed only for the autumn festivals (usually held in September). Originally a light lager of high alcoholic content available only on draft for serving at the festival, it is now readily found year round in bottles, but Oktoberfest beer differs very little from the regular export lager, including the alcoholic content.

Bock beer is believed to have originated in the once famous beer capital of Einbeck. A heavy dark beer with a slightly sweet malt flavor and strong hop background, bock is brewed in the winter for consumption in the spring. True bock derives its color from the heat treatment given the barley in the malting process and may have as much as ten percent alcohol by weight. Many artificial bocks are produced today that are colored and flavored by a prepared syrup containing caramelized sugar.

Throughout Europe, local breweries produce beer with an alcohol content in excess of ten percent by means of extended fermentation and other methods. Such beers are rarely available outside their home grounds, usually because they are not pasteurized. The beer with the reputation for the highest alcohol content comes from Kulmbach, Germany. Some Kulmbacher beers are reported to have as much as fourteen percent alcohol, but those exported to the U.S. fall far below that figure.

Steam beer, another bottom-fermented brew, originated on the West Coast of the United States directly as a result of the desire for malt beverages and an extreme shortage of ice. It is a development in beer brewing that is peculiar to America. Fermentation proceeds at a relatively high temperature (60°–68°F.) and barley malt is used exclusively. Within twelve to eighteen hours after the yeast has been added to the wort in the fermenting tubs, the beer comes into "krausen," where it is kept from six to eight hours. It is then run into the clarifier for two to three days (depending on the ambient temperature) for completion of fermentation. If fermentation has been proper, at the end of this stage the beer shall have undergone a reduction of fifty to sixty percent and be quite clear in appearance. From the clarifier, the beer is racked directly into barrels, where it receives an addition of about twenty percent of krausen, together with some fining. In four to six days the beer has raised a sufficient amount of "steam" in the barrels (some fifty pounds per square inch), and some bleeding of pressure must be done. In olden times these barrels were shipped to saloons, rested a few days, and then tapped for the trade. Steam beer is made today by only one West Coast firm and the product is bottled. Total refrigeration may not be necessary because of the strength of the brew, but it must be kept cool for it is not pasteurized. Steam beer has a golden brown color, sharp hoppy taste, full body, and a lingering malt finish.

Ale Types

Ale is more vinous in nature, possesses a greater percentage of alcohol (four to five percent by weight) and extract than a lager, is more aromatic, more full-bodied, and has a more pronounced hop flavor and tartness.

Prior to the rise of lager beers in the midnineteenth century, all brewing was done with top-fermenting yeast and the beers so made were commonly called ale. Ale types have retained their great popularity only in Britain and in parts of the British Commonwealth, particularly in Canada and Australia. Even in the latter countries, lagers are gradually supplanting the top-fermented brews, and soon Britain will be the last stronghold of great ales in the world.

Ale is fermented at a higher temperature than lager for a lesser period of time and, when maturing is stored at temperatures in the range of 40° to 45°F. (as opposed to lager, which matures at temperatures near 32°F.). Ale requires additional aging in the bottle to develop its best strength and flavor.

There are a number of different types of ale produced today. Common or stock ales are characterized by lower levels of carbonation. Cream ales and sparkling ales have relatively high levels of carbonation, resulting in a rich foam and strong effervescence. The "bitter" of England is brewed from pale-ale malts, with corn and rice added in small amounts to make the beer clear and brilliant. It is more heavily hopped than "mild," the other staple of British pubs, a brown-hued smooth ale beverage with a dominant malt flavor.

The strong or brown ales are quite dark and may be tawny brown, ruby red, or brown with a reddish tinge in their coloring. Some are highly carbonated; others have just the slightest touch of bubble. The alcohol level is usually quite high, some approaching the equivalent of a wine. These will keep for several years in a bottle, just like a wine. All have the characteristic full malt flavor and a vinous character, and some will be hopped quite heavily. Included in this type are the barley wines, which are notably vinous and well hopped.

Stout has a dark color (some almost black), a rich malty flavor usually combined with a rather strong bitter hop taste and a high alcohol content (5 to 6.5 percent by weight). Stout usually has low to medium carbonation and is best served at temperatures above 45°F. The main ingredient is roasted barley.

Porter originated in England about 1722 to satisfy the market that had arisen from a public demand for a brew that was drawn equally from casks of ale and beer. Originally it was a heavy beverage, but is more lightly brewed today and has a more bitter and dry taste than it had in the eighteenth century. Porter is made with charcoal or colored malt and is a dark brown, heavy-bodied malty flavored brew with a slightly sweet taste and a less pronounced hop flavor than ale. It is usually about five percent alcohol by weight.

Malt Liquor

Malt liquor is a term that probably resulted more from alcohol beverage regulations than from a need to designate an actual separate variety of beer. Beers exceeding five percent alcohol could not be called beer in several countries; but one accepted form was malt liquor. Usually a lager type, malt liquor is marked by a darker color and a more bitter flavor than traditional domestic lagers—and, of course, more alcohol. Because of laws governing the labeling of alcoholic beverages, one can label a brand malt liquor simply because it has more than five percent alcohol. Lately, in the U.S. malt liquor has become the name associated with products intended to counter the popularity of "pop" wines; several U.S. brewers are in fact marketing beer and wine or beer and soda combinations as malt liquor.

Weiss Bier

White beer or wheat beer was first made in England but developed its major market in Germany. It came into prominence in Hamburg as Hamburg Wheat Beer in the sixteenth century. Made from wheat and barley malt, it has a distinctive sharp yeasty or bready aroma and a taste by itself. Hence it is usually only served with a fruit syrup, often raspberry, whereupon it becomes more like a lightly flavored, pleasant effervescent liqueur. It is white colored and cloudy with a rich foam.

Other Beers

There are a number of other types of beers or beerlike cereal beverages available which are favored locally or are for special diets. Some examples are Faro and Lambic beers of Belgium, which are fermented with wild yeasts and are very acidic; Malta, a popular beverage in Puerto Rico; and various malt tonics and near-beers that either have no alcohol or have alcohol of less than 0.4 percent. They are made in most countries of the world. Another brewed product is sake, the Japanese beverage that tastes more like a semidry white wine. To make sake, rice is steamed and fermented to produce germination, as in malting, with a yeast prepared from rice straw.

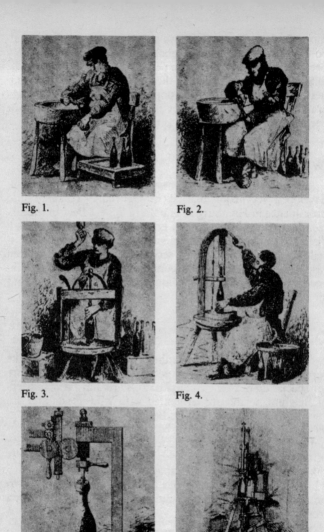

Fig. 1.

Fig. 2.

Fig. 3.

Fig. 4.

Fig. 5.

Fig. 6.

Early Bottling Methods
Figs. 1, 2 - Filling   Figs. 3, 4 - Corking.   Fig. 5, 6 - Later Devices

4. The Great Experiment

Several wine tasters, sitting around after a tasting, were discussing various subjects of common interest, and the subject of the Schmidt's versus Coors TV commercial came up. This led to the idea of a beer tasting that would, of course, include the Schmidt's-Coors comparison. A few weeks later the event was held and was a tremendous success. It was such an entertaining feature, with unexpected educational benefits, that it was decided a second one should be held. The success of the second led to a third and fourth. By this time, close to one hundred different beers had been tried and no one could say that any two were the same. Thirty-five tastings later, over five hundred beers had been tried, and the best of them were submitted to a double-elimination competition to decide which were the best of the best.

The Taste Panel

The judging panel was a diverse group in occupation, background, and taste. There were lawyers, stockbrokers and real estate brokers, engineers, schoolteachers, salesmen,

a chemist, administrators, career military men, housewives, and blue-collar workers. Ages ranged from midtwenties to late fifties. There were twice as many men as women. A wide representation of regional tastes was involved; tasters from New England, the Northwest, the Middle Atlantic States, the Midwest, the Plains States, the Deep South, and the West Coast were on hand. Also involved were foreign nationals from Canada and Australia. In all, some thirty-five tasters participated in the trials.

Each taster was requested to provide background information on himself, including data on beer-drinking experience, and general and specific beer preferences. Tasting schedules were adjusted so that these avowed preferences could be challenged and tested.

Serving the Beer

Beers were served in pairs at all times, the items being matched as closely as possible with regard to color, aroma, and flavor (in that order of priority). Only one person knew which beers were being served and by transferring the beers to a decanter and having the second person pour them into the tasting glasses, no one present knew what beer was in which glass. Beers were poured down the side of the glass for uniformity and to retain head control. Some brewers recommend that their beer be poured straight into the center of the glass, claiming that the beer tastes different otherwise. To pour in this fashion could result in a glass full of foam.

French pilsener stemware was used exclusively so that serving and tasting temperature could be maintained at a standard. A mug would have affected the serving temperature because of its thickness and chilling the mug would have been too time consuming. A standard "beer glass" allows the heat of the hand to warm the fluid too easily. Only stemware—which can be held by the stem if the drinker wishes to keep the beer cool or by the bowl if the beer needs to be warmed up slightly to fulfill its potential—gave the required personal control. Also these glasses have a slightly closed opening, which gathers aroma and bouquet, even from beers that are not particularly well endowed with those features.

The beers were refrigerated to 36° to 40°F., which is actually a bit too cold for serving (although the National Brewing Co. has always recommended a serving temperature of 38°F.). But with the two-step decanting and pouring, this low temperature was required so that the test items would be in the appropriate temperature range (40°–45°F.) when served (as recommended by Heineken and many other brewers). Some items, such as the English brown ales, were served at slightly higher temperatures (50°–55°F.) since they are brewed according to that custom and their flavor is lacking severely when served 10° cooler.

After trying several variations of style, it was found that the tasters preferred testing a variety of flavors spread over the twelve pairs of beers, to testing just one style for the entire evening. The palates became dulled after more than a dozen similar beers; one beer became indistinguishable from another. Likewise, only a very few of the heavy or flavorful beers, like the dark English ales, could be appreciated in one sitting.

Tasters had to be exposed to the beers in a very specific manner to avoid confusing their palates. The lightest styles of beers had to be tasted first, followed by increasingly flavorful beers. The heaviest or strongest flavored items had to be tasted last since anything of lesser flavor tasted subsequently resulted in an invalid reaction. There had to be a respite in between each major change of style as well, to allow the tasters to clear their palates.

The Criteria Used

The tasters were asked to make their judgment on appearance, "nose" (the bouquet and aroma), taste, and aftertaste.

The appearance of the beverage had to be attractive, with color and color density appropriate to type and style, and reasonably devoid of particulate matter. Cloudiness can be a good omen (when it is the presence of yeast, as in some imports like Hansa Fjord, which imparts an excellent flavor), a bad sign (when it is caused by large protein molecules or lactic acid bacteria, which is detrimental to flavor), or have little to do with the product (served too cold).

Dark beer should be a rich gold brown or amber, but reddish-brown hues can be equally attractive. Stouts may be almost opaque. The dark color usually comes from roasting the malt, but there are other techniques, such as adding color or licorice.

Light beers (lightly colored, not low-calorie) come in various intensities of yellows and golds, separately, and in combination, sometimes with a greenish cast.

The nose of a beverage consists of two elements, aroma and bouquet. The aroma is the nasal sensation produced by the ingredients of the product and the bouquet results from the by-products of fermentation.

The aroma should be characteristic of the type and style of beverage being judged. For example, a pilsener beer should have a subtle hop aroma, whereas an English brown ale should have an aroma that is predominantly malt.

Positive features are related to cleanness, purity, "beeriness," appropriate presence of hops, malt, etc. Negative features are excessive yeastiness, sourness, lactic acid, staleness, and skunkiness (believed caused by exposure to light-photosynthesis).

As to flavor, tasters judged on the first sensation, the middle taste (while swallowing), and the aftertaste (once swallowed). Ideally, the taste is present all the way through, start to finish. A beer that lacks any taste feature deprives the drinker of much of the potential enjoyment and must be deemed faulted. Likewise a watery or unpleasant taste leaves the drinker with an unpleasant memory of the brew, especially if the fault is reflected in the aftertaste.

The beer should have sufficient body. Too little is to be watery, lifeless, and unsatisfying. Too much may be cloying or prematurely filling. If you are enjoying beer with a meal, you don't want the beer to fill you up before you have stopped enjoying the food.

Sweetness in a beer is best appreciated at the beginning of the taste. The sweet sensing buds are located on the tip of the tongue, and one of the impressions a beer drinker expects when he takes that first tiny trial sip is given by whatever unfermented sugar is in the brew. Too much sweetness on the palate at this point is a fault, and should the sweetness extend across the palate, the results may range from flabby to cloying.

The bitter hop flavor should also be present at the first sip, but should gradually disappear as the beverage is swallowed. There should be little or none remaining in the finish. The degree of hop bitterness in the flavor will be good or bad only according to personal taste. In beer, what to one is bitter gall to another is a good full-flavored brew.

Malt is the heart of the beer flavor, and its distinctive characteristic taste will determine, to a great extent, the taster's over-all evaluation of the beverage. Modern beer making uses barley malt, but to a lesser extent than in the past. Malt adjuncts, such as corn and rice, are becoming more and more common as prime ingredients. These adjuncts impart a flavor of their own, depending upon the amount used, but their main purpose, or effect, is to reduce aroma and flavor when used in place of barley. They are also cheaper to use, which fact speaks loudly as to why their use has become so prevalent.

Other flavor factors or palate sensations to consider are the degree of carbonation, style of carbonation, alcohol content, fermentation by-products, effects of mishandling, and brewery "house flavors."

If the beer is overcarbonated, like too many American beers (and some foreign beers brewed for the American market), the bubbles mask whatever subtleties of flavor may be present. Instead of the desired pleasant piquancy, the beer is gassy. Too little carbonation and the beer is flat, dull, and weak. The preferred condition is small bubble carbonation, as in fine champagne, a happy state which can be reached only by methods of natural carbonation. Large bubbles, as in soft drinks, are not half so pleasing and are the usual result of carbonic injection.

The amount of alcohol in a beer seems to be a factor that many tasters find difficult to assess. If there is too little alcohol, the beer will seem thin. If there is too much, it will be winy, which is not unbearable, unless it is obtrusive. So-called low-calorie beers necessarily will have less alcohol and must be judged accordingly.

Products of fermentation should not be present in the flavor. If they are, they are usually deemed faults. Similarly, mishandling almost never improves a beer. If it is too old, it gets stale, woody, or acidic. If it has been overheated, it may seem too old or may take on other unpleasant flavors, like metallic sensations. Beer that has been frozen is usually lifeless when served. Exposure to light may bring about photosynthesis resulting in a skunky aroma and taste. Beer bottles are colored deep green or brown to protect against this fault. Certain well-hopped beers, like Molson Ale, seem to be particularly susceptible to skunkiness and it is commonly enough encountered to give the belief that there are more reasons for this fault than simply exposure to light. Another fault is excess yeast cells disintegrating in the beer. This causes a "dirty" flavor, as opposed to the clean beeriness desired. Similarly, residual tannin from excessive malt extraction can cause the beverage to be rough or scratchy when swallowing.

Many brewers have their own house flavors, made of their own recipes. Often the recipe has a secret ingredient (like juniper berries). The taster may or not appreciate the house flavor. In many instances, continued use of such recipes tends to create something very unlike beer.

All of the aspects of flavor taken together are the taste of the beer. The relationship among the factors is called the balance. It is a very important aspect of the overall taste impression and where all other factors are equal but different, the discerning beer drinker will invariably select the better balanced brew.

The last part of the taste is the finish, the consideration of how well it ends and what taste is left in the mouth thereafter. If the beer has no aftertaste or a very brief one, it finishes poorly. If the aftertaste is sour, metallic, or bitter, it finishes badly. As you swallow, the palate sensation should be mostly of malt, with some faint sweetness, and even fainter bitterness from the hops. An ideal brew has balance throughout, with a taste remaining in the mouth that is pleasant in all respects. It may be the only recollection of the entire experience.

Rating the Beers

Tasters were asked to comment upon each of the beers sampled. Each gave his impressions of the aroma and taste, particularly when the effects were not obvious or when choice of words was difficult. Tasters were also required to provide a numerical score as follows:

13–15 **Excellent.** Characteristic of the best of type. No faults. No offensive features. All components of aroma and flavor in harmony. Aroma, flavor, and aftertaste all present to the appropriate degree.

10–12 **Very good.** True to type. No significant faults. No offensive features. Well balanced. Aroma, flavor, and aftertaste all present to the appropriate degree, but short of excellent.

7–9 **Good.** Typical of type. Faults are small and forgivable. Good balance for the most part.

Pleasant and enjoyable but nothing special. Good serviceable beer for thirst quenching and casual enjoyment at a good price.

4–6   **Fair.** May not be true to type. Some noticeable faults but not unpleasantly so. Poorly balanced. May have bitterness or sourness in the aftertaste, or no finish at all. May be thirst quenching and nothing more. Not a beer you would normally purchase a second time.

0–3   **Poor or bad.** Atypical of type. Has definite faults. Has definite unpleasant features. Flawed aroma or taste or both. Badly mishandled. Gone off with age. Improperly made. Contains unforgivable features. Undrinkable, or tastes like nothing more than carbonated water or a soft drink. A beer you would not buy a second time in almost any circumstance.

To ensure that there would be no bias from unusually high- (or low-) scoring groups of tasters, scores were normalized. The highest single score and the lowest single score for each item were discarded. The total of the remaining scores was adjusted to an equivalent score for six raters, and the midrange score set to 45, the middle value of the scoring range. The remaining scores were then adjusted accordingly. Extreme scores were further subjected to inspection for any remaining bias, and adjusted or retried, if appropriate.

A final score of 73–90 could thus be adjudged excellent, 55–72 very good, 37–54 good, 19–36 fair, and 0–18 poor, based on the taster's scoring criteria.

Foods at Tastings

Beer tasters, like wine tasters, need some means of clearing their palates after sampling their subject, and a wide variety of food was tried. We found very early that greasy foods, like potato chips, have an extreme deadening effect on the palate. It took a bit longer to realize that pretzels, because of their saltiness, also impaired taste sensitivity. Some other traditional beer foods, like liverwurst, produced a mixed reaction, enhancing the taste of some beers and clashing with others.

The best devices for clearing beer palates in a tasting situation we found were unbuttered and very lightly salted popcorn, unsalted saltine crackers, and French bread. From this one can draw useful conclusions. If you are going to enjoy a few beers and intend to eat some oily or salty foods, save some money by drinking good inexpensive beverages rather than some high-price brew, at least after the first one. The potato chips, pretzels, corn chips, and salted nuts will so dull your taste that to you one good beer will taste about the same as any other good one.

A Colonial Ale-House.

5. The Beers

In the following pages you will find the sensory descriptions of most of the beers in North America. To be sure, the list is not one hundred percent complete; there are obscure regional brews marketed only locally. Some cannot be found further than twenty miles from the brewery. Until recently an effort to gather the brands listed herein was barely possible. Thousands of labels existed, but most were marketed in tiny geographical areas. By the time a reasonably complete set of such labels could have been gathered, many of them would have been obsolete, what with the reduced number of breweries and marketed brands.

The advent of beer-can collecting, however, has made some small brands available in large metropolitan areas, thereby giving them a public exposure not otherwise available.

Some of the beers listed herein may not now be available. Domestic brands that sell poorly on introduction may be discontinued after only a few months. They may appear later, or may appear under the banner of another brewing firm. Some imports are in short supply, especially those

Fermenting vats at Urquell Brewery in Pilsen, Czechoslovakia

brought in for can collectors. One label, I heard, was brought in by a Washington, D.C. liquor store in a quantity of six dozen.

The sensory descriptions given include all features worthy of note. The impression on eye, nose and palate of the drinker is recorded. The nose of the brew includes the aroma and bouquet, the factors detected by the sense of smell. In the mouth the palate sensations recorded usually indicate the total effect, including the change in sensation as the brew crosses the sweet, sour, and bitter detectors located in different sections of the tongue. "Textural" notes are provided when meaningful. Particular attention has been given to the ending sensations (finish) and the aftertaste.

Whenever it was suspected that a sample had been mishandled or was otherwise different from that which the manufacturer intended, additional samples were obtained and the beer retasted. If a "good" sample could not be obtained after three separate efforts to do so, the report of such may be regarded as a valid reflection of the beer as you can expect to find it in America, but not necessarily of that beer under the proper conditions or in its country of origin.

Beers are reported under their country of origin and, within that classification, listed by manufacturer. Where information on the company was available, it is provided in brief. Corporate names are given when known, as well as data on marketing area, distribution, and brand history.

With a very few exceptions, all the beers reported herein were tasted in packaged form; that is, in can or bottle. Some beers are known to be far inferior in package form than on draft. One notable example of this is Iron City. Even company literature makes that note. However, I know of no beer that is better in a can or bottle than on draft. We who like to enjoy a beer at home should be grateful that there are recipes and techniques for beer making that enable brewers *very nearly* to produce a beer in package that equals the same product on draft. My home is so much more comfortable than most of the dingy bars we have available in this country that I am more than willing to put up with the slight loss of flavor.

In reaching out to the far corners of the country for the obscure regional brands, it could be that many brands were tasted under circumstances to their disadvantage. Brewers know that each recipe has a limited shelf life, and for most of the lighter pilseners the generally agreed figure is three months. For some of the very light brews, however, the viable peak performance period may be as short as a few weeks. Thus the Van Merritt and Hudepohl that performed so poorly in our trials could be quite good if tasted from a fresher source. The fault conceivably could lie in the length of time it took for me to obtain the beer and subject it to the taste panel. Also, the poor performance could mean that the beer is very fragile, and it is not uncommon to obtain "defective" samples close to origin. Probably the day will come when the can or label of your beer will bear a production date so that you can be reasonably assured of freshness, but very few do it now. Coors does, and in doing so qualifies for my vote as the brewer with the most conscience and greatest pride in the quality of product.

If, in performing your own taste teşts, you come up with results substantially different from those reported herein, I would appreciate learning of them. Although alteration in recipes is relatively rare, brewers do adjust them to the ideas of marketing personnel. And brewing techniques are in a constant state of flux. A change in the master brewer at a facility can have a significant effect on the entire product line.

In the future, I hope to continue the testing effort until every product available in North America is scrutinized. And there is no reason why everyone interested cannot participate.

United States of America

The earliest settlers in America brought with them a thirst for malt beverages and as soon as there were communities, there were brewhouses. Since they also brought with them the Puritan ethic, the production and the dispensing of malt beverages were highly regulated from the very start.

As the first arrivals were English, the first brews were ales, and brewing in America followed closely the evolution of malt brewing in the United Kingdom. Early in the nineteenth century, immigrants from the European continent began to arrive in great numbers. They thirsted for the beers of their tradition. As might be expected, among them were men who had the know-how to produce these brews. These new Americans tended to settle in ethnic pockets and thus instantly created a viable market for the brews they favored. Pennsylvania and Wisconsin still contain such pockets, having their own regional tastes satisfied by small independent brewers.

In the beginning the brews were all top-fermented and of four basic styles: ale, porter, stout, and Weiss (for the rapidly growing German population). By 1840, the majority of American brewers were of German origin and closely following the development of their art as practiced in their native land. When bottom-fermented brews were introduced, American brewers were quick to join in. Always at the forefront of the technology of the time, the American brewers converted their plants or built new facilities to produce the new lager. They were also the first to employ artificial refrigeration on a grand scale.

Except for the West Coast, where ice and refrigeration were unavailable (and where steam beer was developed as a workable and popular alternative), the new lager caught on rapidly. It soon began to supplant the traditional ales in the American culture. The popularity of the brews gave the industry a tremendous boost. With the rapidly growing population, over four thousand breweries were operating in the United States by centennial year 1876.

As an outgrowth of that Puritan ethic (which was big on denial), there had always been a strong temperance movement in America. Since all aspects of alcoholic beverages had been regulated from the very beginning, widespread drunkenness had never been a problem in the U.S. as it had elsewhere, but this did not deter the zeal of the temperance folk.

That some states would vote for Prohibition was inevitable, for even today there are large pieces of "dry" real estate in the country. It is doubtful, however, if national Prohibition would have occurred without the shortage of grain and (more important) the strong anti-German sentiment as a result of World War I.

National Prohibition became effective on 16 January 1920, one year after the thirty-sixth state legislature ratified the Eighteenth Amendment to the Constitution. States usually went dry, however, as they ratified the amendment, some as early as 1918. The Eighteenth Amendment banned the manufacture and sale of intoxicating beverages and the Volstead Act passed by Congress declared that any beverage containing more than one half of one percent alcohol was intoxicating.

Prohibition lasted thirteen years and history records it as a disaster for temperance. It was unpopular, unworkable, and unenforceable. It established a financial base for organized crime in America that guaranteed its existence unto perpetuity. During Prohibition more people were involved

An early example of Budweiser print advertising

in the manufacture and sale of alcoholic beverages than in any other period in the history of the world. Most breweries stayed alive throughout the thirteen years by producing the malt, yeast, and ice needed by the millions of home brewers.

When the nation had had enough, 3.2 percent beer was legalized by the Cullen-Harrison Act, which simply raised the definition of *nonintoxicating* to that level. This bill was passed by Congress and signed by President Roosevelt on 7

Massacre made military and advertising history – Custer's last fight, the Sioux massacre of the 7th Cavalry at Little Big Horn, took place June 25, 1876. The same year, Adolphus Busch introduced Budweiser, the brew that would go on to become the largest selling beer in the world. By coincidence and uncanny marketing instinct, Busch acquired the right to this now-classic painting of the slaughter. In 1895, Busch commissioned F. Otto Becker, a Milwaukee artist, to copy the work for lithographic reproduction. Anheuser-Busch made one million prints of the painting. Most of them were displayed in American saloons, and were credited as an early breakthrough in mass marketing and product merchandising – one of many that paralleled the rise of Budweiser.

April 1933. It essentially ended Prohibition for the breweries, which reopened, producing "3.2" for an eager public. But of the thousands shut down by Prohibition, only some seven hundred fifty breweries reopened, and many of those rested on badly weakened financial foundations.

Following World War II came a drastic change in American beer-drinking habits. Whereas most beer drinking before the war had taken place at the neighborhood taproom, Americans now wanted their beer at home. In 1948 television was introduced to the public at large and by 1952 most families had a set. For the next ten years few of them left their homes except to work or obtain provisions. Movie theaters died by the scores, and taprooms survived only because of regulars who would watch their TV from the bar. The packaged-beer industry followed and was here to stay. The beer can, which appeared in 1935 but was deemed only a fad item for ten years, came into its own and soon was augmented by the nonreturnable bottle, which first showed up in quantity in 1953.

Television's impact on American beer drinking went beyond the packaging considerations, however. National advertising gave an edge to those who chose to take the expensive gamble. Packaged beer had become a supermarket item, and the housewife who included beer on the shopping list tended rather to buy the more familiar well-advertised national brand than the local regional brew. Regional brewers were less efficient in production, had higher distribution costs, and were (in general) less well known to this new beer customer.

The formula for success in the industry was clear to many, and the brewing giants of today made their well-considered moves. They increased the advertising budgets to all media, with advertising costs often exceeding beer production and distribution costs. They expanded nationally to reduce distribution expenses and thus were able to offer their brands at a price even with or below that of local competitors. Regional independent breweries folded or were absorbed at a furious rate. Fortunately, many of the better regional labels have been continued by their new owners.

One aspect of this upheaval, one of great concern to the true lover of beer in America, is that mediocrity has been steadily overtaking the product line of most U.S. brewing firms. More and more, corn and rice adjuncts are being used to produce brews that cost less to make, while more and more money is being spent to convince the public that these tasteless beers are not only good, but a virtue as well. The American taste, used to soft drinks, a habit arising from a generation of Prohibition, accepts the products under the constant urging of the TV, which promotes lightness and mediocrity as a virtue in malt beverages.

The beers introduced in the past decade are very pale, have fewer and fewer calories, and less and less flavor. They are beers for people who really don't like beer. They would

Budweiser

At the Top
Because of Quality and Purity

Bottled with crowns or
corks only at the Home
Plant in St. Louis

The Anheuser-Busch Brewery

Covers an area of 140 acres of ground, equal to 70 city
blocks, upon which are located 110 individual buildings.

CAPACITY			TRANSPORTATION FACILITIES		
Brewing Capacity	-	2,500,000 barrels per year	Refrigerator freight cars	-	1,500
Malting Capacity	-	2,000,000 bushels per year	Horses at home plant	-	143
Bottling Works	-	1,000,000 bottles daily	Wagons at home plant	-	78
Grain Storage Elevators	1,750,000 bushels		Auto Trucks at home plant	-	74
Stockhouses (for lagering)	600,000 barrels		Horses at Branches	-	483
Steam Power Plant	-	12,000 horse power	Wagons at Branches	-	430
Electric Power Plant	-	4,000 horse power	Auto Trucks at Branches	-	41
Refrigerator Plant	-	4,000 tons per day			
Ice Plants	-	1,200 tons per day	EMPLOYES		
Coal used	-	325 tons per day	At St. Louis Plant	6,000 people
FREIGHT			At 36 Branches	1,500 people
Inbound and outbound	-	50,000 cars per year			

Total Sales, 1911—1,527,832 Barrels
Budweiser Bottled Beer Sales, 1911—173,184,600 Bottles

The King – even then

really rather have soda pop in a container that was recognizable as being beer.

Despite the trend, excellent beers are still available in America today. The standard-bearers of the giants are usually at least acceptable as beer. Some, like Budweiser and Michelob, are very good, and scattered about the country are excellent regional brews like Perfection from Horlacher, Augsburger from Huber, and Maximus Super from West End. These should be tasted by all serious beer drinkers, and if enjoyable, supported by their trade lest they should disappear from the scene.

Anchor Brewing Co.
(San Francisco, Calif.)

The original Anchor Brewery in Oakland, California, was founded in 1894 by Charles H. Kramm. Only steam beer was produced there beginning in 1896. The present Anchor Brewery (or Steam Beer Brewing Co., as it is called on the labels—Treasury Bulletin ATF P 5130.1 lists it as Anchor) continues the steam-beer tradition alone of all American breweries.

Up to 1965 steam beer was produced only for draft service, but since then it has been sold in bottles that require refrigeration. The president and brewmaster is the energetic Fritz Maytag, who has made his mark with excellent cheese (Maytag Dairy Farms of Newton, Iowa—try their blue, it is super) and who has dabbled in California premium wines (Ridge, I believe).

The five-thousand-barrel annual capacity of this small brewery (next to the smallest in the country) is marketed almost solely on the West Coast, the exception being a test market in New Jersey.

Unfortunately, the New Jersey batch sat in a warehouse for the better part of two years while some marketing wrinkle was being worked out, and we feel those samples were adversely affected by old age. We tried several bottles from different stores with similar (and progressively worse) results, which contradicted the fine reputation of the beer from West Coast trials conducted in the same time frame. In late 1977 we were provided samples that were supposed to be newly arrived on the East Coast, but the results were not really better; probably we have never sampled an "unharmed" bottle. What is reported below is what you can expect in New Jersey:

ANCHOR STEAM BEER—deep tawny brown color with red hues, foamy texture, malty piquant aroma, big intense malty flavor, too sweet on the perfumy side, similar to some ales, flavor carries through the finish with a bit too much persistence. Second trials found a similar result but with an additional bitter backtaste that came through very strongly in the finish. At a later test, the aroma had degraded to a smell like a damp basement, and the bitter overtones had become sour and metallic, particularly in the finish. The best of the above was the first tasted in late 1976, the worst was the last tasted in late 1977. There is good reason to believe that the bottle tasted was going over the hill, as was true of the two bottles sampled subsequently A fresh bottle obtained in San Francisco in early 1978 was tasted and found to be exactly like the first one tasted above.

ANCHOR PORTER—opaque deep brown, foamy-creamy texture, rich burnt coffee-malt aroma, short on body, mostly just bitterness on the palate, poorly balanced, and seemingly artificial. This could be too old as well.

Anheuser-Busch, Inc.
(St. Louis, Mo.; Newark, N.J.; Los Angeles, Calif.; Tampa, Fla.; Houston, Tex.; Columbus, Ohio; Jacksonville, Fla.; Merrimack, N.H.; Williamsburg, Va.; Fairfield, Calif.)

In 1850 a primitive brewery was established in St. Louis by a Mr. Schneider. He was succeeded shortly after by the firm of Hammer & Urban. This business failed in 1857 and the principal creditor, Eberhard Anheuser, bought the plant and continued the business with moderate success. In 1865 Anheuser's son-in-law, Adolphus Busch, bought an interest in E. Anheuser & Co. In 1873 the firm was incorporated as the E. Anheuser & Co. Brewing Association, Anheuser was president, and Busch was secretary and general manager.

Ten years later the name was changed to the Anheuser-

Early horseless vans made for more efficient delivery of Budweiser early in the 20th century.

Busch Brewing Association. When Anheuser died in 1880, Busch became president. Under Busch the business developed very rapidly. Year after year, new structures were added to keep pace with ever-increasing sales. By the turn of the century, the brewing plant covered sixty acres, the equivalent of some sixty city blocks in St. Louis. Annual production stood at one million barrels by 1900 and the company operated its own railroad and had forty-two branches in various cities.

Today Anheuser-Busch is the world's largest brewer, with 29.1 million barrels produced in 1976 (35.2 million in 1975, a world's record) and for the twentieth consecutive year led the brewing industry in sales. Under the continuing leadership of the Busch family, the company continues to expand and modernize. Its shipping capacity of forty-two million barrels exceeds that of the next largest brewer by fifteen million barrels.

Since 1951 Anheuser-Busch has developed a coast-to-coast system of breweries which has worked great econo-

One of Adolphus Busch's original "Budweiser Girls." He was always aware of the primary market for his Budweiser.

An array of the "best beer" medallions won by Budweiser between 1876 and 1904 in competition at major expositions against beers from throughout the world.

mies on their expansion across the American market. The expansion began in 1951 with construction of the Newark, New Jersey, plant. Later, Los Angeles (1954) and Tampa (1959) were added. The late 1960s saw a rapid expansion with Houston (1966), Columbus (1968), and Jacksonville (1969) being added. New England obtained an Anheuser-Busch facility (and the famous Budweiser Clydesdales) in 1970 with the opening of the Merrimack (N.H.) plant. The latest additions have been Williamsburg in 1972 and Fairfield (Calif.) in 1976, the latter not reaching full production capability until 1977. The largest plant is still the St. Louis facility (the original but greatly expanded plant), which has an annual production capacity in excess of ten million barrels.

Anheuser-Busch commands about twenty percent of the American market, and a great deal of that is because of the popularity of its primary brand, Budweiser—the king of beers. Budweiser was introduced in 1876, but Anheuser-Busch did not obtain the rights to the name until 1891. Until that time, the label belonged to Carl Conrad, who, with Adolphus Busch, had developed the formula. Anheuser-Busch brewed Budweiser, but Conrad bottled and sold it.

Anheuser-Busch has never compromised the quality of the original Budweiser formula. Only the purest of natural ingredients are used and have been listed on the label long before it was popular to do so or required by law. The recipe calls for the more expensive Western two-row barley, pure hops (rather than extract), rice adjunct, natural carbonation through krausening, and "beechwood chip aging" for a full

One of Adolphus Busch's "calling cards." He bestowed these and other ornate promotional curios on friends and strangers alike to create awareness of and an image of his prized beer. A look in the peep hole, right, revealed the image of Adolphus himself. The original artifacts now are rare and valuable.

Brewing milestones – August A. Busch, Jr. and August A. Busch III observe Anheuser-Busch production of ten (upper left), 30 (lower left) and 20 (right) million barrels in a single year, most of it Budweiser, in these historic photos. Anheuser-Busch was the first brewer to reach each plateau – in 1964, 1970 and 1974, respectively. Mr. Busch, Jr. is now chairman of the company's Board of Directors. Mr. Busch III is president and chief executive officer.

month. Beechwood chip aging is a process of lagering in tanks containing a lattice of beechwood strips to clarify the brew and to absorb bitterness. All this means a more costly but better-brewed product, one that is famous the world over. Budweiser is brewed in all Anheuser-Busch plants, and production of draft Budweiser in quarter barrels has recently resumed.

Another product of Anheuser-Busch is the famous Michelob, introduced as a draft beer in 1896. It was originally a high-malt beer, but since 1961, when it became available in bottles, rice has been used as a means of lightening the flavor. The quality of Michelob is no less than that of Budweiser; only the choicest ingredients, including only imported hops, are used. The bottled and canned product is different from the unpasteurized brew kegged for draft service, being lighter and having less zest. Many feel that draft Michelob is the finest beer produced in America, and to an earlier generation, it enjoyed a mystique much as Coors does today. The youthful beer drinkers of the late 1940s and the 1950s would often travel to another town where Michelob was available. Today Michelob is produced in all Anheuser-Busch plants except Tampa.

Other Anheuser-Busch products include Busch Bavarian and the new Natural Light and Classic Dark beers. Bavarian, popular in the South, was introduced in 1955. It is made with corn grits as an adjunct but is otherwise brewed like Budweiser. It is produced only in St. Louis, Los Angeles, Tampa, Jacksonville, and Columbus. Natural Light was introduced in early 1977 in several test markets to compete in the low-calorie segment of the market. As with the other products, only natural ingredients and processes are employed in making Natural Light. It is made in St. Louis, Williamsburg, Columbus, Los Angeles, Houston, and Tampa. The new Classic Dark draft beer was introduced in 1976. It is produced in all plants except Tampa and Merrimack.

Anheuser-Busch has a long history of successful advertising that has made its mark on American life. Most Americans are familiar with the Budweiser Clydesdales and earlier generations sang the words "Come, come, drink some Budweiser, under the Anheuser bush." In 1976 a theme developed for a commercial on radio and TV became a hit recording. In this decade, family memories of many Americans include Anheuser-Busch from days spent at Busch Gardens amusement parks in Tampa (the "Dark Continent"), Williamsburg (the "Old Country"), and Los Angeles.

Anheuser-Busch also produces baker's yeast, syrups, and starches (for the paper industry), and whereas many breweries may support local professional athletic teams, Anheuser-Busch owns the St. Louis Cardinals baseball team. Number One is a big, big company.

BUDWEISER LAGER BEER—pale, light but good malty hop aroma, good hop and malt flavor, very well balanced, a dry, good-tasting finish. Certainly one of the best of the big national brands, if not the best.

MICHELOB BEER—golden color, hops notable in the aroma, smooth and beautifully balanced, good body, fine hop-malt taste, finely balanced aftertaste with hops remaining only faintly. An excellent beer and worthy choice for serious beer drinkers. The draft version is similar but better.

MICHELOB LIGHT—134 calories, rather high for a lo-cal, light color, fragrant malty aroma, highly carbonated but the bubbles are small, good tasting light malty flavor with plenty of character, good finish of medium duration. Maybe it is the calories that make a beer taste good.

BUSCH BAVARIAN—pale yellow color, faintly sweet aroma, sweet malty flavor that fades rapidly. Good for hot weather thirst quenching but stick to "Bud" for flavor and depth.

ANHEUSER NATURAL LIGHT—pale color, faint yeasty nose, very faint malty taste, almost no flavor, no aftertaste.

Blitz-Weinhard Co.
(Portland, Oreg.)

Henry Weinhard was born in Lindenbrom, Wurttemberg, Germany, in 1830. After learning the brewing trade in Stuttgart, he migrated to the U.S. in 1851. First employed in breweries in Philadelphia, Cincinnati, and St. Louis, he settled down as foreman of the Muench Brewery in Vancouver, Washington. In 1859 he purchased the brewery and continued the Henry Weinhard Brewery until 1864, when he sold out and moved to Portland. In 1862 Weinhard had formed a brewing partnership with George Bottler in Portland. In 1866 Weinhard became sole proprietor.

Arnold Blitz appeared on the scene in 1909, when he purchased the Portland Brewery, a Weinhard competitor. The present company of Blitz-Weinhard was formed in 1928 when the two firms merged. Today, Blitz-Weinhard is the

oldest continuously operating brewery west of the Mississippi.

Blitz-Weinhard has stayed alive in the highly competitive brewing industry by segmenting its products for tiny niches in the market and by keeping its costs low. With annual sales of 850,000 barrels, Blitz offers five different labels, including a light, a dark, a malt, and its most recent offering, a premium called Henry Weinhard's Private Reserve.

Costs for labor have been held to three cents per can (compared to fifteen cents for some other companies); Blitz avoids excessive advertising costs, relying on customers to pass the word.

Blitz labels and cans can be obtained from ESP, Inc., 1629 Vancouver Way, Livermore, Calif. 94550.

BLITZ-WEINHARD BEER—dull malty aroma, highly carbonated, salty flavor.

OLD ENGLISH 800 MALT LIQUOR—a strange "pop" drink much like Malt Duck. It has a weird aromatic flavor that lasts interminably and is not done well at all. The brand began as Olde English 600 made by the Bohemian Brewing Co. of Spokane. It has been made for the East Coast market in various locations (Newark and Cleveland) and is presently being made in Philadelphia by Henry F. Ortlieb.

TIVOLI LIGHT PREMIUM BEER—very pale color, faintly skunky-brackish aroma, brackish flavor, bitter in the finish, aftertaste weak and salty-sour, a poor performer. The Tivoli label originated with the Tivoli Brewing Co. of Denver and was made later by Falstaff of San Francisco.

BUFFALO PREMIUM LAGER BEER (made by Blitz-Weinhard for the Buffalo Brewing Co. of Sacramento)—aroma of brackish water, dull salty flavor. Label claims that Buffalo was established in 1890 in Sacramento. *100 Years of Brewing* says that Buffalo was incorporated in 1888 and produced its first brew in 1890. Buffalo beer was once a big seller in California and Nevada and enjoyed additional success as an export to Central America, China, and the Philippines. It has appeared under the Buffalo corporate name (1939) and that of the Southern Brewing Co. of Los Angeles (1950).

HENRY WEINHARD'S PRIVATE RESERVE BEER (Bottling No. 10)—medium to light gold, light hoppy aroma, hoppy flavor, light body, nothing after the initial burst of flavor.

HENRY WEINHARD'S PRIVATE RESERVE BEER (Bottling No. 15)—light gold, light hoppy aroma but more than above, nose overall more intense, less hops in the flavor, a little bit sweeter, and lasts longer (a longer-lasting finish and more of an aftertaste).

Carling National Breweries, Inc.
(Baltimore, Md.; Baltimore-Highlandtown, Md.; Belleville, Ill.; Frankenmuth, Mich.; Phoenix, Ariz.; Tacoma, Wash.)

The Carling origins of this firm are found in London, Ontario, Canada, where Thomas Carling founded a brewery in 1840 (see Canada, Carling O'Keefe, Ltd.). Carling products appeared in the United States in 1933 with Black Label

Beer and Red Cap Ale produced in Cleveland. Expansion began in 1954 with the addition of a plant in Belleville, Illinois. The International Breweries, Inc. plant in Frankenmuth, Michigan, was added in 1955. A plant was built in Natick, Massachusetts, in 1956 and another erected in Atlanta in 1958. The West Coast was reached in 1958 with the acquisition of the Heidelberg Brewing Co. in Tacoma. And in Baltimore a plant was established in 1961.

The National Brewery was built in 1872 and was so named in 1885 when it became part of the firm of Joseph L. Straus & Brother. In 1899 it was one of sixteen breweries that formed the Maryland Brewing Co. with the then massive annual production capacity of 1.5 million barrels. In 1901 eight of the sixteen breweries were closed in a reorganization that renamed the syndicate the Gottlieb-Baurenschmidt-Straus Brewing Co., and one of the surviving plants was the National Brewery.

Before joining Carling, National had also begun an extensive expansion program with plants in Detroit and Saginaw, Michigan, and in Phoenix.

Carling National is a subsidiary of Carling O'Keefe, Ltd. of Toronto, operating six plants, including two in the Baltimore area. Annual brewing capacity is listed as 6.9 million barrels. The current product line for each plant is given as follows:

Baltimore (Beltway)—Black Label, Tuborg Gold, Red Cap Ale.

Baltimore (Highlandtown)—National Bohemian, Colt .45 Malt Liquor, Malt Duck, Van Lauter, National Premium. This is the old National Brewery.

Belleville—Tuborg Gold, Columbia, Black Label, Stag, Colt .45, Malt Duck. This is the former Griesedieck–Western Brewing Co. plant.

Frankenmuth—Black Label, Tuborg Gold, Colt .45, Altes.

Phoenix—Dutch Treat, Colt .45, Van Lauter, A-1. This is the former Arizona Brewing Co. and Dutch Treat Brewing Co. facility.

Tacoma—Columbia, Black Label, Heidelberg, Tuborg Gold, Colt .45. This is the former Heidelberg–Columbia Brewing Co. plant.

The Detroit plant (the old Tivoli Brewing Co. plant from 1897 to 1948, then the Altes Brewing Co., and finally the National Detroit Brewery) was closed in 1973. The Miami facility (formerly the American Brewing Co.) was shut down in 1974 and Carling's young modern plant in Natick Massachusetts, closed its doors in 1977. The original Carling plant in Cleveland is now operated by C. Schmidt & Sons, Inc., of Philadelphia.

Carling Brewing Co. The Carling products, Black Label Beer and Red Cap Ale, date back to 1840 in their Canadian heritage. Although they had been available as imports, both appeared as U.S. domestic brews in the 1940s, being produced in Cleveland, by the Brewing Corporation of America, which later became part of the Carling Brewing Co. Today Black Label is produced in four Carling National breweries in the United States, in ten Carling O'Keefe breweries across Canada, and in England by Bass Worthington as Carling Black Label Lager. Red Cap Ale is not sold as extensively, being made at only one U.S. plant and at three Canadian breweries.

CARLING 71 LIGHT PILSENER—pale gold, almost no aroma, light and watery, very little flavor, unbalanced, slightly bitter and sour aftertaste. Contains 71 calories, 3.2 percent alcohol.

CARLING'S BLACK LABEL BEER—pale gold color, big head, big malty hop aroma, some hops in the flavor, good balance, better than average, good at its price.

CARLING'S ORIGINAL RED CAP ALE—deep gold color with tawny tones, big malt-hop aroma, strongly flavored, big body, bittersweet style, good of type, may be a bit too strongly flavored for those who are used to pilsener types of beer, similar to some of the true malt liquors.

STAG BEER (Stag Brewery)—clean fresh aroma, good body, big flavor at the start, family resemblance to Black Label quite noticeable, big head. Originally appeared in 1851 as a brand of Griesedieck-Western.

COLUMBIA EXTRA MELLOW PALE BREW BEER—
flowery malty aroma, foamy with small bubbles, watery
weak body, not much flavor.

HEIDELBERG ALL NATURAL BEER—extremely faint
nose, almost none at all, faint malt and hop flavor, light
body but not watery, sort of flat and no finish.

National Brewing Co. National Bohemian, first brewed in
1885 in "the land of pleasant living," and National Premium have been continuously produced in Baltimore since repeal, and with expansion they were also made in National
plants in Michigan, Arizona, and Florida, according to
package labels. Today these two beers are produced only in
Baltimore, the center of their market. Brands acquired in
the National expansion usually continued to be produced
"in place" for their established market, except for A-1 and
Altes, which were made for a brief time in Baltimore, and
Van Lauter, which was made earlier in Detroit and Phoenix.
A Colt Beer and Colt .45 Stout Malt Liquor were in the National repertoire in recent years, but are no longer marketed.

A-1 LIGHT PILSNER BEER—medium gold, appetizing

malt aroma, malty taste with some zest, medium body, somewhat filling.

NATIONAL BOHEMIAN LIGHT BEER—good clean malty aroma, sprightly clean taste, some underlying sweetness, good finish, good balance throughout, no offensive features. Good beer at a good price, but may be light-bodied for some palates. Very good for the type.

NATIONAL PREMIUM PALE DRY BEER—good malty aroma, pleasant taste with a slight hop flavor, good balance, pleasant aftertaste.

COLT .45 MALT LIQUOR—very malty aroma, too sugary sweet taste, heavy body, strong but sweet, like most American malt liquors.

VAN LAUTER BAVARIAN LAGER BEER (Van Lauter Brewery)—pleasant malty nose, light-bodied, moderately pleasant flavor, not much character or zest.

ALTES GOLDEN LAGER BEER—supposedly reminiscent of the "Fassbier" (kegged lager beer) of Germany, Altes has a light clean malty aroma, a pleasant malty slightly sweet

taste, and a reasonable lingering fresh tasting finish. Altes was originally a product of the Tivoli Brewing Co. and later, in 1948, of the successor company, the Altes Brewing Co. It first appeared under the National label in 1955.

Tuborg Breweries, Ltd. Tuborg is produced by Carling National under license and authority of Tuborg Breweries, Ltd., of Copenhagen. Tuborg beer has been produced in Denmark since 1873 and marketed worldwide. It was the first European brand beer to be produced in the United States. Tuborg Beer is no longer listed in the Carling National literature and seems to have been replaced with Tuborg Gold, a new package offered in 1977. At the time the taste trials began both Tuborgs were available and included.

TUBORG BEER—medium gold color, good hopped nose and flavor, clean yet complex, lingering well-balanced pleasant aftertaste. A very good beer but not up to the quality of the Danish version. Two-row barley from European strains, corn grits, and domestic and imported hops are used. It is a bargain at its price.

TUBORG GOLD EXPORT QUALITY BEER—light gold color, hops faintly in the aroma, light faintly sweet taste, very pleasant lingering finish. Similar to and as good as the Tuborg Beer described above. Probably the same recipe.

Champale, Inc.
(Trenton, N.J., and Norfolk, Va.)

Champale, America's most widely advertised malt liquor, is produced in New Jersey by Champale, Inc., on the site of the former premises of the Peoples Brewing Co. of Trenton, and by Champale Products Corp. of Norfolk, in the old Jacob Ruppert (and Century Brewing Co.) plant. When Champale was first introduced, the corporate name of the brewery was the Metropolis Brewing Co. of Trenton, New Jersey.

At Trenton, Champale, Pink Champale, Metbrew (a near beer from Metropolis), and Black Horse Ale are produced. Former products included Cherry Hill Beer (still being produced by the Metropolis Brewing Co. of Trenton) and Trenton Old Stock Ale, but according to Champale, Inc., these are no longer in their product line. The Norfolk facility produces only Champale for the southern and southeastern markets.

SPARKLING CHAMPALE EXTRA DRY MALT LIQUOR—pale gold color, sweet aroma, sweet almost cloying taste; tries to hard to be like Champagne and fails to be either beer or champagne. As a malt liquor, it is of a very winy style, and there are several better.

PINK CHAMPALE FLAVORED MALT LIQUOR—artifically colored a pale pink, artificially flavored (strawberry?) as well; aroma like a Cold Duck, which I suppose it is imitating; sweet taste, brief finish. Much like a pop wine.

BLACK HORSE ALE (Black Horse Brewery of New Jersey, Champale, Inc., Trenton, N.J., a subsidiary of Iroquois Brands, Ltd.)—cloudy deep yellow-brown color, robust English style, excellent burnt caramel flavor, excellent balance, long pleasing finish. A smooth beer yet one with great character. Best domestic ale tasted and a low-priced bargain. This label sells quite well in the New England and Middle Atlantic States areas. It is also made in upstate New York by the Koch Brewery. A Black Horse Ale was originally seen in Canada and today's U.S. Black Horse may be a descendant of the Black Horse of Dow's of Montreal and Toronto. The Black Horse of Canada was widely marketed in the northeastern U.S. in the 1940s, and in the 1950s a Black Horse Ale was made in one of the Lawrence, Massachusetts, brewing plants. The current Black Horse bears the same logo as the one that was years earlier made in Lawrence.

CHERRY HILL PREMIUM BEER (Metropolis Brewery of Trenton, N.J.)—dusty vegetal nose, lots of flavor with good hop-malt balance in the middle, flawed at the end with a bitter finish. Sells fairly well with regional customers in the Cherry Hill–Willingboro, New Jersey, area south of Trenton. Marketed in returnable bottles only, at a very low price. Although Champale has written to say that it no longer produces this beer, the returnable cases are marked Champale, Inc.

Cold Spring Brewing Co.
(Cold Spring, Minn.)

"Ist Das Nicht Ein Schnitzel Bank? Ja, Das ist. Ein Schnitzel Bank!" Or Schweiger Mutter, Grosse Stein, and (of course) Kegle Brau—and so goes the Cold Spring promotional piece.

The Cold Spring Brewing Co. had its origins in a plant constructed by a George (or Michael) Sargel, who began brewing lager beer there in 1874. The business was incorporated by John Oster, Ferdinand Peters, and a Canadian brewmaster named Eugene Hermanutz in 1900. It was reincorporated in 1930, still under the control of the Peters and Oster families. In 1942 Myron C. Johnson was brought in to run the company and two years later he acquired it. With Mr. Johnson's energetic efforts, this small independent annually sells over fifty thousand barrels amidst an industry of giants.

About ninety percent of its output is marketed in Minnesota, but some is sold in Wisconsin, Iowa, and the Dakotas. The primary brand is Cold Spring Beer, available in both cans and bottles. A premium Kegle Brau is marketed in cans and returnable bottles. Kegle, the German word for bowling, ties in with a major Cold Spring promotional effort, "Johnson's Cold Spring 'Kegle' Handicap Bowling Tournament."

Popular-priced brands include Northern (acquired from the Northern Brewing Co. of Superior, Wis.), Western (acquired from Dakota Brewing Co. of Bismarck, N. Dak.), Arrowhead, and Minnesota 13. All except the last are available in both cans and bottles. Minnesota 13 is available only in returnable bottles; it supposedly recalls a beverage of Prohibition days made secretly by Minnesota residents.

Cold Spring also brews a German-style beer according to an old formula supplied by the Amana Colony of Amana, Iowa. It is labeled Gemeinde Brau (Gemeinde meaning community). It is a private label owned by Paul Zimmerman of Amana and is brewed especially for the community. By special arrangement, Gemeinde Brau does have some limited "outside" availability.

Although not mentioned in literature provided by the company, additional Cold Spring products have been found in the Minneapolis—St. Paul area. These brands include North Star XXX, White Label, Fox de Luxe, Karlsbrau Old Time Beer, and a Cold Spring version of Billy Beer released in early 1978.

In accordance with Minnesota law, beer is available in 3.2 percent and regular (called Strong) alcoholic content. All Cold Spring products sampled were in the Strong category.

Cold Spring also handles the distribution of Schlitz products for the central Minnesota area.

COLD SPRING STRONG—malty aroma, clean spring-water taste through to the finish, somewhat on the mild side, clean, and very drinkable.

KEGLE BRAU (the classic beer)—very faint slightly sweet aroma, tastes like sour sparkling water with a faintly sweet foretaste, and bears some family resemblance to Cold Spring.

WHITE LABEL—faint malty apple aroma, very little flavor at all. White Label was produced previously by White Label Co., Minneapolis, Storz of Omaha, and Kiewel Brewing Co. of Little Falls, Minnesota.

FOX de LUXE BEER—clean aroma and very fruity like an apple wine, apple-beer flavor, tangy flavor but watery otherwise, very much like a soda pop and finishes with an artificial sweetness. This label has knocked around the Midwest for some time, made by Fox de Luxe Brewing Co. of Marion, Indiana, and Grand Rapids, Michigan; Fox Head of Waukesha, Wisconsin; Peter Fox Brewing Co. of Chicago; and the Fox Head division of G. Heileman, LaCrosse, Wisconsin. It was not listed in recent Cold Spring literature, but was found in Minneapolis in late 1977 under its label.

GEMEINDE BRAU—aroma of slightly fermented apples with a pilsener-like background, very good malty hop classic pilsener flavor up front, but after several sips, the taste tends to flatten out and the brew finishes a bit watery.

NORTH STAR XXX—strong vegetal aroma with an apple background, light pilsener flavor with a slight ferruginous character, spring-water finish. This is another well-known Midwest label previously produced by Jacob Schmidt of St. Paul, G. Heileman Co., Mathie Huber Brewing Co. of Wausau, Wisconsin, and Northern Brewing Co. of Superior, Wisconsin.

BILLY BEER—bright gold, sweet malt aroma, light sweet flavor, a bit like a slightly malty spring water, neutral spring-water finish. Tastes like a typical Cold Spring product and certainly a recipe different from that of either the Falls City or the West End Billy Beer.

COLD BRAU EASTERN PREMIUM BEER—pale yellow color, light fresh malty aroma, refreshing spring-water taste, pleasant, very drinkable, low in hops. This brand belonged to Drewry's of South Bend, Indiana.

GLUEK FINEST PILSENER BEER—pale gold color, nice "beery" aroma with noticeable hops, well carbonated, sour flavor with a tangy astringent finish. This was a brand of the Gluek Brewing Co. of Minneapolis (see G. Heileman Brewing Co., Inc.).

NORTHERN BEER (also seen as Northern Premium Beer)—pale gold, faint sweet malt aroma, light sweet malt flavor with a faint sense of hops, a little too sweet. A former label of the Northern Brewing Co., Superior, Wisconsin.

KARLSBRAU OLD TIME BEER—pretty bright gold appearance, sour malt aroma, strong sour flavor, heavily carbonated, lingering sour finish. This label belonged to the Karlsbrau Brewing Co. of Duluth, Minnesota, went to G. Heileman, and thence to Cold Spring (in 1974).

ARROWHEAD BEER—very good sour typical pilsener aroma, good hops and malt, medium dry, clean tasting with a good balanced flavor, pleasant and very drinkable, brief finish.

Adolph Coors Co.
(Golden, Colo.)

If ever a beer had a mystique, it is Coors. The proponents of the beer will go to great lengths (and distances) to obtain it; the opponents sneer derisively and call it Colorado Kool-Aid. Whether you like it or not, the American brewing industry is impressed, for this one product gives Coors the No. 5 ranking in sales in the country and is the leading beer in sales in eleven Western states. The product is available everywhere, sometimes even against the wishes of the company.

Coors was founded in Golden in 1873 when the original Adolph Coors and Jacob Schueler converted an old tannery into a brewing plant. When Schueler sold out seven years later, the firm became Adolph Coors Golden Brewery. In 1913, the company was incorporated and today is America's largest brewery. Coors had to survive seventeen years of Prohibition as Colorado was the first state to vote dry in 1916. During that period Coors made near-beer, malted milk, and buttermilk and skim milk crystals.

Coors is manufactured using pure Rocky Mountain spring water, Coors' proprietary two-row Moravian III brewing barley—which Coors malts itself—rice (for a lighter body), and hops. The hops are used more for flavoring than for bittering and Coors has been importing a fragrant variety from Germany for that purpose. It hopes to convert to domestic hops by 1978 because of recent successes in the quality of home-grown hops. Absolutely no additives or corrective salts are used.

Coors' only product is Coors Banquet, packaged in kegs, cans, and bottles. Coors plans to be the first to package beer in plastic bottles if it can develop a method suitable for beer and conducive to highspeed production. A 3.2 percent Coors is also produced for states so regulated.

Coors is no longer pasteurized. In 1959 Coors began filling in aseptic conditions, even to the point of sterilizing the air entering the room. The operators of the equipment observe the sterilization techniques of a hospital, and sterile garments are worn in the filling room. These techniques obviate the need for pasteurization.

The beer so produced, however, must be kept refrigerated or it will rapidly decline in quality. The beer, aged for an average of forty-nine days, is chilled throughout the entire production process and emerges in its packages very near to the freezing point, which aids the distributors in keeping it cold on its way to the market.

For many years Coors was available only west of the Mississippi. The company felt it could not profitably market Coors so far from the plant because of the need to maintain a refrigerated condition. In the early 1970s, entrepreneurs decided to take advantage of the Coors mystique and truckloads of refrigerated Coors headed for the East Coast where the beer would be sold at unprecedented prices. Eager East

Coast buyers gladly laid down $4 or more for a sixpack, many times the prices in Colorado; in many instances, the beer had been mishandled.

It is understood that Adolph Coors took the matter to court and won his suit to limit the market of Coors to boundaries determined by the company. I view the case and victory for Coors as evidence that it is greatly concerned with making the finest product it can, and with assuring its customers that each purchase of Coors is a worthwhile one.

The Coors seen here on the East Coast has usually been mishandled. Few stores have the refrigeration capacity to keep back stock chilled, and I have seen many stores with a mountain of Coors cases sitting out on the floor without refrigeration and without the prospect of refrigeration for days or even weeks. All beer has a shelf life of finite duration. Every manufacturer knows that old stocks of beer, pasteurized or unpasteurized, do not taste as well as new, and many times reputable firms will trade new for old at stores to protect the good name of the brand. Lighter beers hold for a lesser time than heavier beers or ales. Coors is an extremely light beer and, even if pasteurized, might well be on the lower end of shelf-life expectancy. Since Coors is unpasteurized, it is mishandled if not refrigerated. It will spoil just like milk.

I have tasted Coors many times in Colorado and enjoyed it greatly. Only once did I find it to be of that quality on the East Coast. Coors that is three or four months old by the time it is tasted is a product much inferior to that freshly made, even if faithfully refrigerated.

In performing the Coors-Schmidt's test, I have to agree that, given the condition of Coors on the East Coast, Schmidt's is better. In one test even Old Frothingslosh was better, but the next time you are in Colorado try Coors for yourself. You may love it, or you may call it Colorado Kool-Aid. Even Coors Banquet purchased in New Jersey made the honors list in taste trials.

COORS BANQUET—very pale color, lovely fresh clean aroma, hops barely noticeable, light-bodied, slightly sweet flavor, very refreshing, very lightly flavored, very quaffable. Coors cans seen recently are of a new and apparently unique

Coors design using a press-tab lid. There are two nondetachable round closures; the smaller one is pressed first to relieve the pressure, and then the larger one (one-half-inch diameter) through which the beer is poured.

Dixie Brewing Co.
(New Orleans, La.)

Dixie is the last remaining independent regional brewer in operation in New Orleans. It produces Dixie Beer, Dixie Lager Beer (long aged in natural wooden vats), and Dixie Light, the most recent addition to the product line.

Dixie products are marketed only in the immediate vicinity of New Orleans and are rarely seen outside their normal marketing area. The beers are about average, pleasant with very light hop character, a refreshing brew that suits the regional tastes, similar to Pearl and Jax, the major Dixie competitors.

DIXIE BEER—pale, light beery aroma, slightly soapy, light-bodied, pleasant flavored, very lightly hopped, clean but without zest. Good chilled in hot weather, very quaffable.

Duncan Brewing Co.
(Auburndale, Fla.)

For some time I could not be sure that this brewery was still active. There was even one reference source that indicated it definitely was no longer in operation. Since there had been no response to letters, I assumed that Duncan had joined the list of defunct small independent breweries. But while on business in Florida, I drove out past Winter Haven and found the brewery in full operation.

The Duncan Brewing Co. was founded in 1973 by L. N. Duncan, formerly of the Queen City Brewing Co. of Cumberland, Maryland. The product line includes former Queen City brands Fischer's Ale and Beer, which are made for the Winn Dixie grocery chain, Master's Choice, made for the Albertson's grocery stores, Regal Premium Beer, a label owned by Carling National which Duncan makes only

for sale to distributors, and Dunk's German Style Beer, Duncan's own label.

Duncan brews and packages the beer but neither delivers nor distributes. Local retailers have to pick up supplies at the plant in Auburndale, and many find it easier simply to sell Pabst, Schlitz, and Busch, which are brought to their door.

FISCHER'S OLD GERMAN STYLE BEER—good malt aroma but on the faint side, heavily carbonated, metallic-malt flavor, flattens out rapidly after a very good start, bitterness in the aftertaste. It is a shame that it sags so badly in the middle and ends poorly, for the first taste is extremely good.

FISCHER'S OLD ENGLISH STYLE ALE—good fresh clean malty aroma, good hop flavor at the outset but it soon flattens out to a watery finish. It is not even remotely an English-style ale.

MASTER'S CHOICE BAVARIAN STYLE PREMIUM BEER—light color, slightly sour malty aroma, good hop-malt flavor with some character marred by a background metallic taste that became even stronger in the aftertaste.

DUNK'S GERMAN STYLE PREMIUM SELECT BEER—deep yellow color with a touch of brown, light sour malty nose, light hop-malt flavor with a metallic touch. Very similar to Master's Choice, but lighter.

Eastern Brewing Corporation
(Hammonton, N.J.)

If brewery size were reckoned by the number of brands produced rather than by annual sales, Eastern would be somewhere high in the top ten. Located in the southern New Jersey pine barrens, this company produces a wide variety of brands obtained from now defunct brewing firms over a wide area, plus many of the private labels marketed today. Some are marketed in Eastern's home state, but as many are marketed elsewhere and rarely seen in New Jersey. Should you try to seek them out your task will be further complicated by their use of many corporate names on the packages.

ABC PREMIUM BEER (Garden State Brewing Co.)—fresh clean malty aroma, very light flavor but with some hop character, finishes rather poorly, otherwise would be a delightful beer at a very low price. Previously produced by the August Wagner Brewing Co. of Columbus, Ohio, and the Gold Brau Brewing Co. of Chicago, this product appears now to be made for the ABC chain of liquor stores in Florida. It has been seen only in Florida, except for outlets specializing in sales of "odd" brands, perhaps for can collectors. The can design of ABC is identical to Gold Brau Brewing's 905 brand of twenty years ago, with the ABC replacing the 905. It is possible that it may be the same recipe as well.

ABC PREMIUM EXTRA DRY ALE (Garden State Brewing Co.)—supposedly slow brewed, according to the label, this is a pale clear brew, highly carbonated with small bubbles, with a faint aroma and very little flavor, totally harmless. Again, only seen in Florida. The Garden State name may have originated with the Garden State Brewing Co. of Belleville, New Jersey.

BILOW GARDEN STATE LIGHT BEER (Garden State Brewing Co.)—a cereal nose like Pablum (does anybody remember Pablum?), grainy cereal-barley taste with a very brief finish and no aftertaste. This beer is produced for the Bilow Liquor Stores chain in Monmouth County, New Jersey.

BLANCHARD'S QUALITY PRODUCT BEER (Waukee Brewing Co.)—light malty nose, clean and light malty taste and finish, maybe even with some hops if you think about it hard enough; no zest, no character. This must be what people mean when they speak of computerized beer—no zest, no faults, no anything. Made for Blanchard's Liquor Stores of the Greater Boston area. There was also an Eastern product made for the Kappy's chain of liquor stores in Massachusetts that tasted like this brew, called Kappy's Premium Light Beer. It has not been seen in a Kappy's in well over a year.

CANADIAN ACE BRAND PREMIUM BEER (Canadian Ace Brewing Co.)—very fragrant and malty, light sweet flavor, some hops noticeable in the finish. Reasonably good taste for an inexpensive beer. Seen recently only in half-gallon throwaway bottles with screw caps. This is the former product of Al Capone's Chicago brewery which operated as the Canadian Ace Brewing Co. of Chicago from 1948 to 1958.

CANADIAN ACE DRAFT BEER (Canadian Ace Brewing Co.)—very fragrant aroma but virtually no flavor at all, very foamy. This has also been seen only in half-gallon size NR bottles. Both Canadian Ace products have been seen in New York–New Jersey and New England.

DAWSON LAGER BEER (Dawson Brewing Co.)—strange chemical aroma with an oily "off" flavor. Presuming a bad bottle, I obtained additional lots in both can and bottle. The results were better but there was a chemical element to the nose and the taste was poorly balanced. This brew is marketed primarily in New England where it was originally produced by the Dawson Brewing Co. of New Bedford, Massachusetts, taken over by Rheingold in 1967. Later, Dawson was produced under the Dawson corporate name in Willimansett, Massachusetts, at the Hampden-Harvard-Drewry's-Piels Bros. plant.

FOXHEAD 400 BEER (Foxhead Brewing Co.)—pleasant malt aroma, good beery nose, good taste with zest and very good balance, an inexpensive good-tasting beer that is a super value. Very good with Chinese food. This product probably originated with the Fox-Head Waukesha Corp. of Waukesha, Wisconsin, then produced by Heileman at Sheboygan and by Widemann (for Heileman) at Newport, Kentucky.

FOXHEAD 400 DRAFT BREWED BEER (Foxhead Brewing Co.)—pale and clear, light clean malty aroma, very little flavor, mostly just light carbonation.

MILWAUKEE BRAND PREMIUM BEER (Waukee Brewing Co.)—a very cereal aroma, again like Pablum, but very light; flavor also cereal-like and light in intensity, with a brief finish. A dull beer.

MILWAUKEE BOCK BEER (Waukee Brewing Co.)—opaque brown, sourness briefly in an otherwise faint aroma, brief burnt malt flavor, and no follow-through.

OLD BOHEMIAN BEER (Eastern Brewing Co.)—slightly sour vegetal-malt aroma, slightly sweet taste, brief metallic finish, and aftertaste. The Old Bohemia product line is available in New York, New Jersey, Pennsylvania, but its greatest market is in Maryland, Delaware, and the District of Columbia, where it is sold at a low price.

OLD BOHEMIA ALE—clean malty aroma, light yeasty cardboard flavor, neutral watery finish.

OLD BOHEMIAN LIGHT BEER—pleasant sweet nose, too sweet metallic flavor, dull finish, very foamy.

OLD BOHEMIAN BOCK BEER—tawny brown color without much saturation, faint burnt malt aroma, hardly any flavor at all, just brown colored water.

OLD GERMAN BRAND BEER (Eastern Brewing Corp.)—no aroma and no palate sensation other than carbonation. This is available in the greater New York–Philadelphia area at a low price, which is all that it is worth, if that. There used to be an Old German Brand Ale, but it is no longer available. At times, Old German Brand Beer was produced using the Colonial Brewing Co. corporate name.

POLAR CERVEZA PREMIUM QUALITY PILSNER (Polar Brewing Co.)—faint peppery aroma, coffee taste with a faint metallic background, a strange beer indeed. The *Cerveza* would indicate that this beer is marketed for a Hispanic area. The package resembles a popular Venezuelan product with the same name.

SHOPWELL PREMIUM BEER (Colonial Brewing Co.)—unpleasant "wet-dog" aroma, flat with no taste. Thought to be the result of a bad can, several more samples were tried. Although none was quite as bad as the first, the poor aroma apparently is a regular feature. In better samples the flavor was slightly malty with faint sourness and a sense of metal, but the beer is definitely on the flat side, and very dull. This beer is made for Daitch Crystal Dairies, Inc. of New York City, operators of the Daitch Shopwell grocery chain.

STEINBRAU MALT BEVERAGE (Eastern Brewing Co.)—a near beer with a bready aroma and a sour taste. Typical and awful.

TOPPER LIGHT DRY PILSENER (Eastern Brewing Corp.)—big malty aroma, watery taste, "off" sour-tinny finish, tinny aftertaste. This was a brand of the Standard-Rochester Brewing Co., Rochester, New York, which business shut down in 1970. The label has been seen in New York, Pennsylvania, and, occasionally, New Jersey.

Other Eastern products previously produced, but not seen lately, are: Cee Bee Pilsner Beer (Colonial), Dart Drug Gold Medal (Eastern), made for Dart Drug stores of Maryland and Virginia, Fischer's Old German Style Ale (Fischer) (see Duncan Brewing Co.), Giant Food (Eastern) (see The Lion, Inc.), Grand Union (Eastern) for the Grand Union grocery chain, Markmeister (Eastern), Standard Dry Ale (Eastern), and Wilco Premium Beer (Colonial), produced for the Roger Wilco liquor stores of the Camden, New Jersey, area.

Erie Brewing Co.
(Erie, Pa.)

Charles Koehler had been a grower of tulips in Holland for some years, then in 1840 he sold his lands and sailed to America with his wife. In 1847 he decided that he would become a brewer and established a small plant at 25th and Holland in Erie. He had some success with the business and in passing the brewing idea on to his sons. When he died in 1869, his oldest son, Frederick, together with brother Jackson and partner A. L. Curtze, continued the business as Fred Koehler & Co. Jackson left the firm in 1883 to buy the nearby Kalvage Brewery, and both continued to operate in-

dependently until they decided to merge with the J. M. Conrad and Cascade Breweries to form the Erie Brewing Co. in 1899. The firm is still managed by descendants of Jackson Koehler.

The current product line includes two brews introduced in 1976: Imperial Cream Beer—a blend of choice barley, malt, rice, and hops aged for a full three months for a hearty, robust old-country taste—and Light Lager Beer, a product low in carbohydrates and calories. The traditional Erie product line includes Koehler Beer, Ale, Pilsener, and Lager; Old Pub (a "medium-light" brew); and Yacht Club (another "light"-brewed beer). The Erie market extends from New York to Chicago.

KOEHLER BEER (brewed with the Dutch touch)—pale color, good malty aroma, pleasant barley-malt flavor with some zest, a unique tangy finish, and clean refreshing aftertaste. This is a fine product with a flavor quite different from those of the vast majority of American beers. If you like it, as I did, you may favor it for regular use.

ERIE LIGHT LAGER BEER (96 calories)—slight vegetal nose, a bit off in the aroma, a hint of that vegetable in the taste but a good taste, finish a bit thin with a fairly sweet aftertaste. Despite the weakness in the finish, it is a reasonably pleasant brew when viewed overall. It has more character than most of the low-calorie beers.

OLD PUB TAVERN BREW—aroma and taste of malty cardboard, inexpensive, and just barely drinkable. Only seen in returnable bottles.

KOEHLER LAGER BEER—slightly pale color, light malty vegetal aroma, light to medium flavor, lightly hopped, light body, highly carbonated.

KOEHLER PILSENER BEER—medium to pale color, malty aroma only slightly hopped, hops noticeable more in the flavor than in the aroma, good balance, some hops in the finish, very heavily carbonated.

OLD STYLE BREWER'S LAGER BEER (label says Forrest Brewing Co., Orange, N.J., but these are old labels; the beer is now made by Erie, as indicated by the bottle cap)— medium tawny gold color, austere malty nose, more a palate sensation of carbonated liquid than any real beer flavor, a little sour in the middle and finishes bitter. This product is made in returnable bottles only for the Brewer's Outlet chain of Pennsylvania. It is priced around $4 for a case of pints.

Falls City Brewing Co.
(Louisville, Ky.)

This company was organized and incorporated in 1905 by citizens and tavern owners in the Louisville area. The name of the company was taken from the original (pre-1780) name of Louisville, so called because it is the site of the only large waterfall on the Ohio River south of Pittsburgh. In late 1906 the first draught beer was ready for delivery. Two years later Falls City marketed the first bottled beer in Louisville and spread its sales to nearby Indiana.

During Prohibition the plant continued to operate as the Falls City Ice and Beverage Company, producing soft drinks and near-beer. In 1933 Falls City reestablished itself as a successful regional brewery with its Falls City Premium Brew and today produces one million barrels annually.

In 1972 Falls City introduced Drummond Bros. Preferred Beer, a light, mild beer directed at the twenty-one to thirty-five age group. In late 1977 Falls City introduced Billy Beer, "brewed expressly for and with the personal approval of one of America's all-time great beer drinkers—Billy Carter." The Billy Beer "hype" says that he sampled about nine different recipes and selected this one each time. It was then brewed up specially for Billy—or at least for his endorsement. In early 1978 several other brewers began producing Billy Beer in an identical package for distribution in their marketing area. One of these others was compared to the Falls City product but it was clear that only the package was the same. The beers were from decidedly different recipes (see West End Brewing Co. and Cold Spring Brewing Co.).

The Falls City marketing area now includes Kentucky, Indiana, Virginia, West Virginia, Tennessee, Missouri, Ohio, Illinois, and North Carolina. Its products have also been seen in Pennsylvania, but not on a regular basis.

FALLS CITY PREMIUM BREW—advertised as all grain; aroma of sweet carbonation, malty flavor on the sweet side, faint yeasty finish, a light to medium beer, pleasant but without much zest.

DRUMMOND BROS. PREFERRED BEER—pleasant yeasty aroma, very pale color, pleasant refreshing taste, clean and very light finish, a very refreshing and quaffable brew. Since it is very lightly flavored, overchilling for hot weather refreshment does not seem to impair the flavor. This was the first example seen of a pop-top can with a fold-in tab, a reasonably idiotproof design that could do much to reduce tab litter.

BILLY BEER—pale gold, foamy, heavy malty aroma with faint hops, sweet up front, brackish finish, weak aftertaste. Not worth all the publicity.

Falstaff Brewing Corp.
(St. Louis, Mo.; Fort Wayne, Ind.; New Orleans, La.; Omaha, Nebr.; Cranston, R.I.; Galveston, Tex.)

The Griesedieck family had long been identified with brewing, malting, and liquor industries in St. Louis, and the Falstaff Brewing Co. has roots in two branches of the Griesedieck family.

"Papa Joe" Griesedieck purchased the Forest Park Brewing Co. in 1917 and formed the Griesedieck Brewing Co., which was to become the Falstaff Corporation during Prohibition. The Falstaff name, from Shakespeare's comic character Sir John Falstaff, was obtained from the William J. Lemp Brewing Co., which had made the beer for many years (Lemp was an old company dating back to 1840 and was perhaps the first "national" brewer, being the first to ship its products outside its local regional market area).

Falstaff survived Prohibition making near beer, soda pop, and smoked hams. When brewing was again legalized in 1933, the Falstaff Brewing Co. obtained Permit No. 1. Falstaff was one of the first brewers to begin expansion, beginning in 1935 with the purchase of the Fred Krug Brewery in Omaha; in 1937 the National Brewery of New Orleans was obtained, but World War II delayed further efforts. After the war the Berghoff Brewing Co. plant in Fort Wayne was purchased (with the Berghoff label going to the Walter Co. of Pueblo, Colo.), the Galveston–Houston Brewing Co. plant acquired, and, most recently (1965), the Narragansett Brewing Co. of Cranston obtained, which thrust Falstaff firmly into the New England market. The Ballantine brands were obtained by Falstaff in 1972, but the Newark, New Jersey, plant was closed.

Falstaff has operated other plants during the past decade, all of which are now closed. There were two plants in California, at San Francisco and San Jose. The San Francisco plant was the old Milwaukee Brewery, operated by the

San Francisco Brewing Co. and the Burgemeister Brewing Co. before being obtained by Falstaff. The San Jose plant was formerly run by the Pacific Brewing Co., and later by the Wielands Brewing Co. Falstaff also operated the former Harry Mitchell Brewing Co. plant in El Paso, Texas.

FALSTAFF BEER—light yellow color, fairly rich malty aroma, clean fresh malty flavor with some hops, a good average American beer, perhaps slightly better than average. Pleasant throughout with a good finish.

FALSTAFF FINE LIGHT BEER—pale color, light dank swampy nose, slightly bitter flat taste, not very good at all.

FALSTAFF 96 EXTRA LIGHT BEER—Ninety-six calories, pale color, aroma of yeast and malt, flavor more yeasty than malty with a little sweetness in back, no noticeable hop flavor, watery-yeasty finish, very little aftertaste.

OLD HEIDEL BRAU LAGER (brewed for the Walgreen Co., Deerfield, Ill., by the Great Lakes Brewing Co., Fort Wayne, Ind.; a private label of Walgreen Drugs of the Capital area)—vegetal-malt aroma, thin body, brief taste with no complexity, short finish, no aftertaste.

Lucky Lager Brewing Co. (San Francisco et al.) Through a connection with General, Falstaff produces a selection of the Lucky line of beers and several of General Brewing Company's other brands as well. Lucky products have seen many home breweries over the past years including ones in Ogden, Utah (the former Fisher Brewing Co. plant operated by Lucky), and Pueblo, Colorado (by the Walter Brewing Co.).

LUCKY LAGER BEER (Since 1934)—complex and interesting, a sort of vanilla-cream-soda nose that was reflected into the flavor, would be quite good except that it is a little too sweet. Although it would be better if it were more dry, it is pleasant tasting and quite refreshing, and will seem very good to some palates.

LUCKY BOCK BEER—dark brown color but with little saturation, malty sweet aroma, no faults or high points in the flavor, sweet dull finish, well carbonated.

BREW 102 PALE DRY BEER—supposedly perfected after 101 brews, this beer is very pale yellow, has a clean pleasant fresh aroma with a sweet background, a pleasant slightly sweet flavor, and a pleasing aftertaste. Could be a little drier, but is quite good and very drinkable. This is a former brand of Maier of Los Angeles and is now owned by General.

Christian Feigenspan, Inc. (Newark, N.J.) Feigenspan was a famous East Coast name in brewing. A privately owned corporation, Feigenspan began in Newark shortly before the turn of the twentieth century with the purchase of the old Charles Kolb brewery. Later control was gained of the Dobler Brewing Co. of Albany, New York, and the Yale Brewing Co. of New Haven, Connecticut. By 1939 its lead brand, Pride of Newark, was the largest-selling ale in New York City. In 1944 it was bought out by P. Ballantine & Sons. The Yale Brewery had not opened after Prohibition, but Dobler lasted until 1959 and the Dobler brand names continued into the 1960s, being produced by Piels at Willimansett, Massachusetts. Ballantine reactivated the Feigenspan name in the 1960s as the brewery of record for Munich beer. Falstaff continued the Feigenspan name on the Munich label with Galveston, Fort Wayne, and, most recently, Cranston as the origin.

MUNICH LIGHT LAGER BEER—pale color, light malty nose, very light barely hopped flavor, light body, no faults except for its lightness, inoffensive and could be consumed in quantity, better than average domestic lightweight beer, not noticeably like a Munich beer in style.

P. Ballantine & Sons (Newark, N.J.) Peter Ballantine started his brewing business in Albany, New York, in 1833 with a plant designed for the making of ale. In 1840, he moved the business to Newark where he leased from Morton Bros. Brewers the brewery founded by Gen. John N. Cumming in 1805. Recognizing that the new lager lighter brew was rapidly becoming popular, Ballantine built a lager beer brewery nearby under the name of Ballantine & Company. By the 1880s Ballantine brewing plants had covered twelve acres.

Ballantine maintained its popularity in the greater New York City area and after Prohibition survived for many years. The Ballantine three-ring sign was widely seen and Ballantine beers sold well probably largely because of its being a major radio sponsor of New York Yankees baseball; no other team elicited more interest than the Yankees of the late 1940s and 1950s.

Ballantine produced beer, ale, bock beer, and a fine India pale ale. The last is an authentic India pale ale, made from a recipe used in the nineteenth century in England for beer to be sent to the military forces on duty in India. Since this beer had to travel for many months on a sailing vessel in equatorial waters, it had to be long brewed and long aged else it would perish before it reached its customers far away on remote Indian outposts. It is a strong beer, with all the gusto that other beers only claim. It may be too intense for your palate, but you owe it to yourself to try it before it, like most others of its type, vanishes, in favor of thin, watery, flavorless beers whose only noticeable feature is overcarbonation.

BALLANTINE PREMIUM LAGER BEER—light gold color, clean malty fresh aroma, clean fresh light flavor, medium body, pleasant tasting, lightly hopped, and quite refreshing.

BALLANTINE XXX ALE—deep gold color, yeasty-malty nose, big body, strong flavor with lots of bite, may be a bit much for those who aren't used to strong ale flavor. Those who like their beer strong will love this one, but for most palates there is an overbundance of hops for the level of malt.

BALLANTINE DRAFT BREWED BEER—pale color, flowery aroma of malt, hearty malty flavor, foamy, finish is mostly just carbonation, faint metallic aftertaste. Found in Florida; not seen elsewhere lately.

BALLANTINE BOCK BEER—brown color with little saturation, apple-teaberry aroma, dull taste with a fairly sweet finish and aftertaste, not very interesting.

BALLANTINE INDIA PALE ALE (since 1890)—deep

brown gold, pungent aroma of hops, enormous body for a beer, powerful flavor yet with surprisingly good balance, taste very slightly on the sour side; long, long finish, lingering full-flavored aftertaste. This beer is unquestionably long aged, maybe even in wood, and it shows in the flavor. It may be too intense for many people, but if you claim to be a beer drinker, you should at least try it.

G. Krueger Brewing Co. (Newark, N.J.) In 1865 Gottfried Krueger and Gottlieb Hill purchased the small brewery of Laible & Adam and organized the firm of Hill & Krueger. By 1875, when Hill retired, the annual output of the brewery was 25,000 barrels. By 1889, when the firm was incorporated with sons John F. and Gottfried C. joining the business, annual production had reached 150,000 barrels.

Following Prohibition, Krueger reopened and gained the distinction of being the first firm to package beer in a can, a flat-top Krueger Cream Ale issued in January 1935. Krueger itself survived only a short few years after this achievement, however, with the Kreuger brands being produced in Cranston, Rhode Island, license having been obtained by the Narragansett Brewing Co.

KRUEGER BEER (since 1858)—pale color, good well-hopped nose, hops slightly dominate the flavor, medium body, quite a bit of character, sour malt in the middle, light finish. A good beer, better than average.

KRUEGER PILSENER BEER (in late 1977 renamed Krueger Light Beer)—very pale color, light flavor but good balance between the malt and the hops, no offensive features, a bit weak in the finish but a very pleasant, satisfying and clean-tasting refreshing brew. One of the best lightly flavored beers. The name was changed apparently to provide a means of competing in the "light" market without actually going to the trouble to put out a new beer.

KRUEGER CREAM ALE—sweet aroma, sour malty taste, bitter and perfumy. Not much to recommend this product. It has been seen only in large nonreturnable bottles.

Narragansett Brewing Co. (Cranston, R.I.) This company was organized in 1890 with a lager beer brewery in Arlington, Rhode Island. Following Prohibition, Narragansett enjoyed modest success in southern New England. With its sponsorship of the Boston Red Sox, which became a New England institution in the 1940s, the beer began to sell successfully all over that six-state area. "Hi neighbor, have a 'Gansett" and an accompanying song heralded the start of each Red Sox game on radio and TV and generations of New England youth waited until they would be old enough to do so. In the mid-1960s Narragansett purchased the Haffenreffer labels. Haffenreffer was an old Boston firm dating back to 1890, with a famous brewing family background. Falstaff has continued to produce virtually all of these brands.

NARRAGANSETT LAGER BEER—malty aroma, medium body, flavor mostly malt, a little too light on the hops but still reasonably good, an average American pilsener-type beer.

NARRAGANSETT 96 EXTRA LIGHT BEER—ninety-six calories, pleasant malty beery aroma, faintly sweet up front in the taste, at the end the sensation is like having just drunk a glass of spring water. Very light but refreshing and pleasant. One of the better low-calorie beers.

NARRAGANSETT PORTER—deep orange brown, virtually no aroma, a light artificially sweet flavor that carries into the aftertaste.

CROFT PREMIUM QUALITY ALE (Croft Brewing Co.)—very light aroma of faint malt, sweet aromatic creamy taste. From 1937 to 1954 this brew has been named Croft Cream Ale, Champion Ale, and Banquet Ale.

BOH BOHEMIAN LAGER BEER (Haffenreffer Brewing Co.)—pale, color, very faint malty aroma, almost no nose at all, no taste on the front of the tongue, lingering metallic finish. This label originated with the Enterprise Brewing Co. (Old Colony Brewery) of Fall River, Massachusetts. The

Haffenreffer family had been the active force behind this business and when it closed in 1963 the brand was obtained by Haffenreffer.

HAFFENREFFER PRIVATE STOCK MALT LIQUOR (Narragansett Brewing Co.) (since 1870)—skunky aroma, lightly flavored for a malt liquor, very soft on the palate with a mostly malty flavor, light for a malt liquor.

HAFFENREFFER LAGER BEER (Haffenreffer Brewing Co.)—weak in aroma and body, very lightly flavored, has no real faults but also lacks zest, a slightly better than average light-flavored domestic brew.

PICKWICK ALE (Haffenreffer Brewing Co.)—intense yeasty aroma, soapy taste, creamy and foamy on the palate. This ale appeared in the late 1950s and was billed as "the only blend of lager beer, light ale, and malt liquor ever canned in the U.S." It is packaged only in returnable bottles today.

General Brewing Co.
(San Francisco, Calif. and Vancouver, Wash.)

The early origins of this firm can be traced to a small brewery in Victoria, Vancouver, Canada, in 1858 from which evolved Lucky Lager Breweries Ltd. of Canada and the Lucky Lager Brewing Co. in the United States with plants in Vancouver, San Francisco, and Azusa, California. Lucky Lager was a popular West Coast brew for over half a century and a consistent winner of gold medals at international competitions.

The Lucky plant in Azusa was sold to the Miller Brewing Co., and the Los Angeles plant of the Maier Brewing Co. became part of the firm, renamed the General Brewing Co. in 1963. The old Maier plant is no longer included in General's operations, but most of the Maier labels are still marketed, mostly in California.

In 1958, when Labatt Breweries of Canada acquired Lucky Lager Breweries, it also acquired a forty-seven percent interest in Lucky Breweries, Inc. This interest was sold in 1971 to Paul Kalmonovitz of Los Angeles. During Labatt ownership, General introduced California-brewed Labatt labels on the West Coast.

In recent years General has marketed a wide variety of brands, including Alpine, Amber Brau, Weiss Bavarian, Bohemian Pilsener, Brau Haus, Brown Derby, Bulldog Malt Liquor, Edelbrau, Fisher, Golden Crown, Golden Harvest, Hof-Brau, Keg, Padre, Regal Select, Reidenbach, Spring, Steinbrau Beer, Velvet Glow, Brew 102, and the Lucky Lager line which is produced by Falstaff for the market east of the Rockies. Lucky Lager had earlier been produced by the Walter Brewing Co. of Pueblo, Colorado, and the Interstate Brewing Co. of Vancouver.

Can and label collectors can obtain items from the General product line (and some Falstaff) from ESP, Inc., 1629 Vancouver Way, Livermore, California 94550.

REIDENBACH PREMIUM PALE DRY BEER—faint perfumy malt aroma, overly sweet flabby weak taste, dull neutral finish.

KEG BRAND NATURAL FLAVOR BEER—big malty nose, high carbonation, only quality in the middle is astringency, flavor is lacking until the finish, slight bitterness at the end. Originally a Maier label.

LUCKY DRAFT BEER—big malty nose with hops in the background, slightly sour grainy taste, high carbonation, a little sweetness in the finish, good balance, very drinkable. Lable claims that freshness and clarity comes from a double Swiss and Microfil filtration process.

LUCKY BOCK BEER—dark color, no aroma, thin body, slightly sweet flavor, but most of the palate sensation is carbonation.

LUCKY 96 EXTRA LIGHT BEER—foamy, lovely malt aroma, very light faint malty flavor, very little finish and aftertaste.

PADRE PALE LAGER BEER—pale gold, mild beery aroma, some slight hop character, low carbonation, light sour hop flavor, only slightly malty, lightly hopped finish. Originally a Maier label.

BREW 102 PALE DRY BEER—very pale gold, mild beery aroma, light malt flavor, well carbonated, some zest, a little on the salty side, short finish. Another Maier label.

DE LIGHT BREW MALT BEVERAGE—fifty-five calories, nonalcoholic; deep yellow, slightly cloudy, cereal aroma and flavor, weak and watery.

Genesee Brewing Co., Inc.
(Rochester, N.Y.)

Genesee began in 1878 with an operation by that name selling Liebotschaner Beer in New York. It became part of

the large Bartholomay Brewing Co. in 1889. Following Prohibition, a new Genesee was opened by Louis A. Wehle using the property and plant of the old firm.

Today Genesee is the third largest single-plant brewing operation in the United States and ranks thirteenth in the country with sales of 2.5 million barrels (1976). The bulk of its market is in upstate New York, but there is general availability of its popular-priced products in Pennsylvania, New Jersey, and New England.

The primary product line includes Genesee Beer, Cream Ale, Bock, and Fyfe & Drum Extra Lyte Beer. Genesee also occasionally produces limited amounts of Twelve Horse Ale, heavier and stronger than the Cream Ale. It was produced regularly from 1939 to 1950, but today it is neither advertised nor promoted to any extent.

GENESEE BEER—good malty aroma, well bodied, good malt flavor with a slight hop taste, good balance, very little aftertaste.

GENESEE CREAM ALE—full malty aroma with a slight hop background, good malt-hop balance, well bodied, good taste, a bit weak on the finish.

GENESEE BOCK BEER—very much like Genesee Beer but more malty, medium dark color, big malty aroma, extremely good malty flavor, good body, good balance, pleasant aftertaste, a fine product, best domestic "bock" tasted.

GENESEE LIGHT—pale color, mild malty yeasty aroma typical of many of the light beers, light body with a good dry flavor with some hops.

FYFE & DRUM EXTRA LYTE BEER—very faint malty aroma, light sweet grainy flavor, no hops evident, very foamy finish. Very light overall but not bad for type; one of the better low-calorie beers.

Geyer Bros. Brewing Co.
(Frankenmuth, Mich.)

Although Geyer's product label implies existence since 1862, the claim is not supported by *100 Years of Brewing*, the definitive work on beer at the turn of the century. In fact, there is no mention of Geyer Bros. in the industry up to 1902, so if there is a history preceding that time it is under another name.

In 1900, the Frankenmuth Brewing Co. was formed in that city by a group of farmers. It reopened following Prohibition and operated until 1963. It is presumed that Geyer Bros. added that market to its own. Beers are now produced under the Geyer and Frankenmuth labels.

FRANKENMUTH ORIGINAL DARK BAVARIAN BEER—dark amber color, teaberry aroma, malty teaberry flavor, very mild, a bit too sweet, heavily carbonated, inoffensive but lacks zest. Note: There was also a Frankenmuth beer produced by the International Brewing Co. of Buffalo, New York, in recent years, but with no apparent connection.

FRANKENMUTH ORIGINAL LIGHT BAVARIAN BEER—pale yellow, foamy, malty yeasty nose, rich yeasty malt flavor, long yeasty finish, all in a good sense. Yeastiness is usually not deemed a favorable feature in beer, but it comes off well in this one. A pleasant-tasting brew.

Peter Hand Brewing Co.
(Chicago, Ill.)

In 1890 Peter Hand organized a brewing company in Chicago that still retains his name, and whose same premises have been used for brewery operation since the first beer was released for sale in 1891. The current company was formed in April 1973 when the plant and offices were purchased by the present owners headed by Fred W. Regnery, chairman and president.

Peter Hand is a multibrand brewing company with markets extending westward to California and New Mexico and eastward to New Jersey, but its products are mainly offered in the South and Midwest. All current Hand products

A Vintage Peter Hand delivery truck today serves a role in promotion – and still delivers beer.

are described below, but two new products are planned for early 1978 release. For the packaged-beer market, there will be Peter Hand Select, a "superpremium" (as in the Michelob class and price) aged a full twelve weeks. They promise a beer that tastes like Heineken. For the local draught-beer market, Peter Hand Natural Draft was introduced in Chicago in the late spring of 1978. It is a completely natural beer with no additives or preservatives, and not pasteurized.

Technical data offered by the company state that Lake Michigan water is used in all Hand beers since it is free of mineral content. The hops used for all products except Van Merritt (imported hops used exclusively) are grown in Oregon and Washington, and corn is used as an adjunct for enhanced clarity of brew. The robust flavor of their Old Chicago Dark is due to the use of five separate malts.

For can collectors, M–TY Can Co., P.O. Box 361, Skokie, Illinois 60076, offers Peter Hand brands.

PETER HAND EXTRA LIGHT BEER—pale color, little

aroma, extremely light body and flavor, no zest. A low-calorie beer.

PETER HAND 1891 EXPORT LAGER BEER—faint malty aroma, delicate bittersweet flavor, light body, lightly hopped finish.

OLD CHICAGO LIGHT LAGER BEER—skunky aroma with motor oil overtones, flabby semi-sweet flavor with a bitter finish. Many tried all with the same results. After tasting Old Chicago, I heard this story. When the present management took over the operation, a large batch of this beer was in stock, undistributed. It had exceeded the expected shelf-life limit and should have been destroyed. Brewers regularly remove old unsold stock from store shelves and replace it with new. For whatever reason, runs the story, Hand released the old beer with the predictable results. Old Chicago Light was found wanting by all who tried it during that period. The recipe, however, is a decent one, and new batches of the beer should be given a trial.

OLD CHICAGO DARK BEER—good dark color, medium deep brown with tawny hues, very light malty nose, mildly flavored and pleasant tasting, a little short on aftertaste. This is a good domestic dark beer, one of the best produced in the U.S.

OLD CROWN LIGHT DRY BEER—mild malty aroma, sour taste, dull finish. Old Crown beer and ale are products formerly made by the Old Crown Brewing Corp. of Fort Wayne, Indiana.

OLD CROWN PREMIUM QUALITY ALE (lazy aged)— very light malty aroma, faintly hopped flavor, mostly on the neutral side, little aftertaste. Better than Old Crown Beer for character of flavor.

BRAUMEISTER SPECIAL PILSENER BEER—pale color; light, pleasant malty nose; highly carbonated; light neutral flavor; tasty finish and aftertaste. This brand was previously a product of the Independent Milwaukee Brew-

ing Co. of Milwaukee, and the independent Milwaukee Div. of G. Heileman, Sheboygan, Wisconsin. In 1974 it was produced by both Heileman and Hand. It is widely marketed.

BURGEMEISTER BREWMASTER'S PREMIUM BEER—very malty aroma, light body, nondescript light flavor, little finish. This brand originated with the Warsaw Brewing Co. of Warsaw, Illinois.

OERTEL'S 92 LIGHT LAGER BEER—spicy aroma, highly carbonated, light and sweet at the front of the taste, sour and bitter in the finish. The brand originated with the Oertel Brewing Co. of Louisville and later was produced by the Oertel Brewing Co. Div. of G. Heileman in Newport, Kentucky. It is an old label and the 92 is believed not to refer to caloric content.

VAN MERRITT BEER—virtually no aroma; salty, malty taste; salty finish and aftertaste. According to the label, Van

116

Merritt is "the world's most honored beer" with "imported flavor" and is made from an Old World recipe originated in 1433 and improved through the centuries. It must have been some desperate recipe in the beginning. Van Merritt was a brand of the Van Merritt Brewing Co. of Chicago, Burlington, Wisconsin, and Joliet, Illinois, and later, of the Old Crown Brewing Corp.

ALPS BRAU BAVARIAN STYLE PREMIUM BEER— faint grainy malty aroma, very little flavor, even less aftertaste. This brand was obtained from Old Crown and originated with the Centliver Brewing Co. of Fort Wayne, Indiana.

OLD GERMAN STYLE BEER—no aroma detectable, pale color, neutral flavor, highly carbonated, sour aftertaste. This brand was obtained from the Renner Brewing Co. of Fort Wayne.

ZODIAC MALT LIQUOR—faint sweet aroma, deep yellow-brown color, sweet fruitlike taste with acidic follow-through.

**G. Heileman
Brewing Co., Inc.**
*(LaCrosse, Wis.; St. Paul, Minn.; Evansville, Ind.;
Newport, Ky.; Seattle, Wash.)*

The Heileman story begins in 1850 with the firm of Gund and Witzel, which leased a small brewery in Galena, Wisconsin. Shortly thereafter, John Gund sold out and moved to LaCrosse, where he built a brewery on Front and Division Streets. He was joined by Gottlieb Heileman in 1858 and the partnership of Gund & Heileman continued to 1872, when Gund retired. When Gottlieb Heileman died in 1878, his wife, Johanna, assumed proprietorship and became president of the firm when it was incorporated in 1890.

The company survived Prohibition and slowly grew from a 160,000-barrel capacity at the turn of the century to one of about one million in 1966. When the great upheaval in the brewing industry came in the next decade, with the onslaught of massive advertising campaigns by the large national brewing companies, Heileman set out to build a multibrand house of regional beer brands—each brand having the name, following, and quality to hold its own.

While hundreds of regional brewers were strangled by the national brands' inroads in their markets, Heileman's approach proved successful, even spectacular. By 1977, it had reached seventh in sales in the nation, and with the recent acquisition of Rainer in Seattle, the top six must be hearing footsteps.

Part of the Heileman success has been a concentration on building a massive wholesaler network, and it is now trying to increase sales in the forty-six states of its market by injecting G. Heileman "home" products into the newly acquired regional markets.

HEILEMAN'S SPECIAL EXPORT BEER—gold color, hops dominate the nose and taste, good character and zest, quite European in style, finish is too bitter.

HEILEMAN'S OLD STYLE LIGHT LAGER BEER—very perfumy aroma, tutti-frutti flavor, aftertaste mostly neutral with some background bitterness. Hard to imagine this as a popular item, even at its low price.

HEILEMAN'S LIGHT PREMIUM BEER—Heileman's ninety-six-calorie beer. I had some difficulty finding a supply of this that was not bad (too old, or mishandled, or made wrong—I don't know which). The bad ones had an unclean aroma, flavor of gasoline, and were not enjoyable in any way. Best ones found were quite frail in aroma, taste, and finish, and there were elements of the bad sensations present in the background. Try it for yourself but beware, the recipe might be unusually susceptible to damage from mishandling and age.
and age.

Blatz Brewing Co. (Milwaukee) Founded in 1851 by Valentin Blatz in Milwaukee, the firm was incorporated in 1889 as the Valentin Blatz Brewing Co. In 1890 the firm was merged into the Milwaukee and Chicago Breweries, Ltd. Only Blatz emerged from the gloom of Prohibition and in 1958 was sold to Pabst. The U.S. Supreme Court ordered Pabst to divest itself of the firm and Blatz was sold to G. Heileman in 1969. Blatz has long been a favorite in many areas outside Milwaukee and is marketed in thirty-five states.

BLATZ, MILWAUKEE'S FINEST BEER—pale color, lightly scented, faintly malty, very light-bodied and very light-flavored, an ordinary beer that will offend no one, and not satisfy real beer lovers.

BLATZ LIGHT CREAM ALE—medium yellow, sweet fruitlike aroma; pungent flavor with lots of hops; some sourness in back; aftertaste has some unpleasant components.

George Wiedemann Brewing Co. (Newport, Ky.) George Wiedemann founded this firm in 1870 and became sole proprietor in 1878. The present name of the company was adopted upon incorporation in 1890. Wiedemann's Bohemian Special is a strong regional favorite throughout the South and Midwest and is still brewed to the original Wiedemann recipe. Heileman has extended the market of this brew from coast to coast. I have seen it in Maine and California. Wiedemann is now the Wiedemann Division of G. Heileman and the Newport facility is still operated as one of the Heileman plants.

WIEDEMANN BOHEMIAN SPECIAL FINE BEER— light color, fresh malty aroma with some hops, light but good flavor, finely balanced, a good-tasting fresh pilsener-type beer that has enough zest to give pleasure while it quenches thirst. A very fine beer whose only weakness is a slightly neutral finish. It should be more than satisfactory for most American palates. Recommended for everyday use.

F. W. Cook Brewing Co./Cook's Brewing Co. (Evansville, Ind.) This company was included in the Associated acquisition. The most notable brands acquired were Cook's 500 Ale, which was distributed only for Indianapolis 500 Races during the 1950s, and Cook's Goldblume, which is still marketed by Heileman in a few midwestern states.

COOK'S GOLDBLUME PREMIUM BEER—medium to light malt aroma, refreshing but watery, dank aftertaste.

John Hauenstein Brewing Co. (New Ulm, Minn.) A Sioux uprising in 1862 occasioned the establishment of this firm. John Hauenstein, a cooper employed at a New Ulm distillery, was put out of work when the Sioux attacked and destroyed the building. His solution to unemployment was to found the Hauenstein Brewery in 1864 with a partner named Andrew Betz. In 1881 a cyclone destroyed the newly remodeled plant, but the beer, stored underground, was saved and used to finance the rebuilding of the brewery. The firm was incorporated in 1900 as the John Hauenstein Brewing Co. Heileman obtained the rights to this label just prior to 1974 and closed down the New Ulm facility.

HAUENSTEIN NEW ULM BEER—medium to light color, clean malty aroma with some hops, clean bright taste, a little too heavily carbonated. Still, an enjoyable little brew.

Drewry's Ltd., U.S.A. (South Bend, Ind.; St. Paul, Minn., et al.) The Drewry firm began in 1860 with the partnership of Drewry & Scotten founding the North Star Brewery. The firm became Drewry & Grieg in 1864. Drewry left his partnership in 1867 and founded Drewry & Sons of St. Paul. In the 1950s Drewry's operated the old Edelweiss Brewing Co. plant in Chicago, and for a time owned the Hampden-Harvard plant in Willimansett, Massachusetts. In the early 1960s, Drewry's became part of Associated and thus passed to Heileman. Heileman is beginning to market the Drewry label over a much wider area and in early 1978 the lead label, Drewry's Beer, appeared in New Jersey and New York.

DREWRY'S BEER—light sweet aroma, sweet taste with some hops faintly in the background, completely inoffensive, but lacks zest.

DREWRY'S BEER DRAFT FLAVORED—light brackish

aroma, salty taste, very little aftertaste. This beer was obtained in Wisconsin in late 1977, at which time we heard that it was no longer being made. That has not been confirmed by Heileman, but it is not included in that firm's most recent product list.

Minneapolis Brewing Co. (Minneapolis) Since 1891 this firm has produced the very popular Grain Belt beers for the midwestern market. Over the years the Grain Belt Beer label has seen a great number of adjectives, including: special, friendly, golden, premium, and golden premium. When the firm was purchased by Heileman, it had been renamed Grain Belt, Inc.

GRAIN BELT BEER—pale color, sweet aroma, lightly flavored, highly carbonated, harmless, and uninteresting.

GRAIN BELT PREMIUM (strong)—pale color, faint malty aroma, very lightly hopped, taste on the sweet side with vegetal overtones. Not a particularly good-tasting beer for one that supposedly sells very well in Minnesota, where beer has been a favorite drink since early settlers continued their heritage of brewing fine European-style brews.

Jacob Schmidt Brewing Co. (St. Paul) In his younger days Jacob Schmidt had been employed by Miller, Best, Schlitz, Schell, and Blatz. When he bought out the Milwaukee Brewing Co. in 1884, he was foreman of the Hamm Brewery. His North Star Brewing Co. operated until 1901, when it was incorporated in the above name and the business was moved to the recently (1900) purchased St. Paul Brewing Co. facility. Billed as the "beer that grew with the great northwest," this local Minneapolis–St. Paul brew has featured a series of labels that depict the fauna and activities of the area. Can collectors have been treated to moose, Canada geese, antelopes, pheasants, pike, ice fishing, bobsleds, and about a dozen more scenes. Schmidt became part of the Associated Brewing Co. complex shortly before its acquisition by Heileman in 1963 and the Schmidt plant operates as the Heileman St. Paul facility.

SCHMIDT BEER (3.2 percent by weight)—light color, fragrance of hops, medium body, good in the middle, some greenness typical of very youthful "3.2," watery finish.

SCHMIDT EXTRA SPECIAL BEER (labeled strong, denoting, in Minnesota where the sample was obtained, normal alcohol content instead of being 3.2 percent)—very pleasant fruitlike aroma, too sweet a taste, a bit cloying. A beer should be drier than this. This can, purchased in late 1977, indicates that the beer was made in Sheboygan, a Heileman facility that was closed in 1976. Either this was old beer or Heileman is still using up old can stock. Sheboygan has also been listed recently on some Wiedemann cans.

SCHMIDT SELECT NEAR BEER—very pale, faint malty nose, watery, flat dusty flavor, also noticeable lack of alcohol.

Kingsbury Breweries Co. (Manitowoc and Sheboygan, Wis.) The Kingsbury brands were obtained by Heileman early in its expansion program; for a time Heileman operated the Sheboygan plant and produced the Heileman brands there. The primary labels obtained from this firm are Kingsbury Beer and Kingsbury Brew Near Beer. Interestingly, G. Heileman is the United States' largest manufacturer of near-beer, producing Kingsbury, Schmidt Select, and Zing.

KINGSBURY BREW NEAR BEER (63 calories)—very pale color, very faint malty nose, watery, grainy flavor, easy to recognize the absence of alcohol.

KINGSBURY WISCONSIN'S ORIGINAL BEER—bright gold, faint sweet aroma, very little flavor, little more than carbonation. Can notes the Kingsbury origin in 1847.

Gluek Brewing Co. (Minneapolis) This firm was founded in 1847 by Gottfried Gluek and operated as G. Gluek & Sons until 1894, when it was incorporated as the Gluek Brewing Co. Its products were Gluek's Beer or Gluek's Pilsener Beer and Gluek's Stite Malt Liquor, claimed to be America's first malt liquor, "the original malt liquor, pale and dry as champagne." After Gluek was purchased, it operated for a time as the Gluek Division of G. Heileman. Recent label have dropped the Gluek name.

STITE SPARKLING MALT LIQUOR (strong)—pale color, faint sweet pilsenerlike aroma, medium body, pilsenerlike taste as well, but poorly balanced sour and sweet flavors. It is pale all right, but you can hardly call it dry.

Pfeiffer Brewing Co. (Detroit) This brewery was established by Conrad Pfeiffer in 1890 and was operated by him in his name until he was succeeded by the Pfeiffer Brewing Co. in 1902. Sixty years later Pfeiffer merged with the E & B Brewing Co. of Detroit to form the beginnings of the Associated Brewing Co. At that time, the E & B plant was shut down and brewing continued at Pfeiffer. A Pfeiffer plant in Flint, Michigan, operated for a time but closed before the merger with E & B. The Pfeiffer labels of the 1960s indicate a South Bend facility, but it is likely that this was an Associated plant, and not necessarily a producer of the Pfeiffer brands. The Pfeiffer label has been maintained since the purchase of Associated by Heileman, but the Detroit plant was closed.

PFEIFFER FAMOUS BEER—sweet malt nose, neutral taste, little character, unbalanced at the finish, also a bit "rough" after the initial palate sensation, some scratchiness in the throat on swallowing.

Sterling Breweries, Inc. (Evansville, Ind.) Sterling was merged into the Associated Brewing Co. complex during the 1960s and acquired by Heileman from there. The primary brands involved were Sterling Premium and Mickey's Fine Malt Liquor, the latter becoming a primary Heileman label.

STERLING PREMIUM PILSNER BEER—pale color, faint aroma that was barely noticeable, faint and nondescript taste, little more than thirst quenching. This beer could be served extremely well chilled without impairing the flavor since there is so little to begin with. This is a popular beer in Kentucky, Indiana, and some southern states.

MICKEY'S FINE MALT LIQUOR—pleasant malty beery aroma, fresh and malty flavor, bittersweet and slightly perfumy taste like most U.S. malt liquors, some bitterness in the finish of some samples, but not in those that were fresh. Malt liquor drinkers should try this one, the No. 1 choice of the rating panel.

Rainier Brewing Co. (Seattle) This famous brewing company of the West Coast was obtained by Heileman in the spring of 1977 for $8 million, marking the passing of another big name from the ranks of the strong, independent regional brewers.

Rainier originated in 1878 with the Bayview Brewery, on the site where today's Rainier Brewery is still located. From that time Rainier Beer was the premium brand produced at that place. In 1893 the Georgetown Brewery produced beer under the Rainier label, and by 1916 the plant was the sixth largest brewery in the world.

Following Prohibition, the Bayview was purchased by Fritz Sick and his son Emil, who, after converting it back from a feed mill (which it was throughout Prohibition), formed the Century Brewing Co. and obtained rights to the Rainier name in Washington and Alaska. In 1957, when the owners obtained rights to the Rainier name throughout the United States, the company name was changed from Sicks' Brewing and Malting Co. to Sicks' Rainier Brewing Company.

Although several smaller breweries were obtained along the way, all operations were eventually consolidated into the present brewery. With the formation of the Rainier Companies, Inc., in 1970, Rainier added an interesting property, the Robert Mondavi Winery of Oakville, California, one of the foremost makers of fine wines in the Napa valley.

Rainier products include Rainier Beer, Ale, Light (a ninety-six-calorie beer), Rhinelander Beer and, from the Heileman product list, Mickey's Malt Liquor. For can collectors and lovers of breweriana, Rainier has the largest assortment of goodies ever seen. Write for a price list to: Beeraphernalia, c/o Rainier, P.O. Box 24828, Seattle 98124.

1878 – Home of Rainier Beer

1900 – Rainier Brewery on Airport Way

1978 – Rainier Today

Beercentennial Bottle – limited number produced during the summer of 1978. Authentic shape Circa 1890.

RAINIER ALE—beautiful amber color, slightly cloudy, lovely well-hopped aroma, big body, pungent yet sweet taste, pretty good as American ales go, and a lot more authentic than most domestic brews so labeled.

RAINIER MOUNTAIN FRESH BEER—pale gold, very hoppy aroma but there are very few hops in the flavor, taste is mostly just salty carbonation and the finish is light and brackish.

Other Heileman Products Heileman also obtained other small breweries or brands in the Midwest, including the

Fox-Head Waukesha Corp. of Waukesha, Wisconsin and Heidel Brau from the Sioux City Brewing Co. These small firms and labels were gathered up in the Associated purchase. Fox de Luxe Beer was produced by Heileman for a while but has since been sold to the Cold Spring Brewing Co.

HEIDEL BRAU PILSNER BEER—faint malt nose, light-flavored, very quaffable, pleasant but no zest, very little aftertaste.

SGA LIGHT BEER—pale color, clean malty aroma, slight hop character to the taste, some bite on the palate that eases toward the finish. A good beer at a low price, slightly on the light side.

Horlacher Brewing Co.
(Allentown, Pa.)

Horlacher began in Allentown in 1897 with the founding of the Allentown Brewing Co. Four years later it was succeeded by the newly incorporated Horlacher Brewing Co., operated by George and Fred Horlacher.

Success came with the 1905 introduction of a full-flavored lager called Perfection, a brew that was aged a full nine months. It became a great favorite of the public and was served widely on railroad and steamship lines.

Prohibition brought upon the closing of the brewery until repeal in 1933, when it reopened only to fold six months later. In 1935 the firm was reincorporated under free title. Coburger and Perfection (reintroduced in 1938) were the premium brands of the new company.

Horlacher takes pride in marketing beer that is totally without synthetic ingredients and aims to satisfy local regional tastes, which it feels cannot be accommodated by national brewers.

Horlacher produces Horlacher Premium, Brew II (with a higher alcohol content for regional eastern Pennsylvania tastes), and Imperial Pilsner, and it reintroduced the excellent Perfection Beer in late 1976 and early 1977.

HORLACHER PREMIUM PILSNER—light amber color, light malt aroma with faint vegetal character, light flavor, lightly hopped, sort of dull.

IMPERIAL PILSNER (Hofbrau Brewing Co., Allentown)—light amber color, talcum-powder aroma, sour decayed vegetal taste but not unlike many U.S. pilseners; made with Bohemian hops, grade-A barley malt, and cornflakes.

BREW II—supposedly higher alcohol, but it is not particularly noticeable; sweet aroma with vegetal background, bubble-gum flavor, sour metallic finish.

HORLACHER DRAFT BREWED—clear pale color, very clean malty aroma, very light body and flavor. Label announces it is pasteurized.

PERFECTION BEER—aged for nine months, deep gold color, strong malt-vegetal aroma, big-bodied, big tangy flavor with a sweetness in the background, loaded with character, finishes dry, an excellent beer. Top domestic beer from the taste trials, one of America's best. Extremely long-lived, still good even when approaching two years of age in the bottle, probably the result of the extended aging, which also adds to the production costs. Priced around 45¢ per bottle.

SHOP RITE PILSNER (Old Dutch Brewing Co., Horlacher, Allentown)—Private label for Shop-Rite Food Stores in New York–New Jersey area. Pale amber color, faint malt aroma, light body, lightly hopped (hops barely make it at all and come through only in the finish). Very inexpensive, as with most grocery store brands.

Hudepohl Brewing Co.
(Cincinnati)

This company began in 1855 when a Cincinnati distiller, Louis Hudepohl, and his partner, Fred Kotte, purchased the old (and once famous) Koehler Brewery. Hudepohl & Kotte marketed brands Buckeye (named for the brewery on

Buckeye Street), Muenchener, Dortmunder, and Hudepohl. When Kotte died in 1899, the business became incorporated as the Hudepohl Brewing Co.

During Prohibition the company survived by producing near-beer and soft drinks. Following repeal, public

acceptance of Hudepohl beer necessitated increased production, and in 1934 the Lackman Brewing Co. was purchased as a second plant. Eventually the Buckeye plant was closed and the operation consolidated into an industrial complex on the fringe of Cincinnati's downtown area.

The product line includes Hofbrau, an all-malt beer sold only in draft, Hudepohl, and Hudepohl Draft (which is also packaged in bottles that must be refrigerated). Since April 1973, when Hudepohl acquired the principal assets of the Burger Brewing Co., the product line has included the Burger label. It is worth noting that Burger purchased the old Windisch Muhlhauser Brewery in 1943 and operated it until 1973. The Windisch Muhlhauser Brewing Co., founded in Cincinnati in 1866, was the fifth largest brewery in the United States in 1871–72.

Hudepohl has about one-third of the Cincinnati area market. It also makes its products available in Ohio, Tennessee, West Virginia, Virginia, Indiana, Kentucky, and western Pennsylvania. Its promotions include a Process 14-K, a company-developed process which they believe makes a clearer and brighter beer, and the Cincinnati Reds. The firm also supported the old Cincinnati Royals.

HUDEPOHL PURE GRAIN BEER—interesting spicy aroma, flavor definitely on the salty side, good body, saltiness found to be unfavorable.

Jos. Hube Brewing Co.
(Monroe, Wis.)

One of America's finest independent regional breweries is Jos. Huber, a firm that dates back to the founding of Wisconsin itself in 1848.

Huber products are found primarily in the Midwest, marketed from Indiana to the Rockies, but have been seen regularly in Pennsylvania at Brewer's Outlet stores. The Huber brands include the following: Wisconsin Gold Label, Alpine Beer, Potosi Beer (formerly of the Potosi Brewing Co., Potosi, Wis.), Holiday Beer (formerly of the Holiday Brewing Co., Potosi), Huber Premium and Bock, Wisconsin

132

Club, Bavarian Club, Rhinelander, Bohemian Club, Regal Brau, Hi-Brau, and the very fine Augsburger. All are available in cans except Alpine and Potosi.

REGAL BRAU BAVARIAN STYLE BEER—fresh clean malty aroma, good malt-hop balance in the taste, finish a bit too sweet, sour aftertaste.

HI-BRAU PREMIUM BEER—sweet aroma, sweet and dull flavor, almost no aftertaste.

BAVARIAN CLUB PREMIUM BEER—faint bitter-sour aroma, slightly sour flavor with little zest.

WISCONSIN CLUB PREMIUM PILSNER BEER—malty aroma with decayed vegetal background, neutral dry taste, slightly sour finish, too much carbonation. This label was previously owned by Fox Head of Waukesha, Wisconsin.

RHINELANDER EXPORT PREMIUM BEER—particulate matter in solution, "old" aroma, tastes like toasted bread, low carbonation, little aftertaste. Typical of overaged, stale beer. This beer originated with the Rhinelander Brewing Co., Rhinelander, Wisconsin.

RHINELANDER BOCK BEER—dark color, faint malt nose, pleasant slight hop flavor, good balance, good long finish. An excellent beer worthy of a try, discovered too late to be entered in the finals. Probably would have done quite well.

BOHEMIA CLUB OLD FASHIONED LAGER BEER—light sweet malty nose, taste on the yeasty side, flavor of grain and sweetness, finish a bit flabby. This brand was originated by the Bohemian Brewing Co. of Joliet and Chicago, and was obtained by Huber with the Potosi labels.

AUGSBURGER OLD WORLD BAVARIAN STYLE BEER—golden color, hops dominate the nose, good character, plenty of zest in the flavor, balance very good at the start but dips slightly toward the finish, hops dominate throughout, bitter finish with a trace of the initial sweetness, a big flavorful beer and a very good one. Ranked at the top of the list of all beer brewed in America today.

HUBER PREMIUM BEER—pale color, light aroma, very lightly flavored, no offensive features, overly carbonated. Not a bad little beer at all if you like them lightly done.

HUBER PREMIUM BOCK BEER—deep red-orange brown, foamy, malty aroma, taste gradually becomes increasingly bitter across the palate until it is too bitter at the end.

WISCONSIN HOLIDAY BEER—sweet malty nose, low carbonation, natural with small bubbles, light hops in the flavor, slight cardboard flavor especially in the finish.

WISCONSIN GOLD LABEL LIGHT LAGER BEER—faint malt aroma, very little flavor, flat dull finish.

Hull Brewing Co.
(New Haven, Conn.)

Founded in 1872 by William Hull and his son William H. Hull, this small brewery continues to serve its clientele in the New Haven–Hartford area of central Connecticut. In recent years the product line was limited to Hull's Export Beer and Hull's Ale. The ale has not been seen in the past year and a half, although it is still on the list of beers "authorized" for sale in the state. In fact, the number of stores carrying Hull's Export Beer is decreasing even though the beer is better than most of the national brands that are supplanting it on the shelves.

HULL'S EXPORT BEER—good fresh clean aroma, finely balanced with good lightly hopped character, medium body, very smooth and even pleasant aftertaste, no faults noticeable, one of the best lightly hopped American pilseners.

Jones Brewing Co.
(Smithton, Pa.)

It would seem that fate was in a jolly mood when it arranged for a Jones to establish the brewery in a Smith town. This relatively young company (founded in the twentieth century, unlike most American breweries) caters to regional tastes in the highly competitive beer market area about twenty-five miles south of Pittsburgh.

STONEY'S PILSENER BEER—good malty aroma, salty flavor, salty-sour finish and aftertaste. This is a beer that performs well with food, but shows poorly when tasted by itself, as at a tasting.

ESQUIRE PREMIUM BEER—faint austere aroma, sour metallic taste, sour metallic aftertaste. Needs to be very cold to overcome the tinny nature and the excessive sourness. I cared little for it; it did not perform well in the taste trials. A number of people did like it well enough to ask where they could find more.

135

Fred Koch Brewery
(Dunkirk, N.Y.)

This brewery was founded by partners Fred Koch and Frank Werle in 1888, when they bought the Old Fink Brewery in Dunkirk. A few months later they, and their lone employee, moved to the present site of the brewery on Courtney Street In 1896 a fire completely destroyed the plant. Koch bought out Werle's interest and rebuilt. The brewery was incorporated in 1911. Knowing that Prohibition was just around the corner, Koch purchased the Deer Run Water Co. and the Star Bottling Co. in 1919 and survived the period on spring water, soft drinks, a near-beer called Kobru, and liquid malt syrup.

Reopened as a brewery following repeal, the Koch Brewery expanded throughout the 1930s, 40s, and 50s to a capacity of over a hundred thousand barrels. Sales today are in the range of eighty thousand barrels per year, with forty percent of that as draft, fifty-five percent bottled (thirty percent nonreturnable), and only five percent in cans. The Koch Brewery is still operated by the Koch family, with Fred Koch's grandson John as president and general manager.

The Koch repertoire includes Koch's Light Lager Beer, Golden Anniversary Beer (introduced in 1938 to celebrate Koch's fiftieth), Deer Run Ale, Holiday Beer (every Christmas), and Simon Pure, a label acquired from the William Simon Brewing Co. of Buffalo in 1971.

Koch also produces the Iroquois brands, which were obtained from Iroquois Industries in 1972. This line of labels virtually doubles the number of Koch produced labels on the western New York market. Included are Phoenix Cream Ale and Phoenix Premium Beer (formerly of the Phoenix Brewing Co. of Buffalo), Bavarian's Select Beer (from the Bavarian Brewing Co. of Evansville, Ind.), Iroquois Beer and Draft Brewed Beer (originally of the International Brewing Co. of Buffalo and later of the Iroquois Brewing Co., also of Buffalo), and Black Horse Ale, using the same logo as the Black Horse Ale produced by Champale, Inc. in New Jersey, where it is still listed as a subsidiary of Iroquois Brands Ltd.

Koch products are marketed under various breweries of record; to include the Koch, Simon Pure, Black Horse, and Iroquois names, all identified as being of Dunkirk, New York.

KOCH'S GOLDEN ANNIVERSARY BEER—bright yellow gold, sour malt nose with hops in the background, good fresh flavor at the start but finishes strange and sour, highly carbonated. Tastes very good until you begin to swallow it; something in it aggravates the taste buds on the back of the tongue.

KOCH'S LIGHT LAGER BEER—flowery yeasty nose, light body, not much flavor at all and the finish was quite watery. Best part was the aroma.

IROQUOIS INDIAN HEAD BEER (Iroquois Brewing Co.)—very little aroma, dry lightly hopped and malted flavor, a reasonably pleasant brew in a very pretty can.

BAVARIAN'S SELECT BEER (Iroquois Brewing Co.)—clean yeasty aroma with good malt, taste of sour carbonation with a metallic finish, not too good.

Latrobe Brewing Co.
(Latrobe, Pa.)

In 1893 the Latrobe Brewing Company was founded in Pennsylvania and by 1899 had been absorbed by the Pittsburgh Brewing Company syndicate. Today a small independent brewery by that name cranks out only one beer, Rolling Rock Premium, but does it on a large scale, and in many packages, for its many devoted followers in the East.

Although very few profess Rolling Rock as their favorite, I've never found anyone who said that they out and out disliked it. It is widely sold along the Boston–Washington corridor at popular prices, and has been seen as far north as Maine and as far south as Florida. In Massachusetts some refer to it as the Coors of the East.

Rolling Rock has long been available in returnable seven-ounce bottles called "Little Nips" and was the first beer seen in the new seven-ounce squat cans. It is also available in a variety of twelve-ounce cans and bottle packages.

ROLLING ROCK PREMIUM BEER—pale color, light malt aroma with a trace of hops in the back; most of the flavor is up front where it is fairly zesty; there is some bitterness in the back but it is not offensive. A very good value, worth trying, and worth considering for regular use. Judged to be one of the best beer values in America, and a pretty good little beer for drinking pleasure.

Jacob Leinenkugel Brewing Co.
(Chippewa Falls, Wis.)

In 1867 Jacob Leinenkugel and John Miller founded a brewery in Chippewa Falls. Leinenkugel bought out his partner in 1884 and became sole proprietor and in 1889 the firm was incorporated in the name above. When Jacob died in 1899, the second generation, Matthias Leinenkugel and sons-in-law Henry Casper and John Mayer, took over the firm. Today the fourth generation, in the persons of William Leinenkugel and Paul Mayer, continues to own and manage this fine independent Wisconsin brewery.

The product line includes Leinenkugel's Beer, Bosch Premium Beer and Gilt Edge Premium Beer (both former products of the Bosch Brewing Co. of Houghton, Mich.), Leinenkugel's Genuine Bock Beer, and Chippewa Pride. Leinenkugel products are mild beers using corn grits as an adjunct and Yakima valley hops. Leinenkugel's was called second only to Coors by a recent magazine article, and termed therein the Coors of the East. The magazine had obviously not been written in Boston, where locals have pinned that appellation on Rolling Rock. Since it is doubtful that many Bostonians have tried Leinenkugel's, maybe a test between the principals is in order—or Leinenkugel's could settle to be the Coors of the Midwest, since it is marketed primarily in Michigan, Minnesota, and Wisconsin.

A note for can collectors: Leinenkugel cans are obtainable from the company at 1–3 Jefferson Avenue, Chippewa Falls, Wisconsin 54729, at a cost of $2.00 per pair, including postage and handling.

LEINENKUGEL'S BEER—made with Chippewa Falls water from the Big Eddy Spring; palecolored, faint somewhat dull aroma, slightly grainy flavor with hints of a wood pulp or cardboard taste, surprisingly poor taste for the Coors of anywhere, and the samples came from a fresh source in Minnesota.

CHIPPEWA PRIDE LIGHT PREMIUM BEER—bright gold, very clean malty aroma with a hint of olives, more malt than hops but good character, tart and salty at the start, smooths out to a good dry finish.

CHIPPEWA FALLS (1977 PURE WATER DAYS) LIGHT PREMIUM BEER—bright gold, similar to Chippewa Pride (and it may even be Chippewa Pride) but a little different,

tart saltiness at the start, finish is sweet and brief, overall a very pleasant brew.

BOSCH PREMIUM BEER—pale gold, perfumy malt aroma, at first a bready taste, then a sour malty-cardboard flavor. "From the sportsman's paradise" says the label, formerly belonging to the Bosch Brewing Co. of Houghton, Michigan.

Lion, Inc.
(Wilkes-Barre, Pa.)

The Wyoming valley of Pennsylvania once could boast enough breweries to sate the combined thirst of all its residents. Today most of these local breweries have passed into history in the wake of the overwhelming advertising and production efficiency of the large national brewing companies. Only one, Lion, Inc., remains today brewing its own Gibbons and acquired local brands, Stegmaier and Bartels.

Lion Brewery began in 1906 as Luzerne Brewery, which went into receivership in 1908. Nine years later it was sold in a receiver's sale for $28,100 and named Lion Brewery. This inauspicious start did not portend the finish, however, for when Stegmaier closed down in 1974, Lion was the last surviving brewery in the Wyoming valley.

Lion produces a beer, an ale, a bock, and a porter under the Gibbons name, an ale, a beer, a bock beer, and a porter under the Steigmaier banner, Bartel's Beer, Liebotschaner Ale and Bock, and private labels Home Pilsener, Home Beer, and Giant Food Beer. Lion also recently obtained the Esslinger label from Schmidt's following the latter's purchase of Rheingold.

GIBBONS PREMIUM FAMOUS LIGHT BEER—pale color, very malty aroma, high carbonation, little flavor, neutral finish, a neutrally flavored beer with neither zest nor offense. Available in returnable bottles under $4 per case at Pennsylvania case outlets. Also available in cans and no-return bottles.

GIBBONS FOUR STAR PREMIUM QUALITY ALE—medium tawny color, faint hop-malt aroma, light malty flavor, very light, inoffensive, slightly more character than Gibbons Beer, priced comparably, including the very inexpensive returnables.

GIBBONS PETER PIPPIN PORTER—totally opaque brown, strong malty aroma, light body, light sickish-sweet flavor, faint sweet finish. Not good, but very inexpensive.

LIEBOTSCHANER CREAM ALE—pale color, very malty aroma, sour background to a sweet taste, pleasant-tasting finish and aftertaste. Not really an ale on the palate, more like a pilsener, but quite good, thirst quenching, and slides down easily. Seen only in cans. The Liebotschaner name originated in upstate New York in the 1870s. Genesee made it in Rochester in 1878.

LIEBOTSCHANER BOCK BEER—copper-gold color, light malty aroma, fair burnt malt taste, light-bodied, austere finish, somewhat on the shallow side. Only seen in cans.

GIANT FOOD PREMIUM BEER—pale color, very light malty nose, taste has some faint offensive features, sour finish. This brand is brewed for Giant Food, Inc., Washington, D.C., a private label of the greater Washington area grocery-store chain. It is very inexpensive and about what you would expect for a grocery-store brand beer. Giant Food Premium was produced earlier by Eastern Brewing Corp. of Hammonton, New Jersey, and the Sunshine Brewing Co. of Reading, Pennsylvania.

HOME PILSENER BEER (Pocono Brewing Co., Wilkes-Barre)—pale color, light malty aroma with some vegetal character, sweet light flavor, light sweet finish with some hops, dull, and sort of strange. This brand is made for Astor Home/Home Liquors of New Jersey.

ESSLINGER PREMIUM BEER—light yellow color, light malt aroma, light body, reasonably good flavor with good malt and hop balance. A very good beer at a very good price.

Stegmaier Brewing Co. (Wilkes-Barre, Pa.) Stegmaier was the largest brewery in the Wyoming valley and once was one of the largest independent breweries in America. Charles Stegmaier's first venture into brewing took place in 1851, when he and John Reichard formed a short-lived partnership. By 1857 this effort had failed and Stegmaier had begun again with a new partner, George C. Baer. The Stegmaier & Baer Brewery lasted until 1873, when it went bankrupt. (John Reichard was more successful with his second try, establishing Reichard & Stauff, which was to last to 1939 under the names of Reichard & Son and the Pennsylvania Central Brewing Co.) Charles Stegmaier's third attempt, this time with his sons as partners, was a success. Begun in 1875, the firm was incorporated in 1897 as the Stegmaier Brewing Company and lasted ninety-nine years, closing in October 1974. In its heyday Stegmaier won gold medals at European fairs in 1909 and 1911 and had an annual production of a half-million barrels in 1940.

STEGMAIER GOLD MEDAL BEER—pale color, light

malty aroma, light body, light malt flavor, almost no after-taste, inoffensive.

STEGMAIER PORTER—brown and opaque, faint malty nose, light cloying flavor, sweet finish, too sweet overall, indistinguishable from Gibbon's Porter.

Bartels Brewing Co. (Edwardsville, Pa.) Bartels began in Syracuse in 1886 as the Germania Brewing Co. The founder, John Greenway, sold out in 1893 to Herman Bartels, who reorganized and expanded the company. He operated the Syracuse plant and was a partner in the Bartels Brewing Co. of Edwardsville and the Munroe Brewing Co. of Rochester, New York. The Edwardsville brewery had been erected in 1898 to satisfy local demand for Bartels Beer which, before the building of the new plant, had to be shipped from Syracuse. The Syracuse plant closed down in 1942 and the Edwardsville facility ceased operations in 1968, the Bartels label being acquired by Lion, Inc., in late 1967. Until recently, Bartels Beer was seen only in returnable bottles, but is now regularly packaged in cans as well.

BARTELS PURE BEER—pale to medium color, very faint malt aroma; neutral, rather dull taste: sour finish. Not much of a beer.

Miller Brewing Co.
(Milwaukee, Wis.; Azusa, Calif.;
Fulton, N.Y.; Fort Worth, Tex.)

The Miller Brewing Co. shares its beginnings with Pabst; both were founded by members of the Best family. When Jacob Best, Sr., retired from business in 1853, he was succeeded by his four sons. By 1860 Philip Best (who was to be succeeded by his son-in-law, Frederick Pabst) had become sole proprietor of the Best Brewing Co. At that time two of the sons, Charles and Lorenz, left Best and formed a brewing partnership under the name of Best Brothers and founded the Menomonee Valley Brewery. Included in their accomplishments was the beginning of Milwaukee's "ex-

port" trade, to New York. In 1855 Frederick Miller (who had entered the brewing business four years earlier in Rochester, N.Y.) purchased the firm, and in 1888 a stock company was formed under the name of the Frederick Miller Brewing Co.

Today the Miller Brewing Co. ranks second only to Anheuser-Busch in beer sales. When Philip Morris, Inc., took over Miller in 1970 sales were under five million barrels. In 1977 sales reached twenty-five million barrels, mostly at the expense of the other large brewers, many of whom actually experienced a drop in sales because of Miller's aggressive marketing. The product line is headed by the popular and much advertised Miller High Life ("the champagne of beers"), and Lite, the Miller low-calorie beer evolved from Meister Brau Lite, formerly of the Meister Brau Brewing Co. of Chicago. Both are produced in all four Miller plants. Meister Brau and Muenchener are produced only in Milwaukee for the midwestern market (the latter sold only in kegs). Fort Worth is currently producing a Player's brand, which is being offered only in test markets. Miller Ale and Miller Malt Liquor, earlier Miller products, have been discontinued in favor of Lite and High Life.

The most recent Miller product is Lowenbrau. Import and distribution of Munich Lowenbrau had been handled by Miller for a number of years. In late 1977 manufacture of Lowenbrau Light Special and Lowenbrau Dark Special began in all Miller plants. The Munich import was phased out, with the domestic version as a replacement. The beers are very different, and although the domestic product is priced from one-fourth to one-third lower, the success of the maneuver remains to be seen, for Munich Lowenbrau was very popular. Munich Lowenbrau is made from one hundred percent barley malt and without adjuncts and additives, in accordance with strict Bavarian laws for brewing, is krausened, and is fermented for over six weeks. Miller's Lowenbrau uses corn (about twenty-eight percent, I have heard) and is fermented for a much shorter time. It is a good recipe, but different and less expensive in ingredients and technique.

MILLER HIGH LIFE—pale colored, malty slightly

hopped aroma, light completely inoffensive flavor, no faults but no character to speak of. The so-called champagne of beers come in a clear bottle. It is the only domestic beer so packaged and I have heard brewers warn that such a package makes the product highly susceptible to spoilage from photosynthesis.

LITE (a fine pilsener beer)—Miller's ninety-six-calorie beer, also highly advertised. Very little flavor, no zest, little more than thirst quenching, nothing offensive about it at all, lovely for those who really don't like the taste of beer.

LOWENBRAU LIGHT SPECIAL—light gold color, clean malty aroma, hops dominate the flavor, well balanced, carbonation not overdone. A fine beer, an excellent effort; unfortunately, it is available to us only at the terrible price of losing the Munich Light Special that it replaces. Better to have them both.

LOWENBRAU DARK SPECIAL—deep reddish orange color, fine malty hop aroma, nose similar to Munich Dark Special, flavor highly hopped (relative to the Munich version it is more highly hopped but has much less malt), light body, almost watery at the end, very little aftertaste.

MEISTER BRAU PREMIUM LAGER BEER—malty sour aroma, very little flavor, watery throughout. Meister Brau was obtained by Miller from Meister Brau, Inc., of Chicago in 1970. From 1940 to 1967 the brand was produced by Peter Hand.

New Albion Brewing Co.
(Sonoma, Calif.)

This is the most recent addition to the American brewing scene, a brewery in the heart of the wine country of California. It was incorporated in October 1976, with brewery construction being completed in July 1977. Production of stout and ale began in August 1977 and America's smallest brewery, with an annual production of two hundred barrels, entered the highly competitive industry marketing its brews in the San Francisco Bay Area.

New Albion produces only ale and stout in the British traditions but plans eventually to make a porter. All of its beer is bottled. John R. McAuliffe is president and master brewer and Suzanne D. Stern is vice president and secretary.

Olympia Brewing Co.
(Olympia, Wash.: St. Paul, Minn.; San Antonio, Tex.)

Olympia was founded in 1896 by Leopold F. Schmidt. Twenty years earlier Schmidt had begun the Centennial Brewery of Butte, Montana. On a visit to Olympia in 1894 he found the artesian waters (and surrounding countryside) of nearby Tumwater so attractive that he sold his holdings in Centennial (then Montana's largest brewery) and formed the Capital Brewing Co. in Tumwater.

In 1902 the newly named Olympia Brewing Co. became a pioneer in the multiple brewery concept. Four breweries were in operation by 1909, but none could produce a beer comparable to that of the home plant. To protect the quality of the name, Olympia was brewed only at Tumwater. When Prohibition closed the plant down in 1916, it had grown to the largest in the state.

With repeal, the Schmidt family, which held the copyrights and trade names, built a new brewery. The publicly held company has since been continuously managed by the Schmidt family and today the president of the firm, Leopold F. Schmidt, is the great-grandson and namesake of the founder.

Olympia was one of the first to recognize that consumer interest following World War II had shifted from draft to packaged beer. It decided that a small brewer could not survive the required capital investment, and that it had to expand nationally. In 1970 Olympia was marketed in only eleven western states. With the purchase of the Theodore Hamm Brewing Co. of St. Paul in March 1975 and the Lone Star Brewing Co. of San Antonio in December 1976, Olympia products extended to twenty-six states. In 1976 Olympia was sixth in the nation in sales, and although the company says its market extends only as far as Indiana, at least four of its products are readily available in major East Coast metropolitan areas.

The Olympia product line includes Olympia (packaged and draft), Olympia Gold (a low-calorie product; packaged only), Olympia Dark (draft only), Buckhorn (packaged only), Hamm's (packaged and draft), and Hamm's Dark (draft only). These beers are brewed at both Tumwater and St. Paul. Lone Star, Lone Star Draft, and Buckhorn (Texas saloon version) are brewed only at the San Antonio facility. That brewery, operated as a wholly owned subsidiary, has completed several test brews of Olympia beer and the company expects "Oly" to be produced there sometime soon. Lone Star operates a gift shop of Lone Star branded goodies; write: P.O. Box 2060, San Antonio, Texas 78297.

West Coast's largest Brewery – Overlooking the rapids and waterfalls of the Deschutes River, Olympia Brewing Company's headquarters brewery ranks as one of the biggest tourist attractions in the Pacific Northwest. The company and its best-selling beer take their name from the City of Olympia, the state capital on the southern shores of Washington's Puget Sound.

OLYMPIA BEER—a very pale beer, with very light malt aroma, extremely clean light flavor with some hops noticeable in the finish. Oly has a large following who say it is better than Coors; together these two dominate the western beer scene. Samples we tried were much better when tasted fresh from the brewery; it may be our imagination, but Olympia from Washington tasted better than Olympia from St. Paul.

OLYMPIA GOLD—my samples of this low-calorie product were slightly cloudy, the aroma malty and sour, and the flavor perfumy sweet and very light. Definitely not a beer up to expected Olympia performance.

Theodore Hamm Brewing Co. The original Hamm brewery was built in 1864 by A. F. Keller and purchased by Theodore Hamm in 1865. It was incorporated as the Theodore Hamm Brewing Co. in 1896. "Born in the land of sky-blue waters," Hamm tried expansion to the West Coast in 1953 and 1957, but the move was not successful. Hamm also obtained the Gunther Brewing Co. facility in Baltimore at this time but sold it to the F. & M. Schaefer Brewing Co. when expansion failed.

HAMM'S BEER—pale color, light malty aroma, clean and pleasant tasting but a bit dull; a slightly bitter finish is the only evidence of hops.

HAMM'S DRAFT BEER—pale color, sweet aroma with a touch of vegetable, overcarbonated, a too sweet taste, very brief flavor and aftertaste.

Olympia – the standard bearer of the Olympia Brewery Company. "Oly" has a large following that is growing steadily.

Olympia Gold, The Olympia entry in the low calorie market.

BUCKHORN PREMIUM LAGER BEER—clean malty aroma, clean and pleasant taste, bitter finish, not very interesting. This label originated with the Buckhorn Brewing Co. of St. Paul and was acquired by Hamm in 1973. It is not the same Buckhorn that is produced by Lone Star.

Lone Star Brewing Co. In 1883 a number of prominent San Antonio citizens organized a stock company. The brewery was completed a year later. A new plant was completed in 1896 and in 1902 famed brewer Adolphus Busch of St. Louis was named president. Lone Star operated a plant in Oklahoma City for a time, but closed it in the 1960s.

LONE STAR BEER—malty aroma with strange vegetal background, same strangeness in flavor but all aspects of the flavor faded rapidly in the mouth, ending with a weak watery finish.

Henry F. Ortlieb Brewing Co.
(Philadelphia)

The Ortlieb brewing firm had its start as a Weiss beer brewery founded in the early 1860s by August Kuehl. In 1869 Trupert Ortlieb bought the business but sold it to Charles Blomer in 1885. Blomer's business failed and the plant closed in 1892. A year later the facility was bought by Henry F. Ortlieb and reopened. The company remains in the family; today the chief executive and owner is Joseph W. Ortlieb, who occasionally goes on TV to urge Philadelphians to try "Joe's Beer."

Ortlieb markets its products in southeastern Pennsylvania and in New Jersey and Delaware, the area dominated by Schmidt's, Ortlieb's major competitor. There is also some limited marketing in New England.

Orblieb obtained the Kaier label in 1966 from the Charles D. Kaier Brewing Co. of Mahanoy City, Pennsylvania, which plant closed in 1968 after 106 years of operation. About that time the Neuweiler label was obtained from Louis F. Neuweiler's Sons of Allentown, Pennsylvania, and reintroduced by Ortlieb in 1974. The McSorley Cream Ale brand was obtained in early 1978 was a result of the purchase of Rheingold by Schmidt's. Old English 800 Malt Liquor is produced by Ortlieb in Philadelphia under the Blitz-Weinhard Co. label for East Coast markets.

KAIER'S SPECIAL BEER (Charles D. Kaier Co., Philadelphia and Shamokin, Pa.)—good malty hop aroma, balanced malt-hop flavor with good character and zest, quite good for a low-priced item. Available in cans and returnable bottles at a very low price. This beer has been widely marketed through the Ortlieb subsidiary in Shamokin, Fuhrmann & Schmidt. Since Fuhrmann & Schmidt is still an authorized brewery, the Kaier beer could still be produced there, as could other Ortlieb products. I understand the brewery is closed at present.

IVY LEAGUE BEER (Ivy League Brewing Co., Philadelphia)—the label touts "juniper beer flavor," but the beer's aroma seemed unusual (in addition to being slightly

skunky), the taste was very strange—which I have to attribute to the juniper berries (more commonly an ingredient of gin)—and the beer had a short and strange aftertaste. If this is what is meant by a house flavor, I will pass. This is not a good beer, just strange.

NEUWEILER CREAM ALE (Neuweiler Brewing Co., Philadelphia) (since 1891)—a cloudy brew, carbonated with small bubbles indicating natural carbonation, sweet vegetal-metallic aroma, sweet malt taste with undertones of decayed vegetable material. I understand this beer is made with two-row and six-row choice barley malt with very little use of cereal grain adjuncts, a special Canadian top yeast, and hand skimming to remove all possible astringent bitterness. It is also aged for two full months. It is surprising that it showed so poorly, and additional tests were performed with similar results.

ORTLIEB'S BOCK BEER—medium brown with rosy hues, strange grasslike aroma, sweet and strange, not good at all.

ORTLIEB'S PHILADELPHIA'S FAMOUS BEER—light nose with some hops, sour malty flavor with a bitter finish and aftertaste.

OLD ENGLISH 800 MALT LIQUOR (Blitz-Weinhard, Philadelphia)—one of the beers more like a "pop" wine, strong aromatic flavor that is overdone. Too sweet for a beer drinker. Nor can I think of any food that would go with it.

McSORLEY CREAM ALE—deep tawny brown color, big malty hop aroma, full flavored, good balance, plenty of hops yet not overly bitter, a very fine ale at a reasonable price.

OLD STYLE BREWER'S LAGER BEER (Brewer's Lager Brewing Co., Philadelphia)—pale color sweet clean malty nose, tart "prickly" flavor, sweet in the back, sour in the front, imbalanced. Made by Ortlieb in cans only, a private label of the Brewer's Outlet chain of Pennsylvania.

Pabst Brewing Co.
(Milwaukee, Wis.; Peoria Heights, Ill.; Newark, N.J.;
Los Angeles, Calif.; Pabst, Ga.)

In 1844 Jacob Best, Sr., established a small brewing plant on Chestnut Street Hill in Milwaukee. Together with his four sons, Philip, Jacob Jr., Charles, and Lorenz, he operated the successful Best Brewing Co. until he retired in 1853.

In the next few years three of the brothers withdrew from the business and in 1860 Philip Best became sole proprietor. By this time the Empire Brewery, as it was then known, had secured a high reputation, especially for the new chill-brewed lager beer.

In 1862 a Great Lakes steamer captain, Frederick Pabst, married Philip Best's daughter Maria, and two years later became a partner in the brewery. When Best retired in 1866, he left the operation of Philip Best & Co. to his sons-in-law, Frederick Pabst and Emil Schandein.

Captain Pabst was a businessman of remarkable talent and under his leadership the firm grew rapidly. It was incorporated as the Philip Best Brewing Co. in 1873 with a capital of $300,000. A year later the capital exceeded $2,000,000 and the company was well on its way to being a leader in the American brewing industry. When the output of the brewery passed the half million-barrel mark in 1889, the stockholders voted to change the name to the Pabst Brewing Co. in recognition of Captain Pabst's forward leadership of twenty-five years.

When the brewery of Falk, Jung & Borchert was destroyed by fire in 1892, the business was absorbed by Pabst, increasing the capital stock to $10,000,000 and the annual output to over one million barrels.

From the beginning the firm had attempted to maintain a forward posture in the industry. Philip Best had brewed the first lager in Milwaukee in 1851. Artificial refrigeration had been installed as early as 1878. In 1902 a Pabst brewery was constructed; the first plant in the country equipped with a pipeline system for conveying the beer direct from the brewery to the bottling house.

The pinnacle of these efforts came in 1893 when Pabst

was named "America's best" at the Columbian Exposition in Chicago. Two years later the Blue Ribbon name was added to the Pabst label with an actual blue ribbon affixed to the neck of the bottle. This device, a blue silk ribbon tied by hand and bearing the word "Select," had been used by Pabst for a full thirteen years before achieving the award.

During Prohibition Pabst survived by manufacturing soft drinks, malt syrup, near-beer, and cheese. As Prohibition came to a close, Pabst completed a merger with the Premier Malt Products Co. of Peoria, Illinois, and in 1934 acquired a plant in Peoria Heights. Further expansion occurred in 1945 when a third plant was opened in Newark, New Jersey, and in 1948, Pabst added a fourth by purchasing the Los Angeles Brewing Co. in California. The Blatz Brewing Co. of Milwaukee was purchased in 1958, but the Justice Department obtained a court order requiring divesture of this asset in 1969, so Blatz was sold to the G. Heileman Brewing Co. The most recent expansion was the completion of a new brewery in Pabst, Georgia (so named by a decree of the state) in 1970.

The company's position in the ranks of American brewers (in sales) had slipped to thirteenth in 1958, but under the presidency of James C. Windham (who came to Pabst in the Blatz deal) the firm had by 1973 regained its former position of third, with sales of thirteen million barrels. In 1976 sales reached seventeen million barrels, but this was good enough only for a ranking of fourth in the nation.

In 1975 Pabst acquired the Burgermeister and Burgie beer brands from the Theodore Hamm Co. These are brewed by Pabst only for the West Coast markets.

The Pabst Brewing Co. believes that its philosophy of naturally brewed products with no artificial ingredients is responsible for maintaining its large share of the American market. Pabst uses a high percentage of malt for its brewing process and employs only corn as an adjunct. The yeast used is a pure European strain that dates back to 1887. Real hops (a mix of European and domestic) are used. Fermentation carbon dioxide is liquefied and stored for reinjection into the beer before packaging as a method of natural carbonation.

Today Pabst markets Blue Ribbon, Andeker, Pabst Extra Light, Red White & Blue Special Lager Beer, Pabst Special Dark, and Pabst Blue Ribbon Bock Beer and Big Cat Malt Liquor. Eastside, Old Tap Lager, Burgermeister, Burgie, and Burgie Light Golden are brewed only for the West Coast. Pabst Old Tankard Ale is no longer manufactured.

Pabst is proudest of Blue Ribbon and Andeker and spares no effort to maintain the quality and reputation of these products. When Pabst became the first nationwide brewer to market beer in cans, in July 1935, the product offered was not the famed Blue Ribbon, but a Pabst Export—just in case the can really did taint the beer. Andeker is produced using two-row barley malt, long preferred by Bavarian brewers, and only imported hops. It is double-fermented and aged for over thirty days (not just one to two weeks, like most American-made malt products). The consideration and care show in the consistent quality of these Pabst products.

PABST BLUE RIBBON BEER—light colored, lightly flavored, very clean taste, no mentionable flaws, inoffensive, but lacking in body and character. It is brewed at all Pabst breweries and is available nationwide.

ANDEKER AMERICAN BEER—sprightly and interesting, well-hopped aroma and taste, yet with a high percentage of barley evident, small bubble natural carbonation, very much along the lines of a German beer. Andeker is brewed at all Pabst plants but, though available nationwide, not stocked by all stores because of its higher cost. The good body and fine hop character derive in part from the use of only imported hops and long aging. A good beer, one of the few truly made along European lines.

RED WHITE AND BLUE SPECIAL LAGER BEER—extremely mild, light and clean nose and taste, very quaffable. First brewed in 1899, this product is marketed primarily in the southeastern U.S. at popular prices.

PABST BLUE RIBBON BOCK BEER—very dark color, slightly sour aroma, taste that borders on unpleasant, almost no aftertaste at all. Found with regularity only in the spring, and then everywhere.

BIG CAT MALT LIQUOR—fresh, fruitlike aroma, pleasant taste like the nose, pleasant sweetness soon becomes dull on the palate as it lacks complexity, lacks aftertaste. Not mentioned in Pabst literature, this brew has been seen sporadically in New Jersey and Pennsylvania.

BURGIE! BURGERMEISTER BEER—pale yellow gold, subdued sour malt aroma, light body, dull flavor, sour metallic medicinal quality in the background. Burgermeister was a product of the San Francisco Brewing Co. until 1955, produced under the Burgermeister Brewing Co. label from 1955 to 1965, by Schlitz in San Francisco from 1966 to 1968, and by Hamm in San Francisco while that company was part of G. Heileman (to 1975), from which Pabst obtained the labels. The Burgie! usage on the label appeared in 1970 under the Burgermeister Brewing Co. name, a corporate name of Meister Brau, which had purchased the label from Schlitz when a court-ordered divestiture was effected. This is a brand different from the Burgermeister of Peter Hand and the Burgermeister of the Warsaw Brewing Co. of Warsaw, Illinois (now defunct).

BURGIE LIGHT GOLDEN BEER—deep gold, good beery aroma, light body, on the watery side, very little flavor, salty backtaste, unbalanced, bitter and slightly sour aftertaste.

EASTSIDE LAGER BEER—very pale yellow, dry straw nose, good depth, slight malt flavor with some hops in the background, dull finish. Eastside was a brand of the Los Angeles Brewing Co.

PABST EXTRA LIGHT BEER—seventy calories, pale color, very faint hoppy aroma, light mineral water flavor, slightly sweet, weak and watery, faintly mineral aftertaste.

Pearl Brewing Co.
(San Antonio, Tex.)

In 1885 a group of leading San Antonio citizens purchased the City Brewery, a small brewing plant located on

the site of the present Pearl Brewery. They formed the San Antonio Brewing Association and appointed Otto Koehler as manager.

An established beer formula was purchased from the Kaiser-Beck Brewery of Bremen, Germany along with rights to the product name. The actual name was *Perle*, a German word for little pearllike bubbles, or *Perlens*, that would rise in a freshly poured glass of the brew.

By 1916 Pearl had become the largest brewery in Texas. Even though Prohibition did not become law until the 18th Amendment was ratified in 1920, Pearl had problems beginning with America's entry into World War I and the Food Control Act, which essentially cut off the brewers' supply of grain. Pearl survived until repeal as a creamery, ice plant, sign company, and soft-drink bottler. Pearl was ready to go on repeal, and fifteen minutes after Prohibition officially ended, more than one hundred trucks and twenty-five boxcars loaded with Pearl Beer rolled out of the brewery's grounds, down a street loaded with cheering crowds.

Up to 1952 Pearl was known as the San Antonio Brewing Co. and labels bearing that name were still being seen throughout that decade. Pearl continued rapid growth through the 1950s and in 1961 acquired a famous old brewery, the Goetz Brewing Co. of St. Joseph, Missouri, and with it the Country Club Malt Liquor and Goetz Pale Near Beer labels. In 1970 Pearl merged with the Southdown Corp. of Houston and shortly thereafter, when the Jackson Brewing Co. of New Orleans closed, acquired the rights to Jax, a popular southern beer. In 1976 the St. Joseph Brewery was shut down and all Pearl operations consolidated in San Antonio.

Pearl Beer is made from the waters of the "country of 1100 springs," and corn is used to produce a light-colored brew. In addition to cans and bottles, Pearl produces its main line of products unpasteurized in kegs.

An interesting feature of the Pearl Brewery is the Jersey Lilly Hospitality Center with replicas of the circa 1886 San Antonio courthouse and saloon, reminiscent of the days when Judge Roy Bean dispensed Pearl XXX Beer (and occasionally justice, of a sort) from his original Jersey Lilly in

Langtry, Texas. Believe me, Judge Roy never had it so good as you can at Pearl today.

PEARL XXX FINE LAGER BEER—pale color, fresh malty aroma, mild short-lived malty flavor with just a touch of hops, good balance, no unpleasant features, but very lightly flavored.

PEARL XXX LIGHT FINE LIGHT BEER—extremely pale color, faint yeasty nose, tart flavor, short slightly sweet finish, little aftertaste, faintly malty sweet.

PEARL XXX LIGHT LAGER BEER—pale color, good malty beery aroma, light-bodied, weak and watery. Label says seventy calories; may be a replacement for Pearl Light above.

JAX BEER (a New Orleans tradition since 1890)—yellow color with slight depth, pleasant mild malty aroma, highly carbonated, pleasant and mild flavor with a good hop-malt balance, slightly sweet aftertaste, a fairly good beer with some character and quite refreshing.

TEXAS PRIDE EXTRA LIGHT LAGER BEER—similar to Jax, slightly less aroma, good hop-malt flavor but mostly up front, flattens out in the middle and there is very little finish and aftertaste. Lacks the character of Jax.

COUNTRY CLUB MALT LIQUOR—medium dark gold color, faint grapish winelike nose, very little flavor (which came as a surprise in view of the aroma); most of the flavor comes as a faintly sweet sensation at the very end.

Note: Pearl became in February 1978 the fourth brewer to produce and market Billy Beer, joining with Falls City, Cold Spring and West End in the Billy Carter venture. Pearl will have the largest marketing area for Billy Beer, covering seventeen states throughout the South, Southwest and West.

Joseph S. Pickett & Sons, Inc.
(Dubuque, Iowa)

Iowa's only commercial brewery is the Dubuque Star Brewing Co., according to the U.S. Treasury list of authorized breweries, but the owner, president, and master brewer, Joseph F. Pickett, Sr., assures me that the proper name is the one given above, which is displayed on their labels, and which has been since August 1971.

Joseph Pickett graduated from Duquesne University in 1931 with a B.A. in chemistry and bacteriology. After playing pro football with the Pittsburgh Steelers for two years, he took up the brewing trade, graduating from the Siebel Institute in 1934. For the next eight years he served many breweries, including Tube City, Storz, and Overland, finally becoming assistant brewmaster in Chicago for the Schoenhofer Edelweiss Brewing Co. in 1942. He stayed with the firm through its merger with the Atlas Brewing Co. and its acquisition by Drewrys Ltd. U.S.A., Inc. (South Bend, Ind.), in 1951. When Drewrys merged with the Associated Brewing Co. of Detroit, Mr. Pickett became a vice president of Drewrys.

The Dubuque Star Brewing Co. began about 1898, and when Pickett assumed ownership in 1971, it was in sorry shape. Equipment was geared to the 1930s, with no can production facilities and with only a single bottle production line (returnables only). It was primarily a keg beer plant, an anachronism in the 1970s.

The two company brands, Dubuque Star and Vat 7, could command only a five percent share of the local market with sales of eleven thousand barrels annually.

Under the Pickett ownership an extensive modernization program was begun, and by late 1977 was ninety-five percent complete. The new principal brand, Pickett's Premium, introduced in 1973, already accounts for twelve percent of the Dubuque County market and is now sold in Illinois and Wisconsin.

The Edelweiss and Champagne Velvet labels were acquired in 1972, probably from G. Heileman, which had obtained them from Associated when it folded in the 1960s. Edelweiss should have a sentimental attachment to Joe

Pickett, Sr., for he spent many years with the original brewer, Schoenhofen Edelweiss. Champagne Velvet, a label which originated with the Terre Haute (Indiana) Brewing Co., is produced for markets in Wisconsin and Michigan.

Additional brands produced are Barbarossa Beer, for markets in southwestern Ohio, Weber Beer, for Wisconsin, and Dubuque Star, for distribution in eastern Iowa under the corporate name of the Dubuque Star Brewing Co.

EDELWEISS LIGHT BEER—pleasant malty aroma (maybe cheery beery, as the label once said), medium to light flavor with good balance, almost no finish, no appreciable aftertaste.

CHAMPAGNE VELVET—faint malty nose, sour salty taste, sour finish, disappointing for a beer that was once marketed all over the Midwest and through much of the East. This label was also marketed by the Brewing Co. of Portland, Oregon, and the Atlantic Co. of Chicago in the 1950s.

Pittsburgh Brewing Co.
(Pittsburgh)

The Pittsburgh Brewing Co. syndicate was formed in 1899 when sixteen breweries were consolidated, each agreeing not to engage in an independent brewing business in the Pittsburgh area for a period of five years. The capacity of the combine was a huge 1.5 million barrels and the capital of the company a hefty $19.5 million. Included were the following Pittsburgh breweries: Iron City, Wainwright, Eberhardt & Ober, Keystone, Winter, Phoenix, Straub, Ober Bros., Bauerlein, Hauch, McKeesport, Connellsville, Uniontown, Mt. Pleasant, Latrobe, and Jeannette. Most of the smaller and older plants were closed after the merger. The first three listed above made up the greatest portion of the PBC operating segment.

Iron City roots go back to the year 1861, before the advent of steel, before Andrew Carnegie had ever been heard of, and when Pittsburgh was, indeed, the Iron City. The first

166

barrels of the brew were produced by two Germans, Edward Fraunheim and August Hoevler. They were soon joined by Leopold Vilsack, an experienced brewer, and in 1866 the growing operation was moved to Liberty Ave. and 34th Street, the current address of the Pittsburgh Brewing Co. In 1890 the company name was changed from Fraunheim & Vilsack to the Iron City Brewery, after their popular product. When Iron City joined in forming PBC in 1899, it became part of what was then the third largest brewing company in America.

When Prohibition arrived two decades later, PBC became Tech Food Products and survived by manufacturing ice cream, soft drinks, near-beer, and refrigeration equipment. It reopened as Pittsburgh Brewing Co. immediately upon repeal.

The early post-Prohibition years were not easy for PBC. The famous "beer wars" were touched off by the refusal of the local brewers union to join the Teamsters. Several years of beatings, firebombings, and truck vandalism followed until AFL–CIO affiliation ended the issue. In 1952 the Eberhardt & Ober plant was shut down and the Liberty Avenue facility became the sole PBC brewery. Thirteen years of million-dollar profits began with 1959, but real trouble was in the offing.

In 1971, black tavern owners organized a boycott of PBC products, charging that blacks were underrepresented in the brewery workforce. To assure black leaders that there was no intentional bias in hiring, PBC made a generous agreement with the NAACP on hiring policy. Pittsburgh's white middle class, already disturbed by government civil-rights interference and feelings of uncertainty about the past decade of protest, felt that the terms of the agreement were too generous and reacted with the now famous white backlash boycott of Iron City beers. The boycott was effective; PBC profits began to sag and the workforce was commensurately reduced. Not only were few blacks hired, but few in general were hired. The 1975 operations were down to only six percent of capacity and the few remaining employees agreed to a wage freeze in lieu of further layoffs.

At that time (1975) PBC decided to attempt to counter the damage by becoming a multibrand brewer. A wide variety of labels were acquired, mostly from recently defunct firms that had competed in the PBC marketing area. This approach seems to have turned the fortunes of PBC; the first half of fiscal 1977 actually saw a small profit for the first time in several years. The company attributes some measure of the small success to the diversification. About two dozen labels are in the company repertoire, many enjoying considerable popularity, and PBC is one of America's most prolific producers of beer brands. Two-thirds of its ninety-thousand-barrel output is sold locally, but PBC brands are now well know in the fifteen states of its market.

To the delight of collectors of beer cans and breweriana, PBC supplies a continual stream of juicy items, not the least of which is Old Frothingslosh. This brand first appeared in 1954 when radio KDKA disc jockey Rege Cordic aired a series of zany commercials for the fictitious beer, Old Frothingslosh, The Pale Stale Ale for the Pale Stale Male. Going along with the local gag, PBC put Old Frothingslosh labels on 500 cases of Iron City Beer bottles for friends of the company at Christmas. The next year Old Frothingslosh went "public," appearing at Christmas with a new set of labels. These bottles were quickly sold out as they were greatly appreciated gifts. Each year at Christmas new labels of Old Frothingslosh appeared and by 1962 they were being marketed over a wide area, as far as Washington D.C.

Old Frothingslosh, "so light, the foam's on the bottom," "brewed from hippity-hops on the banks of the Upper Crudney in Lower Slobbovia," etc., made its appearance in cans in 1968 with the introduction of Fatima Yechburg, the 300-pound go-go dancer who became Miss Frothingslosh. A series of cans featuring the Frothingslosh lovely have since followed.

Among other collectibles are series of cans depicting Pittsburgh history, sports, landmarks and local scenes. It is understood that all of the special cans are Iron City Beer. Several have been tasted and compared and there certainly is a family resemblance. The Oyster House and Seven Springs brands are admitted variations of the Iron City formula and are brewed especially for the Oyster House Tavern and Seven Springs Resort.

Most of the current PBC labels originated with the

Queen City Brewing Co. of Cumberland, Maryland, and the August Wagner Brewing Co. of Columbus, Ohio. Except for Old Frothingslosh, which might be found anywhere, PBC products are marketed in Pennsylvania, Maryland, Delaware, Washington, D.C., New Jersey, Ohio, and states adjacent to those named.

PBC beers, particularly Iron City, have a peculiar reputation among beer drinkers. They are deemed sour in the bottle and metallic tasting in cans. Few will argue their merits served from a keg, however, and this "workingman's beer" has a loyal following among the beer-guzzling steelworkers. It is particularly well suited, I am told, to a whiskey chaser. Those who believe in washing away the heat and dirt of the day's work with a mug of "Arn," and then deadening the days troubles with a shot, do so with regularity in Pittsburgh. Needless to say, it is quite unlike some of the smooth modern brews sought after by today's young "sophisticates."

PBC has never been able to capture much of this young (under 35) and female market. Its first try was Hop'n Gator, a pop mixture of beer and Gatorade, which reputedly got the alcohol quickly into your bloodstream. It was a poor attempt, especially disappointing for those who downed several cans and then sat around for hours waiting to "feel it." Robin Hood Ale and Mark V are aimed at this market, but the main hope is with a new all-natural and smooth light beer named Sierra. It should be seen early in 1978.

IRON CITY PREMIUM BEER—light malt aroma with a very faint hops plus ordinary flavor with a slight prickly sensation on the tongue is the most offered. A typical average domestic brew.

IRON CITY DRAFT BEER—labeled "the beer drinker's beer," sweet malty aroma, too sweet a taste but probably pleasant enough for most palates, good finish somewhat on the neutral side.

OLD FROTHINGSLOSH PALE STALE ALE—faint grainy aroma, small bubble carbonation, little flavor, light body, watery; of course the taste of this product is really secondary to the package.

AMERICAN BEER—skunky nose, small bubble carbonation, little flavor, less of an aftertaste; most of the palate sensation is CO_2. This is a former brand of the American Brewing Co., Cumberland, Maryland, probably a corporate name of Queen City.

ROBIN HOOD CREAM ALE—light grain aroma, malty, salty, soapy flavor; medium to good body; pleasant. A very good effort. Formerly an August Wagner beer introduced by PBC in 1976.

HERITAGE HOUSE PREMIUM BEER—sweet malty aroma, very little flavor, but with a sweet aftertaste, very ordinary. Formerly a product of the Cumberland Brewing Co. (again, probably a corporate name of Queen City) and was produced on the West Coast under the Falstaff banner at San Francisco in 1974.

SEVEN SPRINGS MOUNTAIN BEER—a better than average-tasting beer, clean grainy nose, good-tasting well-balanced flavor with a pleasing aftertaste. Comes in cans with the same logo in many different colors.

GAMBRINUS GOLD LABEL BEER—malty grainy aroma, light-bodied and light-flavored, a sweet style at first that tends toward sour in the back of the mouth, and a short sour finish. This former product of August Wagner Breweries is named for St. Gambrinus or King Gambrinus, the patron saint of beer (or brewers). Background on Gambrinus is confused. He may have been Dutch or Belgian, or neither; he may have been a king; he may not have existed. The presumption is that he was at least a king, and on this product he wears a crown. Gambrinus may be a corruption of the name of a Belgian nobleman-brewer, Jan Primus. There is also a brand called Gambrinus Gold, described below.

GAMBRINUS GOLD BEER —very similar to Gambrinus

170

Gold Label, but much lighter in flavor, main impression is a taste like a light mineral spring water.

TECH LIGHT BEER—a very pleasant grainy aroma as with most of the PBC beers, light body and flavor, metallic background to the taste with a dull salty finish. The product was marketed earlier by PBC as Tech Premium Beer.

OLD EXPORT PREMIUM BEER—strong vegetal nose, sharp salty bitter taste, astringent brackish finish. A very poor beer tried again with the same results. Formerly a Cumberland Brewing Co. brand.

BROWN DERBY LAGER BEER—faint typical PBC grainy aroma, little flavor; mostly just fresh light carbonation, ordinary and inoffensive. This beer has over the past forty years been made by a host of breweries, including Best of Chicago, Rainier in San Francisco (1939–41), the Los Angeles Brewing Co., Huber of Monroe, Wis., Grace Bros. of Santa Rosa, Calif. (1956), Eastern of N.J. (1958), Storz of Omaha (1970), Maier of Los Angeles (1972), Walter Co. of Pueblo, Colo (1973), Queen City (1973), and General, which still may be producing the brand on the West Coast. Pittsburgh introduced it in 1975.

THE ORIGINAL OYSTER HOUSE BEER—slightly cloudy in appearance with a brown-gold color, vegetal nose, very good slightly salty flavor up front, so-so middle, very dry finish. Really good with those oysters.

AUGUSTINER BEER—very light, pleasant but ordinary aroma, badly balanced bittersweet taste, very foamy, finishes clean. Until 1975 this was an August Wagner product.

MUSTANG PREMIUM MALT LIQUOR—faint sweet malt aroma, big body, well balanced, clean finish, smooth with a long-lasting good-tastingaftertaste. One of the best domestic malt liquors tasted.

MARK V LIGHT BEER—Pittsburgh's ninety-six-calorie

entry. Light pleasant aroma, weak start on the palate, poor in the middle, but finishes very well with good taste and some character. Not the best of type, but respectable. An August Wagner label.

POINT VIEW HOTEL—a special can, more than likely Iron City: medium-intensity malty aroma, very soft and light on the palate, watery finish.

WEIR THE BIG 14 RADIO PREMIUM BEER (brewed and packaged by Pittsburgh Brewing Co. for Pasco Distributing Co., New Cumberland, W. Va., and Iron City Dist. Co., Mingo Junction, Ohio)—mild malt aroma, light flavor with noticeable bitterness in the middle, very brief finish.

THE ORIGINAL OLD GERMAN BRAND PREMIUM LAGER BEER—labeled "the world knows no finer," it has a faint malty vegetal aroma like some foreign pilseners, a bitter taste, but most of the sensation is nothing more than carbonation. Previously a Queen City brand.

BURGUNDY BRAU BEER (Dubois Brewing Co., Dubois, Pa.)—deep red-brown color, salty-sweet aroma, sour-salt flavor backed by a tannin-like sensation as normally found in red wine, a very different sort of brew. The label says it contains a special (unspecified) ingredient. The Dubois Brewing Co., founded in 1897, was bought by PBC in 1967. The Dubois plant was closed in 1972, but the name is still used, at least on this product.

OLD DUTCH BRAND, THE GOOD BEER—a very clean malty nose, but very little flavor of any kind; only a faint sensation of malt with virtually no hops at all. This is another product that has for several decades been made by many brewers, including the Krantz Breweries and International Brewing Co. of Findlay, Ohio, the Old Dutch Co. of Detroit, the Associated Brewing Co. and its successor, G. Heileman, and, most recently Queen City.

STEEL VALLEY BEER—light color, light malty faintly

hopped aroma, seems highly carbonated, slight sourness in the finish. This is probably a special package of Iron City.

WFBG RADIO'S KEYSTONE COUNTRY PREMIUM BEER (distributed by Reliable Beer Co.)—pale-colored; light, mostly malt, aroma; slight bitterness on the palate but otherwise pretty light-flavored and light-bodied; slightly tinny finish; not much aftertaste.

ALT DEUTSCH BRAND DUNKEL BIER DARK BEER—deep copper color, very faint sour aroma, medicinal background to a generally sour flavor; flavor starts out as good roasted malt but soon turns sour and the sourness stays in throughout the finish.

MAGNA CHARTA CREAM ALE (Magna Charta Brewing Co.)—pale gold, good hop-malt aroma, good hoppy taste with a creamy texture marred by a metallic background, highly carbonated. This beer is packaged in a sixteen-ounce can.

DUBOIS BOCK BEER (Dubois Brewing Co., Pittsburgh)—medium dark red-brown coloring, sharp and clear, strong roasted malt and hop aroma, sort of a pleasant burnt-sour aroma, light to medium body, dry flavor of roasted malt and hops with a slightly sour finish, a fairly decent bock and certainly one of the better American efforts.

BRICKSKELLER SALOON STYLE BEER—dusty cardboard aroma, sweet grainy "beer-hall" flavor, almost cloying at the finish.

SIERRA NATURALLY BREWED PILSNER BEER—sour "off" aroma, a sort of "tincan" nose, sour malt flavor, metallic finish, recognizable as a Pittsburgh product.

Prinz Brau Alaska, Inc.
(Anchorage, Alaska)

For the first time in thirty-two years Alaska has a brewery. It is also the only foreign-owned brewery in the

United States. The newly constructed plant, completed in 1976, is wholly owned by the Dr. August Oetker Co. of Bielefield, West Germany, that country's second largest brewer.

The slogan of Prinz Brau is Great Land, Great Beer, taken from the Aleut word *alyeshka*, meaning the great land, from which the name Alaska is derived. Prinz hopes to attain fifteen to seventeen percent of the Alaskan market by the end of 1977. Up to now, Alaskan beer drinkers (a formidable market consuming twenty-one gallons per capita annually) have favored Budweiser (30 percent), Olympia (30 percent), and Schlitz (15 percent), with Miller heading the list of also-rans.

The Oetker Co. was started in 1891 and today is a huge widely diversified firm with more than one hundred fifty companies in the Oetker Group. Oetker's Brewing Division has financial control of twenty breweries in West Germany, second only to Dortmund-Union-Schultheiss. Oetker produces 6.6 million barrels of beer each year in Germany. It also controls four breweries in Italy commanding ten percent of that market, and has plants in Austria, Spain, Botswana, Uruguay, Zaire, and Nigeria. Prinz Brau actually originated in Italy at Oetker's Carisio brewery.

The Alaskan facility is producing two beers: Prinz Brau, a light pilsener type, and Prinz Extra, a strong German type more like a superpremium or import. Prinz Brau is 3.5 percent alcohol and Prinz Extra has 3.9 percent. About equal amounts are packaged in cans and bottles. Half and quarter barrels are now offered, including disposable kegs for isolated bush communities. Both are brewed only from the finest Canadian barley malt without the use of adjuncts and are fermented seven to ten days.

PRINZ BRAU BEER—medium yellow-gold color, strong hop nose, some good hop character to the flavor but harsh and unbalanced, highly carbonated and this adds to the harshness.

PRINZ EXTRA BEER—medium yellow-gold color, well-hopped aroma of medium intensity, similar flavor to above but lighter and smoother, still harsh and unbalanced. One taster said it would be best served with something like a fat liverwurst as it would cut the fatness; after identifying the product, the liverwurst was changed to blubber.

Rheingold Breweries Inc.
(Orange, N.J., and New Bedford, Mass.)

The story of Rheingold is the story of much of the American brewing industry: the modest beginning, the sudden rush of success, constant growth, the struggle to survive Prohibition, recovery, postwar expansion, the economic agonies of the late 1960s and early 70s, and, last, the sale and closing of the brewery with the attendant scattering about of the brand names.

Rheingold's story begins in 1799, when Samuel Liebmann was born in Wurttemberg, Germany. After some forty years of farming, he bought a combination inn and brewery near Stuttgart. The business was successful until the outspoken Liebmann's views on personal freedom angered William I, the reigning monarch. Liebmann then sent his eldest son, Joseph, to America to choose a site for a brewery and in 1854 migrated to Brooklyn.

By 1855 Liebmann and his three sons had purchased a large site on Forrest Street and constructed a brewery. Success followed and S. Liebmann's Sons Brewing Co. was on its way. The father-to-son business, traditional in so many German-American brewing firms, seemed to work especially well at Liebmann. Small brewing firms in the neighborhood were gradually absorbed and the Liebmann facilities were constantly being modernized.

In 1902 Liebmann purchased the famous old Claus-Lipsius Brewing Co. of New York City. The last remaining neighbor, Obermeyer & Liebmann, was absorbed during Prohibition (1924) and the corporate name was changed to Liebmann Breweries, Inc. Liebmann remained in operation throughout Prohibition, producing near-beer and Teutonic (a terrible pun!), a concentrated liquid extract of malt and hops. Obermeyer & Liebmann had survived to 1924 producing similar products, including Lion Tonic.

The Liebmann management did not decide to branch

out immediately following repeal, as did many others. Instead, it waited until after the end of World War II. The next purchase, made in 1947, was the John Eichler Brewing Co. in the Bronx. Three years later it obtained the Trommer Brewery in Orange, New Jersey, home of the once famous Trommer's White Label. In 1954 two California breweries were bought, one in San Francisco and one in Los Angeles, both formerly owned by Acme Breweries. The San Francisco plant (renamed the California Brewing Co.) continued to brew the local brands, Acme Gold Label Beer and Acme Bull Dog Ale. Only Rheingold was brewed at the new Los Angeles Rheingold Brewing Co.

At this time Rheingold had more plants in operation than any other American brewer except Falstaff. All five of these plants operated until 1957, when the Los Angeles plant was sold. Two years later the San Francisco plant was also sold. The Eichler plant in the Bronx was closed in 1961. Rheingold had shrunk to the plants in Brooklyn and Orange.

The Liebmann family sold out to Pepsi-Cola United Bottlers, Inc., in 1964 and the name of the firm was changed to Rheingold Breweries, Inc. Strangely, in 1965 Rheingold was the eighth largest brewer in the nation with sales of 4,236,000 barrels, but it was downhill from that time on. Even with the acquisitions of the Dawson plant in New Bedford, Massachusetts, in 1967 and the Esslinger (1964) and Jacob Ruppert (1965) labels, annual sales by 1973, when PepsiCo gained a controlling interest in Rheingold at a cost of $57 million, had dropped below three million barrels, and Rheingold stood only fourteenth in sales in the nation. The beer business had slipped so badly that the major interest in the 1973 purchase was the very profitable soft-drink operations owned by Rheingold and not their beer.

Within a year, PepsiCo stopped production at the Brooklyn plant, site of seventy percent of the total Rheingold output, and in a grandstand move, designed to emphasize to New York City and Teamsters officials how serious the economics were, dumped 100,000 gallons of Rheingold into the East River, asserting it would be too costly to finish processing and packaging the beer. Rheingold's other plants (Orange and New Bedford) were said to be marginally profitable but insiders indicated otherwise.

With strikes, sit-ins, lockouts, lawsuits, and violence in the offing, a New York coffee company, Chock Full o'Nuts, came to the rescue and purchased Rheingold for the sum of $1 (it was more complicated than that, but $1 was the price tag).

For almost two years Rheingold struggled on, with occasional months in the black, but mostly it was a losing business; the coffee profits supported the beer brewing. In 1976 the Brooklyn plant closed after 121 years of continuous operation.

The Orange and New Bedford plants continued to brew original Rheingold and acquired brands (McSorley's, Gablinger, Esslinger, and Ruppert). The New Bedford plant was quietly closed in early 1977, and on 1 December 1977 the following cryptic note was received from Rheingold: "Effective 10/7/77 all Rheingold brands were sold to C. Schmidt & Sons of Philadelphia, Pennsylvania. The Orange, New Jersey, plant will close its doors tomorrow, December 2, 1977."

Rheingold left its mark on New York City life, for what New Yorker of the 1940s and 1950s could ever forget Miss Rheingold. Even the name Rheingold has it legend. It is said that in 1885 David Liebmann, a true opera lover, paid tribute to Anton Seidel, head of the Metropolitan Opera Company, with a banquet. In honor of the occasion a special brew was prepared, because the last performance of the season happened to be *Das Rheingold*, the beer was named Rheingold. When introduced to the public, it was accepted enthusiastically.

Returning to Miss Rheingold, the first one in 1940 was radio and movie personality Jinx Falkenburg, who was selected by the brewery. For the next twenty-four years, however, Miss Rheingold was elected by ballot-box stuffers (an old New York City custom), and Rheingold-guzzling males fell in love with Rheingold winners and losers alike for over two decades. With candidates smiling at them from hundreds of billboards, posters, magazines, and newspapers, they could hardly resist. Rheingold appointed a final winner in 1965, stating that public interest in the contest had waned, but another theory has been regularly advanced. Rheingold had long been a favorite with the predominantly Jewish New York market. In the 1950s there had been a massive influx of blacks and Puerto Ricans, so much so that a black or Puerto Rican Miss Rheingold became a definite possibility. The Rheingold management was afraid it would lose its white clientele if Rheingold became known as a black beer or a Puerto Rican beer. Yet it was equally concerned with keeping up its sales to blacks and Puerto Ricans, whom management felt it might lose should it keep

178

Miss Rheingold in the traditional mold. Therefore, Miss Rheingold was quietly retired and we were never treated to a dark-eyed senorita or a Nubian princess. Interestingly, the racial aspects of a Miss Rheingold contest on beer sales might scarcely be worth a thought in the New York City of the late 1970s.

RHEINGOLD EXTRA DRY LAGER BEER—pale color, fresh malty aroma with faint hops in back, light-bodied, light-flavored, mostly malt but with some hop bitterness in back. Reasonably dry, as advertised; not bad, but doesn't have much zest or character, though more than most.

RHEINGOLD EXTRA LIGHT—pale color, light malty aroma, slightly sweet flavor with a sour aftertaste. Only eighty-seven calories, this brand appeared in late 1977 and, rumor has it, is lagging in sales.

Forrest Brewing Co. Forrest is a corporate name of Rheingold used on Gablinger products and also found in use on one private labeling. Gablinger was the first widely marketed low-calorie, or so-called weight-control beer, which had its origin with Dawson's Calorie Controlled Ale and Lager Beer back in 1952. Gablinger was introduced in 1967, when there was a problem with the Food and Drug Administration over what could be claimed on the label. Since it was marketed for "special diet use," the label had to state the number of calories contained; however, the Federal Alcoholic Administration Act prohibited alcoholic beverage labeling that disclosed any information regarding calories. In this brewer's Catch 22, Gablinger was in and out of the courts for about two years until the ATF Div. of the IRS decided to allow the label to state, "Has only ninety-nine calories, $1/3$ less than our regular beers."

GABLINGER'S BEER—light color, slight malt aroma, almost no hops at all, light-bodied, light and ordinary flavor; little more than thirst quenching but good for that.

GABLINGER'S EXTRA LIGHT BEER—deep gold color, good "soapy" aroma, very light in body and flavor but very pleasant nevertheless, very drinkable, better tasting than Gablinger's above. Contains only ninety-five calories, reduced by a longer brewing process.

BREWER'S LAGER (private label of Brewer's Outlet chain of case lot beer outlets of eastern Pennsylvania.)—yellow-gold color, dull brackish aroma, slightly sweet taste, flat in the middle, slightly salty faint finish. Only available in returnable sixteen-ounce bottles at a very attractive price and of acceptable value because of that low price.

McSorley's Ltd. Another Rheingold corporate name, used only in producing McSorley Cream Ale. This brand was originally produced by the Fidelio Brewing Co. of New York City, founded in 1852, later by the Greater New York Brewing Co. (1939) for McSorley's Ale House, an Eastside New York pub that permitted only male patrons for over one hundred years.

McSORLEY CREAM ALE—deep color, great malty hop aroma, full flavor without excessive bitterness, great balance. A fine ale.

Dawson Brewing Co. (New Bedford, Mass.) Founded by Benjamin and Joseph Dawson in 1889, this firm specialized in ale and porter before Prohibition and converted to lager only after repeal, at that time building up a solid trade in New England. Everyone in New England during the 1940s and 50s was familiar with the Dawson jingle, a humorous fanciful note from history followed by:
> Our history might be askew, but one fact is very clear;
> When you want a better brew, call for Dawson's ale or beer—
> Time out for Dawson's.

Beer aficianados in Boston found the Dawson's Draft Light and Special Dark particularly attractive at Jacob Wirth & Co., a German restaurant on Stuart Street, even though most of them never knew the brew by anything other than Jakie's Light or Special Dark. After Rheingold took over the Dawson plant, it continued to produce the Rheingold beers in New Bedford, but sold the Dawson label to the

Eastern Brewing Corp. of Hammonton, New Jersey, which continues to produce Dawson Beer for a dwindling New England market. The fine Dawson draft beers, produced on draft in New Bedford, were still available at Jacob Wirth's as recently as late 1977. The Dawson plant was closed in 1977.

Esslinger Brewing Co. (Philadelphia) This firm was founded in 1868 by George Esslinger. From 1937 to 1953 separate ale and lager plants were operated, and in 1961, when the venerable Wm. Gretz Brewing Co. of Philadelphia closed, Esslinger bought the rights to the brand name. Esslinger itself only survived three more years, closing in 1964. Its labels were all sold to Rheingold.

ESSLINGER PREMIUM BEER—light color, light malt aroma, light body, reasonably good flavor with good malt-hop balance. A very good popularly priced beer.

Jacob Ruppert Brewing Co. (New York City) Franz Ruppert, who had been a grocer for ten years in New York, purchased the Aktien Brauerei in 1850. He renamed it the Turtle Bay Brewery and was joined in the business by his son Jacob. In 1867, two years before Franz was to sell his share of the business, Jacob Ruppert struck out on his own, himself cutting the timber, and clearing it from the site of his brewery.

In the first year he produced 5,000 barrels in the new brewery, and by 1874 had erected an entire new plant. Huge ice houses were built in 1877 and 1880. Ruppert grew rich before Prohibition and easily survived it. He began an expansion program immediately following World War II, but expansion did not prove successful. The Baltimore plant was a short-lived venture and the Norfolk, Virginia, plant operated under the Ruppert name only from 1948 to 1953. Since 1954, it has been the southern home of Champale.

For years the Ruppert name had been a New York City fixture. Even those who did not enjoy an occasional beer could relate to the owner of the Yankees, who had been purchased by Jacob Ruppert, Jr. In 1965 Ruppert came to an end in New York City; the plant was closed and the brand name sold to Rheingold, which continued to market beer under the once proud Ruppert name.

KNICKERBOCKER NATURAL—malty aroma, smooth, soft malty flavor with good hop balance, light body, good-tasting long aftertaste, very respectable brew, worth trying. This beer was previously called Ruppert Knickerbocker Beer. The Knickerbocker name was first used in 1892 by the Bartholomay Brewing Co. in upstate New York. This beer is very popular in New England, its major market.

JACOB RUPPERT BEER—pale color, light malty aroma, clean nose, quite yeasty and very light-bodied sour flavor with a little bitterness. Not much of a beer but very inexpensive. This beer appeared in late 1977, between the closing of the New Bedford plant and the closing of the Orange plant, which was listed on the label as its place of manufacture.

Postscript: After Schmidt's closed the Rheingold plant in Orange, it began producing Rheingold, Rheingold Extra Light, and Knickerbocker at the Schmidt facilities in Cleveland and Philadelphia. The Esslinger label was sold to Lion, Inc., Wilkes-Barre, Pennsylvania, and McSorley Cream Ale was sold to Henry F. Ortlieb, Philadelphia.

F. & M. Schaefer Brewing Co.,
(Lehigh Valley, Allentown, Pa.; Baltimore Md.)

Frederick and Maximilian Schaefer founded this firm in 1842 when they purchased the Sebastian Sommers Brewery in New York City. In 1848 they became one of the pioneers in the manufacture of lager beer in America. The stock company that began the present company name was organized in 1878.

Following Prohibition, Schaefer operated only from its plant in Brooklyn, which provided Schaefer products for the New York metropolitan area until 1977, when a transfer of operations to the new Lehigh Valley plant was completed. A second facility, the old Gunther plant in Baltimore, was purchased from the Theodore Hamm Brewing Co. in 1969,

along with the Gunther label. Schaefer purchased the Beverwyck Brewing Co. plant in Albany shortly after World War II but gave it up in the late 1960s. Schaefer also operated the old Standard Brewing Co. plant in Cleveland as Schaefer of Ohio during the late 1950s and early 60s. Newark, New Jersey, was listed on Schaefer products as late as 1976, but it is not known if Newark ever housed more than corporate offices for the firm. In recent years, Schaefer has also produced the Piel Bros. brands.

Schaefer has been a staunch supporter of Metropolitan New York sporting events and the "Schaefer Circle of Sports" sponsors a wide variety of athletic endeavors through direct sponsorship, or through radio and TV coverage. Some of the product popularity is known to be the result of fan appreciation.

Schaefer is a big seller in the New York City area, in upstate New York, and in Pennsylvania. It has been well received in the Baltimore area and there is little else available on the Delmarva peninsula. Schaefer is eighth in sales in the U.S.

SCHAEFER BEER—golden color, good malt aroma, fine taste up front with plenty of zest and character, good body, flavor all the way through; this would be an excellent beer except that it suffers from excessive bitterness in the aftertaste.

SCHAEFFER BOCK BEER—brown with red-orange hues, malty aroma, taste a brief touch of strong hops, then it flattens right out, poor balance, scratchy in the throat, slightly foamy.

Gunther Brewing Co. This firm dates back to 1900, when it was founded by George Guenther (Günther—the umlaut got lost in Americanization), who earlier had been a co-founder of the Bayview Brewery in Baltimore, which was absorbed by the Maryland Brewing Co. (see Carling National). Gunther Beer is now made at the Lehigh Valley plant as well as at Baltimore and is being marketed over a much wider area than before, including upstate New York and New England.

GUNTHER LIGHT LAGER BEER—pale color, faint malty aroma, little character and no zest, not much of a beer, too light for real beer taste.

Piel Bros. (Brooklyn, originally) Brothers William, Gottfried, and Michael Piel founded a large brewery in Brooklyn in 1883 and became successful as Piel Bros. After reopening in Brooklyn following Prohibition, Piels enjoyed many good years before suffering economic ills in the mid-1960s. Before being absorbed into Schaefer, Piels operated for a brief time in the Hampden-Harvard-Drewrys plant in Willimansett, Massachusetts. Piels will be long remembered for a series of commercials featuring Bert and Harry Piel (voices of Bob Elliott and Ray Goulding) which were particularly entertaining. Curiously enough, there was a similar series of commercials using Bob and Ray as the voices of Godfrey Gunther, Sr., and Godfrey Gunther, Jr., in the Capital area in the late 1950s. Piels breweries of record during the 1948 – 74 period included New York City, Brooklyn, Staten Island, and Stapleton, New York, and Willimansett, Massachusetts.

PIELS LIGHT BEER—light gold color, light malty aroma, pleasant tasting but with little zest and personality; a very long and pleasant aftertaste. A good beer, one of the better light domestic pilseners; no faults except a lack of character, a common trait in American beers. It is similar in style to Hull's Export. Inexpensive and worth trying. Thirst quenching and pleasantly so.

PIELS REAL DRAFT PREMIUM BEER—unpleasant faint background to the aroma, perfumy aromatic quality to the taste, overdone in this respect, not dry enough to enjoy with food.

August Schell Brewing Co.
(New Ulm, Minn.)

The New Ulm brewery of August Schell has had an extremely colorful history, at least in its early days. A young German immigrant, August Schell began producing beer in the small brewery that also served as his home. The property was some distance from the main settlement and deep in the heart of Indian country. Curious Indians had always been welcome at the Schell homestead and treated to food and the traditional good German hospitality. When the famous Sioux uprising led by Chief Little Crow took place in 1862, the Schell family fled to New Ulm for safety. Over the next several weeks there was considerable loss of property and human life, but when the Schells returned to their home and brewery they found the buildings intact, even though there was much evidence of Indian presence during the period of absence. The Indians had not forgotten the kindness of the Schell family.

August Schell became an invalid in 1877 and was succeeded by his sons, Adolph and Otto. The brewery was incorporated in 1902 as the August Schell Brewing Co. and remains so to this day, operating as one of the remaining few fine small breweries in America. The beautiful Schell Gardens and Deer Park offer tourists and local citizens a peaceful and calm environment for tasting the Schell beers.

The product line includes Schell's, a higher-priced

186

Schell's Export, Fitger's Rex, and low-priced Twin Lager and Steinhaus. These beers are primarily marketed in Minnesota and have not been seen elsewhere.

SCHELL'S ITS A GRAND OLD BEER—winelike aroma, taste very much like a dry white wine, tends to flatten out toward the finish, a good beer, especially for a wine lover, excellent beer for meals, especially with seafood.

SCHELL DEER BRAND EXPORT II BEER—sour aroma, salty sour taste, sour finish, bitter-sour aftertaste, not a pleasant brew. This was one of two old Schell beer formulas recently found in excavating the property. The two were marketed to a limited extent and the public choice was to become Schell's Export, an import-type beer. Without having tasted the Export I, I was willing to lay odds on it after trying this one. At the end of 1977, Schell announced that Export I had been judged the best and will now be offered as Schell's Deer Brand Export Beer.

Joseph Schlitz Brewing Co.
(Milwaukee, Wis.; Los Angeles, Calif.; Tampa, Fla.;
Winston-Salem, N.C.; Memphis, Tenn.; Longview, Tex.;
Baldwinville, N.Y.; Honolulu, Hawaii)

The firm of Joseph Schlitz began in 1849, when August Krug erected a small brewhouse on Chestnut Street in Milwaukee, just three years after the city was incorporated. When Krug died in 1856, Joseph Schlitz took charge of the business, and in nine years doubled the brewery's capacity and sales. The stock company, Joseph Schlitz Brewing Co., was formed in 1874. The next year Joseph Schlitz died in a shipwreck off the coast of England while on a voyage to visit his native Germany. By order of Schlitz's will August Uihlein and his three brothers, all nephews of August Krug, assumed control of the business with the stipulation that the company name remain unchanged. The company continued to grow under the leadership of the Uihlein family. By the turn of the twentieth century, the brewery's capacity had exceeded one million barrels annually. The Uihleins have managed the company since then, and still retain eighty-two percent of the company stock.

Schlitz expanded from a one-plant company with purchase of the George Ehret Brewery in Brooklyn in 1949, and three years later was the leading brewer in America with a record 6,347,000-barrel output. Although the Brooklyn plant was to close in 1973, Schlitz continued expanding, the most recent addition being the Baldwinville, New York, plant (near Syracuse), which opened in 1977. The Hawaii Brewing Co. of Aiea, Oahu (Honolulu) is also a division of Schlitz, producing Primo, the beer of Hawaii. All brands are available in packaged and keg draft form. Schlitz now ranks third in beer sales in America and has a substantial investment in four Spanish breweries.

SCHLITZ (The Beer that made Milwaukee famous)—pale color, malty nose with faint hops, light flavor, lightly hopped, inoffensive on all counts, very pleasant tasting but lacks zest.

SCHLITZ LIGHT BEER—pale color, vanilla nose, light malty vanillalike sweet taste, pleasant but with little zest, some family resemblance to Schlitz above. This label was introduced in 1975.

OLD MILWAUKEE BEER—very much like Schlitz Light, but with a wild cherry and burnt bramble flavor and with a yeastiness in the finish that is quite noticeable when aspirated.

SCHLITZ MALT LIQUOR—hearty malt aroma, good lusty malt flavor at the start, flattens out somewhat in the middle but leaves a good malty aftertaste. Quite good for the type. Introduced in 1964.

PRIMO HAWAIIAN BEER—According to the package, "island brewed since 1897," but prior to 1974 the wort was shipped to Hawaii from the Schlitz plant in Los Angeles. That year a new brewhouse was opened and Primo was once again island brewed. The beer itself is a sorry affair, greatly lacking in flavor. Primo is very pale in color, has a faint

sweet aroma, and its predominant feature of flavor is carbonation, yet the beer itself is not highly carbonated. Schlitz acquired the Hawaii Brewing Co. in 1964. Primo is also now being made in Memphis, but it is not known where this production is being marketed.

Note: Schlitz markets four of the nine American brands in national distribution, more than any other brewer.

C. Schmidt & Sons, Inc.
(Philadelphia, Cleveland)

Christian Schmidt, in 1859, founded a modest brewery on Edward Street in Philadelphia and put out about five hundred barrels of ale and porter each year. The brewery did not begin the manufacture of lager beer until 1880, quite late in the industry, but at that time remodeled the plant for that purpose and increased the annual output to 125,000 barrels.

In June 1892 the firm name was changed to C. Schmidt & Sons, the new members being Henry C., Edward A., and Frederick W. Incorporation was effected in 1902 as C. Schmidt & Sons Brewing Co.

Edward Street in Philadelphia is still the home of Schmidt's, but the operation takes place on a much grander scale, the firm having acquired many famous eastern Pennsylvania brand names and expanded to a second brewery in Cleveland, the old Brewing Corp. of America plant bought from Carling National.

The Schmidt's product line is quite extensive:

BRANDS	PLANT
Schmidt's Beer	Philadelphia
	Cleveland
Schmidt's Tiger Head Ale	Philadelphia
Schmidt's Bock Beer	Philadelphia,
	Cleveland
Schmidt's Oktoberfest Beer	Philadelphia,
	Cleveland
Kodiak Cream Ale	Philadelphia

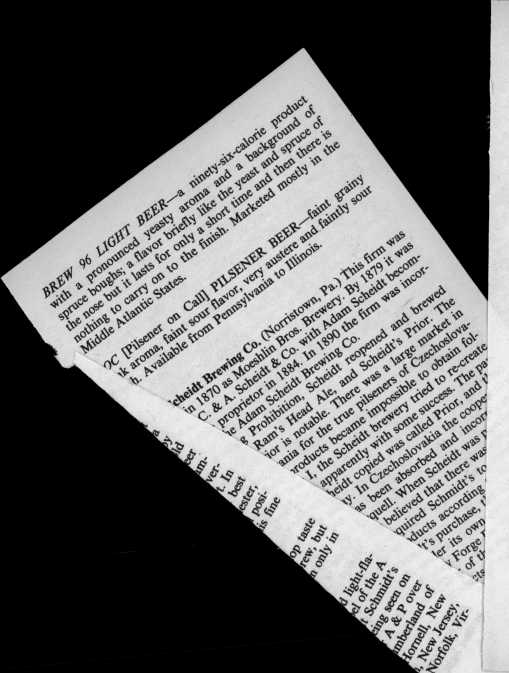

Valley Forge Old Tavern Beer — Philadelphia
Ram's Head Ale — Philadelphia
Prior Double Light Beer (Prior Brewery) — Philadelphia
Prior Double Dark Beer (Prior Brewery) — Philadelphia
Duke Beer (Duquesne Brewing Co., Duquesne, Pa.) — Philadelphia
Schmidt's Bavarian Beer — Philadelphia
— Cleveland
POC Beer (Pilsener Brewing Co., Pittsburgh) — Cleveland
Duke Ale (Duquesne Brewing Co.) — Cleveland
Brew 96 (Pilsener Brewing Co.) — Philadelphia
Reading Beer (Reading Brewery) — Philadelphia
Bergheim Beer (Reading Brewery) — Philadelphia
Tudor Beer (Valley Forge, Philadelphia) — Philadelphia
Tudor Ale (Valley Forge, Philadelphia and Cleveland) — Philadelphia, Cleveland
Duquesne Bavarian (Duquesne Brewing Co.) — Philadelphia, Cleveland

In a recent advertising campaign, Schmidt's challenged the Coors mystique with its primary brand, Schmidt's of Philadelphia, which accounts for ninety percent of its sales. The firm has had considerable success with this ad campaign in calling attention to their product, a good one that apparently appeals more to regional tastes than does Coors. Schmidt's has since taken on Bud, Schlitz, and Miller on a one-on-one basis under the aegis of the independent Consumer Response Corp. of New York. In five major cities it claims victory. Our tests showed similar results repeatedly among different groups of tasters. Schmidt's is a good product.

SCHMIDT'S OF PHILADELPHIA—deep gold color, good malty aroma with hops noticeable only in the background, a bright and crisp beer with lots of character, good hop-malt balance, clean and zesty, a good aftertaste. A good lively beer that should have widespread appeal.

SCHMIDT'S TIGER HEAD ALE—deep gold color with a tinge of brown, very little aroma, light taste and slightly on

the bitter side, great bitterness in the finish. Not unpleasant, and reasonably good for the type, but not very alelike. Available irregularly through most of the northeastern U.S.

SCHMIDT'S BOCK BEER—very dark brown, sw̶ aroma, almost no flavor at all, and very little afte̶ Available only in season.

SCHMIDT'S OKTOBERFEST BEER—tawn̶ roasted malt aroma; light but very pleasant ma̶ in hops; very good for quaffing; light, almost̶ A pleasant little brew that is worth a try.

SCHMIDT'S BAVARIAN BEER—ver̶ ly sour taste with a brief bitter finis̶ ment of Duquesne Bavarian. Alt̶ different, the package has the̶ Schmidt's replacing Duquesne.̶ varian seen up to early 1977,̶ ly converted to Schmidt's̶ where both were seen.

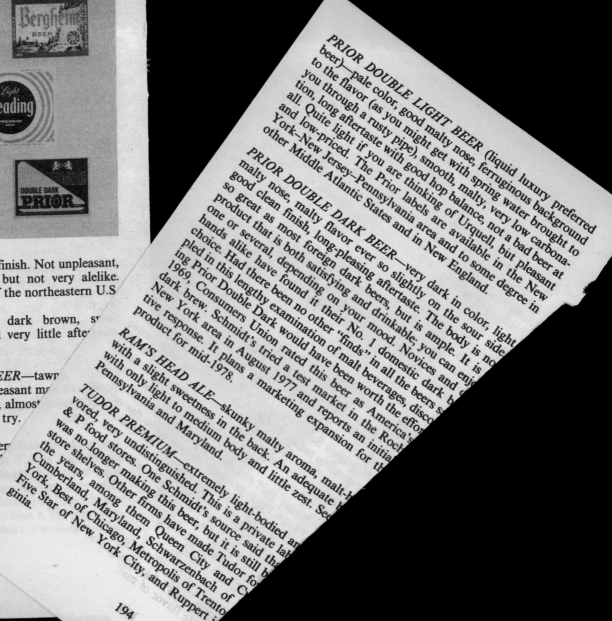

PRIOR DOUBLE LIGHT BEER (liquid luxury preferred beer)—pale color, good malty nose, ferruginous background to the flavor (as you might get with spring water brought to you through a rusty pipe), smooth, malty, very low carbonation, long aftertaste with good hop balance, not a bad beer at all. Quite light if you are thinking of Urquell, but pleasant and low-priced. The Prior labels are available in the New York–New Jersey–Pennsylvania area and to some degree in other Middle Atlantic States and in New England.

PRIOR DOUBLE DARK BEER—very dark in color, light malty nose, malty flavor ever so slightly on the sour side, good clean finish, long-pleasing aftertaste. The body is no̶ so great as most foreign dark beers, but is ample. It is̶ product that is both satisfying and drinkable; you can enj̶ one or several, depending on your mood. Novices and̶ hands alike have found it their No. 1 domestic dark b̶ choice. Had there been no other "finds" in all the beers s̶ pled in this lengthy examination of malt beverages, disc̶ ing Prior Double Dark would have been worth the effor̶ 1969. Consumers Union rated this beer as America's̶ dark brew. Schmidt's tried a test market in the Roch̶ New York area in August 1977 and reports an initia̶ tive response. It plans a marketing expansion for th̶ product for mid-1978.

RAM'S HEAD ALE—skunky malty aroma, malt-h̶ with a slight sweetness in the back. An adequate̶ with only light to medium body and little zest. Se̶ Pennsylvania and Maryland.

TUDOR PREMIUM—extremely light-bodied a̶ vored, very undistinguished. This is a private la̶ was no longer making this beer, but it is still b̶ & P food stores. One Schmidt's source said th̶ store shelves. Other firms have made Tudor fo̶ the years, among them Queen City and C̶ Cumberland, Maryland, Schwarzenbach of̶ York, Best of Chicago, Metropolis of Trento̶ Five Star of New York City, and Ruppert̶ ginia.

TUDOR ALE—cloudy yellow, good malty aroma, very light body, watery, flavor disappears in the middle, poor and unbalanced aftertaste. Also A & P private label.

Duquesne Brewing Co. (Duquesne and Pittsburgh) This company was founded in Pittsburgh in 1900. For many years it was a major Pittsburgh area brewer, commanding a substantial share of that market, but began to falter in the 1960s. It was acquired by Schmidt's in late 1975 or early 1976.

DUKE BEER—mild malty aroma, taste all up front, light body, clean and pleasant aftertaste. The "prince of pilseners" is seen most regularly in the southeastern corner of the country. The brand, bearing Duquesne on its label, was seen as recently as early 1977. Earlier Duke was made in Pittsburgh as well as Duquesne. This leads to the suspicion that Schmidt's may have acquired the POC and Brew 96 labels in the Duquesne purchase.

DUQUESNE BAVARIAN BEER (made by Duquesne Brewing Co., Duquesne and Pittsburgh; then Duquesne alone; then Philadelphia; then Philadelphia and Cleveland)—soapy aroma, light body, light taste, minimal hops, not Bavarian style in any way, a very uninteresting beer.

Reading Brewing Co. (Reading, Pa.) The Reading brands were obtained by Schmidt's in 1977, at which time the Old Reading Brewery was closed and production transferred to Philadelphia. Reading was successor to an old firm established in 1886 and with roots tracing to 1843.

READING LIGHT PREMIUM BEER—pale color, light malty aroma, pleasant malty taste with some hops, clean tasting, light-bodied, refreshing and with no offensive qualities. A good average beer that should be considered for regular home use, especially with its low price. Generally available in the Northeast.

BERGHEIM BEER—very faint and slightly sweet malt aroma; light, delicate flavor of malt and faint hops; almost no aftertaste. Inexpensive but offers little. Found only in eastern Pennsylvania.

In late 1977 Schmidt's purchased the Rheingold Brewery in Orange, New Jersey, the last surviving facility of the firm of Rheingold Breweries, Inc. The Rheingold plant was closed by Schmidt's in December 1977. The transaction included the Rheingold, Forrest (Gablinger), Jacob Ruppert (Knickerbocker), and McSorley labels. By early 1978, Rheingold, Rheingold Extra Light, and Knickerbocker Natural were appearing under the Schmidt's banner and the Esslinger label had been sold to Lion, Inc. of Wilkes-Barre, Pennsylvania. The McSorley label was dealt to Henry F. Ortlieb.

Schmidt' cans and bottles of Rheingold and Rheingold Extra Light are being produced by the Rheingold Breweries, Philadelphia and Cleveland. The Gablinger line is using the Ruppert name as the brewery of record (Ruppert Brewery, Philadelphia and Cleveland). For a description of these products, see Rheingold.

Schoenling Brewing Co.
(Cincinnati)

The Queen City has been a haven for brewers for over a century. In the late 1800s it was the home of the fifth largest brewery in the nation and of over a dozen smaller firms. After Prohibition, no fewer than ten brewers opened for business.

Only two of these remain in operation today and independents Schoenling and Hudepohl struggle to maintain their share of the area market with the onslaught of the other two Ohio brewers, Anheuser-Busch and C. Schmidt & Sons. Schoenling commands the smallest share of the Cincinnati market, but its products are shipped outside the state and have been seen in Pennsylvania and in some southern states. Both Schoenling products reported below have been seen only in no-return bottles. They are well-made, good-tasting products that deserve a try.

SCHOENLING CREAM ALE—deep yellow gold; clean burnt malt aroma; mellow with mildly tart flavor. A good-tasting brew that is available in convenient seven-ounce bottles called "little kings."

SIR EDWARD STOUT XXX SPECIAL BREW—medium yellow-gold color, nice "beery" aroma, fresh and malty, very light flavor, slightly sour finish. It is a light pilsener type, not a stout.

Spoetzl Brewery, Inc.
(Shiner, Tex.)

Founded and built in 1909 by the Shiner Brewing Association, a stock company of local citizens, the business faltered until 1914, when Kosmas Spoetzl, former brewmaster of the Pyramid Brewery in Cairo, Egypt, leased the brewery with option to buy. Early in 1915, after making several improvements to the brewery facilities, Spoetzl began producing a draft Bavarian-style beer made from pure malt and hops by his own recipe. The Shiner citizenry, mostly of Czech and German extraction, acclaimed the new beer. Spoetzl purchased the brewery outright that year only to face Prohibition in 1918 (Texas was one of the first to go dry). He tried brewing near-beer, but the public never purchased enough of it to ensure survival of the firm, but the plant could make a living supplying ice to all those Texans who were brewing their own alcoholic beer at home.

In 1933, 3.2 percent beer was legalized in Texas and Spoetzl fortunes began to turn. The new Texas Export Beer, later named Shiner Texas Special, was a success in south Texas. Throughout the 1940s the popularity of Shiner Beer encouraged continual expansion and modernization of the brewery.

When Kosmas Spoetzl died in 1950, his daughter Cecelie became sole proprietress, and the only proprietress of a brewery in the United States. For sixteen years Miss Celie, as she was known by friends and business associates, operated the firm, selling out in 1966 to former San Antonio brewmaster William Bigler. Bigler formed a stock company retaining the Spoetzl name. The brewery has since changed hands but the name remains.

Spoetzl products are marketed on a limited basis in major Texas cities, but most of them are sold close to home in Sublime, Sugar Land, and Sweet Home, Texas. Only one brand, Shiner Texas Special, is sold in package and on draft.

Stevens Point Beverage Co.
(Stevens Point, Wis.)

The Stevens Point Brewery was started in 1857 by two men named Ruder and Whale. It was bought in the early 1860s by Andrew Lutz and his brothers, who ran it until 1897, when it was sold to Gustav Kuenzel. Kuenzel ran the facility as the Gustav Kuenzel Brewing Co. until it was sold in 1901. It was incorporated as the Stevens Point Brewing Co. in 1902. During Prohibition the name was changed to the Stevens Point Beverage Co.

Only Point Special Beer and, in season, Point Bock Beer are produced for sale in a seventy-five mile radius around Stevens Point. I have not had the opportunity to taste Point Special, but Michael Weiner described it in *The Taster's Guide to Beer* as being light with distinctive hop aroma and no aftertaste.

Straub Brewery, Inc.
(St. Mary's Pa.)

The nation's third smallest brewery, with an annual production of about fifteen thousand barrels, is an independent. In fact, it is one of the most independent breweries in America. There is no advertising; no public relations office exists; not even a salesman is heard.

Sixty-two-year-old brewmaster Gibby Straub was recently quoted in a local newspaper: "We only make so much and that's it. All the Straubs like to hunt and fish too much; to hell with making all this money. Besides, we're selling all we make now."

All they make is for the north central Pennsylvania

area around St. Mary's with its population of 7,500. Forty percent of Straub's output is on draught, and the remainder is bottled. Sold only as far away as Emporium and Johnsonburg, Pennsylvania (a 100-mile sales region), the product line has been regularly turning a profit (since 1872). Straub has little fear of the industry behemoths.

The Straub product is not cheap, $5.50 by the case at distributors, for the company never cheapened their formula. It believes that you can't make good beer with cheap ingredients and production shortcuts. It concentrates on making good beer, not in competing with cheap beer.

The Straub recipe calls for two tons of barley malt and one ton of untoasted cornflakes mixed into a 143-barrel batch with water in a mash tub. It is mashed, blended, and simmered in a giant copper kettle built in 1901. Dried hops from Washington, Oregon, and Idaho are added at three different times in the brewing (which takes twelve hours at Straub) and the wort is cooled for its long (six-to-seven-week) fermentation. The Straub Brewery may be the only one in the U.S. still using a porous Lampson carbonating stone to carbonate the beer naturally.

Since the beer brews and ages longer, it is slightly higher than most domestic beers in alcohol, and a slight bit lighter than many in carbohydrates and calories. Locals are often heard to order a Straub's beer by asking for a bottle of high test.

Straub has no public relations staff, but does invite visitors to stop by any afternoon (except Wednesday) to enjoy its fine brew, as long as the guests are twenty-one and wash their own glasses.

STRAUB BEER—pale gold with a well-developed firm head, light and clean grain taste; extremely dry at the start, eases a bit in the middle, then finishes dry, as it started. This is the driest domestic beer I have ever tasted and there was not a single sour note. Straub is a really fine beer, and should be excellent with all food. A sample of the beer was obtained too late to be entered in the finals but there is little doubt that it would have been a contender. The people of St. Mary's and environs are indeed lucky to have such a fine local brew.

Stroh Brewery Co.
(Detroit)

Stroh, the oldest brewing firm in Michigan, was founded in 1850 by Bernard Stroh. It was called the Lion Brewery in 1870, when the lion crest of Kyrburg Castle in Kirn, Bohemia, was adopted as the Stroh emblem; the crest remains on the Stroh label to this day. In 1882 the name was changed to the B. Stroh Brewing Co. and finally to the Stroh Brewery Co. in 1909.

The major Stroh product is Stroh's Bohemia Style Beer, which is said to be "America's only fire-brewed beer," patterned after the practice of the Municipal Brewery of Pilsen, Bohemia. Brewing over direct fire was an innovation implemented by Stroh in 1912.

National Prohibition did not begin until January 1920, but Michigan went dry in May 1918. The "Stroh Products Co." survived the fifteen years by making ice, ice cream, soft drinks, near-beer, and malt extract. Stroh thrived in the post-Prohibition era, reaching annual sales of a million bar-

COURTESY STROH BREWERY

Stroh Brewery, Detroit, Michigan

rels for the first time in 1953. Growth from that time was even more rapid, and by 1976 Stroh was seventh in the nation with sales of 5.75 million barrels, and sixth nationally in single-brand sales. Sales in 1977 passed the six million mark, but Stroh slipped to eighth place in sales (because both Olympia and Heileman purchased additional breweries, adding substantially to their production capacity and sales).

The Goebel Brewing Co. of Detroit was acquired by Stroh in 1964, and since that time Stroh has produced the Goebel labels, brands well known in the Midwest.

Stroh markets its products over a seventeen-stage region bounded by New York, Iowa, Missouri, and the Carolinas. Some form of national recognition may have been obtained when Paul Newman downed several cans of Stroh's beer in the movie *Slap Shot*, which took place in Johnstown, Pennsylvania.

STROH BOHEMIAN STYLE BEER—light malty aroma, an ordinary beer with most of the taste in the back, almost nothing up front. It has a flavor very similar to Blatz.

STROH'S OWN BOCK—medium dark brownish color, aroma of teaberry, sweet malt taste, light body, short finish, little aftertaste.

GOEBEL GOLDEN LIGHT LAGER—pale gold color, faint malty nose, lightly flavored, but a good balance between the malt and the hops. One fault: there is more hop bitterness in the finish than in the middle. Not a bad beer though, and better than the Stroh; also better than the average American beer. Goebel was formed as the Goebel Brewing Co. Ltd. in 1889 by an English syndicate, which acquired four Detroit breweries at the time. Of the four plants, only the Goebel brewery operated after 1894. Before it became part of Stroh, Goebel operated a second plant in Muskegon, Michigan, in the 1950s.

Walter Brewing Co.
(Eau Claire, Wis.)

John Walter moved to Eau Claire in the early 1880s and founded the John Walter Brewing Co. Operation was continuous to 1916, and has been continuous since 1933, when the brewery reopened following repeal. The brewery remains healthy today, even in the face of increasing competition from the large national brewers; its sales approach 100,000 barrels annually.

Products include the traditional Walter's Beer; Breunig's Beer, originally brewed by the Rice Lake Brewing Co. of Rice Lake, Wisconsin; Old Timer's, originally brewed by the West Bend Lithia Co. of West Bend, Wisconsin; Bub's Beer, previously a product of the Peter Bub Brewing Co. of

Winona, Minnesota; Master Brew; and several private brands.

As far as can be ascertained there was no connection between this firm and the now defunct Walter Brewing Company of Pueblo, Colorado. An interesting note concerns the West Bend Lithia Co. This old firm, which dated back to 1849 and ended in 1972, was obtained by Martin F. Walter in 1911. It obtained its unusual name during Prohibition when production changed from beer to a type of water, lithium carbonate. Prudence suggested deletion of "Brewing" from the corporate name in favor of "Lithia."

Most sales are within a radius of seventy-five miles with other concentrations in Minnesota, Chicago, and southeastern Wisconsin.

BREUNIG'S LAGER BEER—pale gold, big malty aroma, dry malty flavor, a good beer that is even flavored all the way through; no real highs but no faults. Breunig's was a label of the Rice Lake Brewing Co. of Rice Lake, Wisconsin until obtained by Walter.

BUB'S BEER—medium gold, very little nose at all, at first a brief taste of hops then the flavor is a very light sour malt with a neutral ending. The motto of Bub's is Makes It Fun to Be Thirsty. This label came from the Peter Bub Brewing Co. of Winona, Minnesota.

WALTER'S BEER (design of can common to Walter's of Eau Claire for the period 1967 to present)—bright gold, nice malty nose, foamy, flavor starts out sweet but soon turns to malty sour, salty and bitter aftertaste.

WALTER'S (design of can identical to that traditional to Walter Brewing Co. of Pueblo, Colo., before its demise)—bright gold, austere slightly hopped nose, sweet malt taste without any hops noticeable, very drinkable with a long pleasant finish. Lacks character because of the lack of hops in the flavor, but still good tasting.

MASTER BREW—bright gold, very faint malt aroma, light and very sweet, no character, sour finish. A poor beer.

OLD TIMER'S LAGER BEER (same can logo as Master Brew)—pale yellow, slightly "off" light malty aroma, light yeasty-grainy taste, highly carbonated.

WISCONSIN OLD TIMER'S LAGER BEER (The Best of the Better Beers)—pale gold, light malty aroma, light clean malty flavor, smooth, neutral finish with a tinge of sweetness. This can had the same logo as West Bend Old Timer's Lager Beer produced by the West Bend Lithia Co., West Bend, Wisconsin, as recently as the early 1970s.

West End Brewing Co.
(Utica, N.Y.)

In 1856 Charles Bierbauer founded a brewery that became the Columbia Brewing Co. in 1885 and was to become the West End Brewing Co. under the Supervision of F. X. Matt two years later. The brewery was so named because, of the twelve breweries then in Utica, it was the one that primarily serviced the west end of town. This rather provincial name remains in use today.

The corporate name of F. X. Matt Brewing Co., used on the widely marketed Maximus Super, is named for the company founder and grandfather of the present third generation of company management. Matt's Premium Lager is also produced under the F. X. Matt corporate name. A Maximus Regular, introduced as a less alcoholic companion to Super, was not a market success and is no longer made. With the current interest in light beer (now reportedly accounting for eight percent of beer sales in the country), it may yet make another appearance.

Only Utica Club Pilsener Lager and Cream Ale are marketed under the West End corporate name. An Old English Ale has been marketed in the Utica area but only on draft and in limited quantities. It may no longer be available.

A Fort Schuyler brand was purchased from the Utica Brewing Co. in 1959 and is now produced by West End, attributed to the Fort Schuyler Brewing Co., to compete in the low-price end of the market. West End also began brew-

ing and distributing its version of Billy Beer in early 1978
(see Falls City Brewing Co. for the story on Billy Beer).

The West End products are found regularly only in up-state New York and parts of New England, although they are marketed in fifteen states. We have seen them in Connecticut, Maryland, Massachusetts, Pennsylvania, New York, and New Jersey. The excellent Max Super has been seen in many places outside the West End marketing area; it has a scattered but very loyal following. It was seen as far south as North Carolina.

Correspondence from Mr. F. X. Matt, vice president of the West End Brewing Co. and namesake of the founder, makes a point with regard to the term *lager*, a commonly misused word: "*Lager* comes from a German word meaning 'to age' and, historically, it was the Germans who added the refinement of aging to beer making. All modern beers are aged, even if *lager* does not appear on their label, although aging practices vary widely from brand to brand. The term *pilsener* refers to a type of pale-colored and milder-tasting beer which was first brewed in Pilsen, Czechoslovakia, and which represented quite a difference from the Munchener heavy, dark beers which were made in Munich, Germany. Today, practically all beers are of the Pilsen variety, and thus are known as pilseners." Notwithstanding its uselessness as a descriptive term, the word *lager* has become so popular among beer drinkers and label designers that nothing short of a cosmic catastrophe will diminish its popularity.

UTICA CLUB PILSENER LAGER BEER—aroma of Concord grapes and corn, light malty vegetal flavor, light neutral finish, no aftertaste.

UTICA CLUB CREAM ALE—malty nose of sweet caramel but not cleanly done, bitter-sour vegetal flavor.

MAXIMUS SUPER BEER—deep golden color, complex aroma of malt and hops, clean taste with an excellent balance of malt and hops, very Germanic in style, notable similarity to Andeker from Pabst only slightly better, good flavor and good aftertaste. One of the better American beers.

MATT'S PREMIUM LAGER—slightly skunky aroma that carries into the taste, metallic flavor, aftertaste of grain. *Note*: Both rice and corn are used as adjuncts in this recipe.

FORT SCHUYLER LAGER BEER—grainy barley aroma that reflected the taste that followed, some hops underlying the grainy flavor, very dry, brief finish. A fairly good beer at its price. It is called "the beer drinker's beer," a claim that has got to be one of the more pretentious on a U.S. label (the prize, however, goes to "the expert beer drinker's beer" [Courage Draught of Australia]).

BILLY BEER—bright yellow, sour malty well-hopped nose, faintly skunky in back, very dry, doubtful balance, short metallic finish. Totally different from Billy Beer of Falls City, this brew seems slightly similar to fort Schuyler.

D. G. Yuengling & Son, Inc.
(Pottsville, Pa.)

In 1903, stated *One Hundred Years of Brewing*, D. G. Yuengling & Son was "one of the oldest brewing establishments in the country in continuous existence." That claim is still true; Yuengling is the oldest brewery in the United States for continuous operation (even during Prohibition) and for continuous ownership of the same family (since 1829).

David G. Yuengling was born in Germany in 1806 and came to America in 1828. After residing in Reading and Lancaster for one year, he moved to Pottsville and established the brewery, becoming one of the first in the country to make the new "lager" beer.

In 1873 Frederick G. Yuengling was admitted to the partnership, and the same year David G. Yuengling Jr., established an ale brewery in New York City. The New York operation was extended to a second plant manufacturing lager beer, but neither of these ever became successful, and each required continual financial support from Pottsville. They were finally closed down in 1897. A second abortive attempt at expansion was initiated about that time with a firm in Richmond, Virginia, under the name of Betz, Yuengling, & Beyer.

Members of the Yuengling family have maintained continuous control of the company; the current president is master brewer Richard L. Yuengling, a direct descendant of the founder.

Throughout the entire period, the firm of D. G. Yuengling & Son, Inc. (incorporated as such in 1914) has remained at the forefront of modern brewing technique, and has maintained an extremely high-quality product line.

Yuengling products are marketed primarily in eastern Pennsylvania, but can be found in nearby New Jersey, Maryland, and Washington, D.C. The product line is headed by the very fine Yuengling Premium Beer. The firm also produces Old German Brand Beer, Lord Chesterfield Ale, Yuengling Porter, Yuengling Bock Beer, and a Bavarian Type Premium Beer, attributed by the label to the Mount Carbon Brewery of Pottsville, Pennsylvania.

YUENGLING PREMIUM BEER—light gold color, good malt aroma with a subtle hop background. For flavor few beers start off as well as this one. The first few mouthfuls are incredibly clean and fresh with plenty of good hop character and a bright zesty flavor. Then, inexplicably, the flavor sags and becomes quite ordinary after several more sips. That initial effect is very pleasant, however, and sufficient to ensure that this beer be ranked high on the list of America's finest. Try it by all means; it has been seen from Washington to Boston, but not regularly at any one place. This beer is made without any artificial ingredients; only the finest barley malt, corn grits, hops, and natural spring water are used.

OLD GERMAN BRAND BEER—darker color than the premium, deep yellow gold, aroma of burnt baked potato, sharp hop taste, bitter finish.

LORD CHESTERFIELD ALE—yellow gold, good sweet malty aroma that faded quickly, perfumy sweet and bitter ale taste, plenty of body, lingering aftertaste. Good value for its type; priced quite reasonably in returnable bottles; seen only in Pennsylvania.

YUENGLING DARK BREW PORTER—deep copper-brown color, rich malty coffeelike aroma, coffee flavor, finish on the bitter side, lingering afttertaste. Pretty good beer of its type and very reasonably priced in returnable bottles. Seen only in returnables and in Pennsylvania.

BAVARIAN TYPE PREMIUM BEER—medium color, sweet malty aroma with hop background, most of the initial flavor is hops, then flavor flattens out in the middle and the finish is quite bitter.

Australia

Australia ranks fourth in per capita consumption of beer (trailing Czechoslovakia, Germany, and Belgium), downing about twenty-five gallons each year, but the inhabitants of Darwin in northern Australia are the world's recordholders with a staggering annual consumption rate of over sixty gallons.

Beer in Australia is more than a way of life; it is almost a religion. It is a symbol of manliness, the totem of the rugged individualist, the drink of the frontiersman. It is said that much of the beer drinking in Australia today may be caused by doubts concerning that rugged individualism, for Australians now cluster in cities, for the most part, involved in factory or office jobs, which can scarcely be deemed the milieu of the rugged individualist. So they drink enormous quantities of their fine beers while watching bruising Australian athletic competition.

Brewing began in earnest in Australia in the middle of the nineteenth century and by the 1880s production was about thirty million imperial gallons, with consumption around thirty-two million. The Australian brewing industry has grown in leaps and bounds since then and today a substantial quantity of beer is exported throughout the world. Several years ago Foster's boasted that its lager was the third largest nationally distributed imported beer in the U.S. It was third immediately following saturation advertising to promote sales of the huge 740 milliliter cans (almost a U.S. quart), but it does make the point.

"Where's the church key?"
A kangaroo yearns for some Foster's Lager

Australian beer is very much like English-style beer, even though the majority of it is light-colored lager. There usually are more hops in the recipe and a higher alcoholic content than in American-style brews.

Carlton & United Breweries, Ltd.
(Melbourne)

Carlton & United is the largest brewer in the Southern Hemisphere, and some say it is among the ten largest brewers in the world. The several roots of this conglomerate trace to the midnineteenth century and to the Foster Brewing Co., originator of Foster's Lager. C & U operates ten breweries in Australia and shares ownership of a brewery in Fiji. It is Australia's leading exporter of beer.

Foster's Lager is the primary export, being shipped to the U.S. in bottles and twenty-five-ounce cans (those cans are 26⅔ ounces in Australia). It is made from all-barley malt, hop extract, and untreated water.

FOSTER'S LAGER—light yellow, often slightly cloudy when served *iced* (as is the practice in Australia), fresh light malt aroma, light body, fresh well-hopped flavor, poorly balanced with the malt component too weak for the hops, and the zest dies in the finish. Being able to obtain the Foster's Lager for the Australian market, I compared the two. There were great similarities, but the nonexport version was much maltier; in fact, it was more intense on all counts. It would seem that the export Foster's has been "adjusted" to American tastes.

VICTORIA BITTER ALE—yellow slightly cloudy, pungent hop-malt aroma, plenty of hops in the flavor, especially up front, big body, sharp aftertaste with sour metal undertones. A big sharp beer for those who like beer powerful.

Castlemaine Perkins, Ltd.
(Brisbane, Adelaide et al.)

There have been a number of breweries in the history of Australia with the name Castlemaine, all stemming from a

parent brewery established at the town of Castlemaine in 1857.

CASTLEMAINE XXXX BITTER ALE—faint aroma of grain and hops, big ale flavor much in the British style, very well balanced, sour hop finish, a really good British-type ale.

PICKAXE (no label, just skimpy information molded into the bottle)—faint apple-cider aroma, small bubbles, touch of sweetness in the mostly malty flavor, brief finish, and no significant aftertaste.

Cooper & Sons, Ltd.
(Upper Kensington, Burnside)

COOPER SPARKLING ALE—cloudy yellow with green cast, spritzy more than carbonated, flavor on the bitter side, very bitter aftertaste. Made at the Upper Kensington brewery.

COOPER GOLD CROWN BEER—fruitlike aroma, good malty flavor at start and at finish, vanished in the middle of the palate, sweet aftertaste. Made at the Burnside brewery.

COOPER BEST EXTRA STOUT—dark brown, faint aroma like the Chinese Hoi-Sin sauce, rich malty flavor, very good finish and aftertaste. A good stout of medium body and complexity. Made at the Upper Kensington brewery.

Courage Breweries, Ltd.
(Melbourne)

Courage is believed to be a subsidiary of Courage of England.

COURAGE DRAUGHT ("The expert drinker's beer," says the label)—cloudy yellow, faintly sour malt nose, light body, sweet and yeasty flavor, taste is brief, no finish to speak of.

CREST LAGER EXPORT QUALITY (Courage Australia Pty., Ltd.)—faintly skunky aroma, a flavor that can only be described as being like an antiseptic gauze (as like bandage). A very poor beer.

Swan Brewery Co., Ltd.
(Perth)

The Swan Brewery, so named because it was situated on the bank of the Swan River about a mile from Perth, was established in 1889. It experienced rapid early growth when gold was discovered nearby at Coolgardie and Kalgoorlie.

Swan has a high reputation among Australians and if offered a single choice, most would agree on Swan. During the Vietnam War, large quantities of beer were shipped from Australia to give Aussie troops a taste of home. The bulk of the beer selected for this purpose was Swan Lager, which was well appreciated by the lads from "down under" sweating it out in Nam. Swan was the best-performing Australian beer in the taste trials conducted for this book.

SWAN LAGER AUSTRALIAN BEER—tawny gold color, very malty aroma, good malty flavor with some pronounced hop bitterness up front, long and good aftertaste. If an Australian tells you this is not a good beer, check to see if he comes from a different region of the country. Australians are very protective of their regional beers and will stick by them even when proven wrong in blind tests.

217

SWAN SPECIAL PREMIUM EXPORT LAGER—tawny gold color; clean malty nose; hefty flavor, but a bit too much on the bitter side; dull, sour metallic finish.

Tasmanian Breweries Pty., Ltd.
(Hobart) (Cascade Brewery Co., Ltd.)

This firm dates back to the early part of the nineteenth century (ca. 1830).

CASCADE DRAUGHT—aroma of marigolds, sour-tin marigold flavor, bad beer. May have been too old.

CASCADE BREWERY SPARKLING PALE ALE—faint and slightly off nose, soapy taste, bitter and sour finish, a poorly balanced brew.

Tooth & Co.
(Sydney)

The first ale in Australia was made in New South Wales in 1795 by James Squire at Kissing Point on the Paramatta River. Fifty years later Tooth & Co. was founded, then known as the Kent Brewery. At the turn of the twentieth century Tooth was Australia's largest brewer.

RESCH SPECIAL EXPORT PILSENER—pale color; light, fresh aroma lightly malted and lightly hopped; good, slightly sweet flavor (yet reasonably dry); finish is clean but brief.

TOOTH KB LAGER—very page color, almost no nose at all, light body, extremely light flavor somewhat on the metallic side of sour. Seen everywhere in the east in the "quart" cans. Not worth its price.

TOOTH SHEAF STOUT—deep dark brown color, almost opaque, toffee-coffee nose, big smoky coffee flavor, medium body, long-pleasing coffee finish. A very good stout of the type.

Austria

Brewing began early in the territories of the Austro-Hungarian Empire. As mentioned, Pilsen (Bohemia) beer stretches back to 1292. In 1378 a brewery of substantial size was built at Dobrau, near Pilsen. Beer was drunk in Vienna as early as 1340. Until late in the sixteenth century only officers of the crown were allowed to brew and they were not permitted to sell their product. At that time these regulations and privileges were abolished and the middle classes were free to engage in the business.

The Dreher family had been brewers from 1632. Two hundred years later we find Anton Dreher extending the Dreher brewing business from Vienna to Bohemia, Hungary, and Trieste. At the turn of the twentieth century, the Dreher breweries represented the largest brewing business on the Continent under one management. Anton Dreher is credited with introducing many of the innovations still a part of modern brewing operations Included among his accomplishments is leading in the development of the bottom-fermentation process and in the application of artificial refrigeration (following the lead of Sedlmayr of Munich) in his breweries. He is further credited with placing Vienna on equal footing with Munich in the quality of its lager beers.

Bruder Reininghaus Brauerei A.G.
(Graz)

Steinfeld Graz lay in that part of Austro-Hungary called Styria and had a brewery as early as 1697. These facilities were purchased by Peter and Julius Reininghaus in 1853. By 1900 the firm was the second largest brewing firm in Austria outside of Vienna and fifth largest in the empire. The Reininghaus and Puntigam labels produced today are both highly respected. Only Puntigam appears to be available at present in the U.S.

PUNTIGAM EXPORT BEER—faint sweet aroma, sour vegetal taste with lots of hops, celery-juice taste, dull finish. The Puntigam name is believed to have been derived from a merger involving the Erste Grazer Brauerei of F. Schreiner & Sons of Puntigam, Styria.

Harmer K.G.
(Vienna) Ottakringer Brauerei

The firm producing the very fine Ottakringer Gold Fassl is believed to be the descendant of the brewing firm of J. & J. Kuffner of Vienna, although there may be any number of other breweries involved through mergers over the years. In any event, the beer now appears regularly in both cans and bottles and it is a real winner!

OTTAKRINGER GOLD FASSL EXPORT LAGER BEER—brownish gold color, lovely malty nose, finely balanced hop-malt flavor of good intensity, medium body, pleasantly finished, a very drinkable beer. Highly recommended.

Gosser Brauerei A.G.
(Loeben-Goss)

Gosser Brauerei A.G. is another well-respected firm with roots going back to the Austro-Hungarian Empire and, like Reininghaus, is located in the area that was known as Styria. The beers are commonly found in restaurants in Austria and two export brands are also now readily available in America.

GOSSER GOLDEN ROCK FAMOUS AUSTRIAN BEER—light malt-hop aroma with a background sweetness that can be best described as deodorantlike; oily metallic malt taste; not at all exciting.

GOSSER BEER—pale and cloudy, malt aroma, unbalanced burnt malt flavor; a strange beer that tasted differently with each sip. Neither of these brands has the quality of the domestic Gosser brews.

Osterreichische Brau A.G.
(Liz)

AUSTRIAN GOLD LAGER BEER—rising hop nose with a sweet background; some sour-metallic unpleasantness in the beginning of each mouthful; otherwise a medium hop taste and a dull finish.

Brauerei Schwechat A.G.
(Vienna)

Schwechat is the original paternal plant of the Dreher brewing empire of Austro-Hungary. It is the plant established by the Dreher family in 1632 and it was once the property of Anton Dreher, who built much of what stands today. The label of their major export, reported below, bears notice that this was the first Vienna lager beer.

STEFFL EXPORT—strong pineapple aroma, sweet malt flavor with a decided pineapple taste, sweet-sour finish. Very disappointing.

Brauerei Zipf Vorm.
Wm Schaup
(Zipf) (Osterreichische Brau, A.G.)

This firm was established in 1858 as Bierbrauerei in Zipf, Upper Austria.

ZIPFER URTYP LAGER BEER—pale gold color, bright hoppy nose, very hoppy taste, unbalanced and overdone, unlikeable bitter-sour finish.

Belgium

The manufacture of beer in Belgium is of ancient origin, having been manufactured in Brussels in the twelfth century. In the fifteenth century, the popular beers were white beers made of wheat and oats called *walgbaert* and *hoppe*. There also were *roetbier* (red) and *zwartzbier* (black). In time, these varieties were replaced by *lambic*, or strong beer, *mais* (small beer), and *faro*, a mixture of the two.

Belgian beers are similar to the beers of France and are rather vinous in nature. In modern times, certain local types have become popular, particularly the white sparkling summer beers of Louvain, the *bieres brunes* of Malines, *saison* from Liege, the *uitzet* of Flanders, *fortes-saisons* of the Walloon provinces, and *arge* from Antwerp.

Beer consumption in Belgium has always been high, with per capital consumption of over thirty gallons ranking it third in the world. Since 1919 the Belgian government has pursued a policy of encouraging beer drinking in order to cut down on the use of stronger alcoholic beverages.

In 1910 there were 3,349 breweries operating in the country. Today the number is under two hundred. The small independents are yielding to the onslaught of giant brewers from within and without, with their more efficient production and distribution. Two hundred is still a large number when one considers the size of the country and the population. Some loss of breweries traces to a decrease in beer consumption, down forty percent since 1925. To spur sales, home delivery is offered by most local brewers.

Standard categories for labeling beer in the Benelux countries have been adopted. "Cat III" is for household beers at 3° (Belgian degrees, which can be roughly equated to percent alcohol by volume). "Cat II" is for 3.0°–4.0° "export" beer. "Cafe" beers at 4.6°–4.8° are "Cat I." Stronger beers are "Cat S" (*superieure*). The last category includes the Belgian versions of English-type ales (5°–7°), abbey beers, and "Scotch" ales, which are 7°–10°.

Brasserie d'Orval

(Villers-devant-Orval)

ORVAL ABBEY'S ALE BIERE LUXE—dark orange foamy appearance, soapy-sweet malt aroma, intense resinous aromatic flavor that fills the senses, sharp and sweet.

This reminds me of a highly alcoholic spruce beer, which is definitely an acquired taste. Years ago an Englishman named Charlie Grimes used to make this in the little French seaside village of River Bourgeoise in Nova Scotia. It was very popular and reputed to have once put the local parish priest back on his feet when he was near death from the flu. I like it, but as I said, it is very much an acquired taste. It is doubtful if Orval can be found outside of Belgium. This beer is made by the Trappist fathers and is considered to be one of Belgium's classics.

Brasserie des Trappistes
(Chimay) (red-cap bottle; about 6°).

BIERE des TRAPPISTES (Cat. S)—foamy brown appearance, sweet apple bubble-gum aroma, strong herbal flavor like a home-made root beer, carbonation only apparent in

224

BREWERIANA

1. Anheuser-Busch Brewing Ass'n beer tray, circa 1900
Courtesy of Anheuser-Busch, Inc.

2.

2. Stroh poster, circa 1900.
Courtesy Stroh Brewery Company.

3.

3. Phillip Best Brewing Company display of 1881 showing gold medals won by Best at Centennial Exposition (1876), the Paris World's Fair (1878) and the Atlanta Exposition in 1881.
Courtesy Pabst Brewing Company.

4.

4. Adolph Coors calendar, late 19th century. Courtesy Adolph Coors Brewing Company.

5.

5. Early Schlitz advertising art. "Schlitz Malt Extract Invigorates the System." Courtesy Joseph Schlitz Brewing Company.

6.

6. Coors 1904 poster. Courtesy Adolph Coors Brewing Company.

7.

7. Stroh serving tray, circa 1900. Courtesy Stroh Brewery Company.

8.

10.

8. Pabst Blue Ribbon famous oysters display. First issued in 1898. This was the second most widely distributed point-of-sale piece in the United States; the first being "His Master's Voice" for Victrola. Courtesy Pabst Brewing Company.

9. Stroh serving tray, circa 1900.
Courtesy Stroh Brewery.

10. Anheuser-Busch Brewing Ass'n beer tray, circa 1900.
Courtesy Anheuser-Busch, Inc.

11. Schlitz Atlas Brau sign, circa 1900.
Courtesy Joseph Schlitz Brewing Company.

9.

11.

12.

13.

12. and 13. Coor's advertisements for Bock beer, circa 1900.
Courtesy Adolph Coors Brewing Company.

14. Pabst's Grand National Championship Six Horse Hitch of 1904.
Courtesy Pabst Brewing Company.

14.

15.

17.

15. The "Schlitz Globe" yacht sailed around the world by Captain Adolph Frietsch bearing the Schlitz banner. Courtesy Joseph Schlitz Brewing Company.

16. "Purity" Early Schlitz advertising art. Courtesy Joseph Schlitz Brewing Company.

17. Stroh poster, circa 1900. Courtesy Stroh Brewery Company.

18. Anheuser-Busch Brewing Ass'n poster for Columbian Exposition, Chicago 1893. Courtesy Anheuser-Busch, Inc.

16.

18.

The photographs on the following two pages are in the collection of Kermit A. Dietrich. In recent years this collection has been open to public view in a museum operating in conjunction with the Bavarian Summer Festival in Barnesville, Pennsylvania. Following its closing in 1978, the museum will move to Kempton, Pennsylvania, a location seventeen miles from Allentown, Pennsylvania and will reopen in August, 1979. Included in the "World of Beer Memorabilia" are a 60-barrel brewing kettle, bottling equipment, 800 trays, 250 calendars, 30 leaded glass windows, a 1904 Reading Brewery Co., wagon, 1922 beer truck, 135-piece set of coopering equipment, a Victorian bar dating to 1885, and a widely assorted collection of Breweriana dating back to 1771.

21.

19.

20.

22.

23.

19. Tray from Casey & Kelly, Scranton, Pennsylvania, 1905.

20. Tray from Seitz Brewing Company, Easton, Pennsylvania, 1905.

21. Circa 1900 tray from The National Brewing Company of San Francisco. National was the first lager beer brewed in the Bay Area.

22. Early 1900s tray from Columbia Brewing Company, Shenandoah, Pennsylvania.

23. Early 1900s tray from Sprenger Brewing Company, Lancaster, Pennsylvania.

24. Self-framed lithographed bin from about 1900. Emmerling Brewing Company, Johnstown, Pennsylvania.

25. Sign from Sunshine Brewery, Reading, Pennsylvania. Pictures Whirlaway, Sea Biscuit and Man O' War.

26. Sign from American Brewing Company of Rochester, New York about 1900. Reverse painted on glass with gold leaf. Only one known.

27. F & M Schaefer lithograph of 1898.

The above mentioned photographs are courtesy of Kermit A. Dietrich Collection.

25.

26.

27.

24.

the finish, good aftertaste. My aunt "Beenie" used to make a root beer that tasted very much like this, and it was great stuff when the bottle didn't explode. Tough to find in the U.S., but possible. All trappist beers are top-fermented with yeast added in bottling to cause a secondary fermentation.

Brasserie Union S.A.
(Jumet)

CUVEE de l'HERMITAGE (Cat. S)—tawny-orange color, rich malt aroma, sweet and bitter toasted-malt flavor, a strong flavor tending toward bitter in the finish, but not overly bitter in the aftertaste. This is real sipping beer, best Belgian beer ever tasted. Technically, this is a strong ale with a sweet palate at about 8° alcohol.

Brasserie Centrale S.A.
(Marbaix-la-Tour)

SAISON REGAL BIERRE LUXE (Cat. I)—pale orange-brown foamy appearance; aroma initially sweet but builds to a sweetness that actually becomes unpleasant, with the hops clashing against the other aroma components; the flavor is an intense sweet cough medicine with a tenacious acetone-like character. This has to be some sort of regional Belgian taste. It is too much for me. This is the best known example of a saison and is top-fermented in the bottle.

Brie Dubusson Freres
(Pipaix)

BUSH BEER STRONG ALE (Cat. S)—foamy orange brown—foamiest thing I ever poured; strong repugnant aroma, sour to the point of being nauseating, taste of gall or sweet bile (think about that for a moment); indescribably awful. This is the worst concoction I have ever experienced. It is so bad that I can't imagine it suiting even a local Belgian taste. There must be some trick to it, or something that has to be mixed in. Unbelievable. Maybe it was spoiled. It is alcohol rated at 10°.

Brasserie de Abbaye de Leffe
(Dinant)

ABBEY de LEFFE BIERE LUX (Cat. S) (6.5 percent)—deep reddish-orange-brown, pure barley malt aroma, very sweet taste but very clean and not cloying; persisting, however, is an aromatic ketonelike background to the flavor that evolves to sourness in the aftertaste. Although brewed by a subsidiary of the giant Artois brewing complex, the beer is highly reputed.

Brouwerijen Artois Brasseries
(Leuven/Louvain)

In a document of 1366 there is a mention of a tiny beer-making plant in a house in Louvain named Den Horen, or the Horn. This little brewery was destined to grow into the Artois Breweries.

In 1717 Sebastian Artois bought the Horn and bestowed his name on it. Later, grandson Leonard enlarged the business by adding two other small breweries to it—the Frase Kroon in 1787 and the Prince Charles in 1793. These three became known as the Artois Breweries.

Belgium did not begin to experiment with lagers until quite late in the nineteenth century and Stella Artois Lager first appeared in 1892. The current recipe dates to 1926. In 1977 the Artois group produced 4.5 million barrels in its ten breweries in Europe, most of it Stella and Loburg. Artois also makes a bock, double bock, export artois, special table beer, Gersten-Orge, and Double Gersten-Orge for the home markets.

STELLA ARTOIS—yellow-gold color with particulate matter in solution, soapy aroma, bitter metallic taste throughout; like a bad can. Difficult to find this beer in the U.S., but it is imported.

LOBURG BIERE LUXE (Cat. I)—yellow gold, well-hopped pungent malty aroma; hops dominate the flavor but balance is good until the finish; slight bitterness in the aftertaste. Difficult to find in the U.S.

Canada

While Canada never suffered a national prohibition, sectional prohibition began as early as 1878. Ontario had prohibition from 1916 to 1927, with beverage rooms not re-opening until 1934. Saskatchewan closed the public bars in

Canadian Beer going on board the Queen's ship during a royal visit.

1915 and had prohibition from 1917 to 1923. Quebec prohibited the sale of liquor for a time but allowed the sale of beer and wine.

Today, laws governing the sale of alcoholic beverages in Canada are a strange lot, and beer, wine, and liquor can be purchased in most provinces only in stores operated by provincial liquor control boards, whose main purpose is to minimize consumption. Prices are inordinately high and there are severe penalties for very simple offenses, enforced by provincial police and the RCMP (Royal Canadian Mounted Police). You may not, for example, have an open bottle or can in your car, even if all you are doing is going to a bring-your-own-beer party. If served in a tavern, you cannot pick up your drink and move to another table. Only a waiter can move your drink. If you open a can of beer on the beach you may be arrested. There cannot be a TV or piano

Page of Canadian Churchman issue of March 31, 1903 with Labatt's India Pale Ale Advertisement.

in a tavern; entertainment with alcohol is not allowed. Citizens have been slapped into jail for drinking a beer on their patio. These laws vary from area to area, but you catch the drift.

Slowly these laws have been changing and they will continue to change, for the youth of Canada, recognizing the asinine nature of the restrictions, are ignoring them more and more. The beer flows freely at rock concerts and even smaller gatherings because there just aren't enough police or facilities to arrest thousands for the heinous crime of drinking beer. Meanwhile, the laws make drinking attractive to the young and immature, and as in the United States during Prohibition, a great deal of drinking (and drunkenness) is prompted by the thrill of countering the temperance forces.

Canada produces some excellent beer. Although most of the beer sales today are lager beers, there is still a considerable market for ales, in part because of the long years of association with Britain and the large numbers of Scots, Irish, and English in the population. The beers of Canada usually have a slightly higher alcohol content that U.S. brews, nominally five percent by volume.

Canadian beer has many loyal followers in the United States. The ales of the Molson and Labatt breweries are especially popular in the U.S. since there is really nothing in the repertoire of American brewers quite in their style. A poll taken of some East Coast U.S. retail outlets finds that sales of Canadian beers regularly exceed those of German beers. Part of this may be because of the lower price of the Canadian imports, but it does indicate that many Americans find favor with the style of Canadian brews.

Although there are forty-six breweries still operating in Canada, most of the small independents have disappeared into the large conglomerates and only seven separately identifiable brewing companies remain These produce 117 labels, of which twelve can be called national brands.

The list of Canadian brewing companies extant in 1978, according to the Brewers Association of Canada, is as follows:

NEWFOUNDLAND
Carling O'Keefe Breweries of Canada, Ltd., St. John's

Canadian Beer arriving in Egypt for Canadian United Nations forces.

Labatt Breweries of Newfoundland Ltd., St. John's, Stephenville
Molson Newfoundland Brewery Ltd., St. John's

NOVA SCOTIA
Moosehead Breweries, Ltd., Dartmouth
Oland's Breweries (1971), Ltd., Halifax

NEW BRUNSWICK
Moosehead Breweries, Ltd., St. John
Oland's Breweries (1971), Ltd., St. John

QUEBEC
La Brasserie Labatt, Ltd., Montreal
La Brasserie Molson du Quebec, Ltd., Montreal
Molson Breweries of Canada, Ltd., Montreal
O'Keefe Brewing Company, Ltd., Montreal

ONTARIO
Carling O'Keefe Breweries of Canada, Ltd., Toronto, Waterloo
Doran's Northern Ontario Breweries, Ltd., Timmins, Thunder Bay, Sault Ste. Marie, Sudbury
Henninger Brewery (Ontario), Ltd., Hamilton
Labatt's Breweries of Canada, Ltd., London
Labatt's Ontario Breweries, a Division of Labatt's, Ltd., London, Toronto
Molson's Brewery (Ontario), Ltd., Barrie, Toronto

MANITOBA
Carling O'Keefe Breweries of Canada, Ltd., Winnipeg
Kiewel-Pelissier Breweries, Ltd., St. Boniface (Labatt's)
Labatt's Manitoba Brewery, a Division of Labatt's, Ltd., Winnipeg
Molson Brewery Manitoba, Ltd., Winnipeg
Uncle Ben's Breweries (Manitoba), Ltd., Transcona

SASKATCHEWAN
Carling O'Keefe Breweries of Canada, Ltd., Regina, Saskatoon
Labatt's Saskatchewan Brewery, a Division of Labatt's, Ltd., Saskatoon
Molson Saskatchewan Brewery, Ltd., Prince Albert, Regina

ALBERTA
Carling O'Keefe Breweries of Canada, Ltd., Calgary
Labatt's Alberta Brewery, a Division of Labatt's, Ltd., Edmonton
Molson Alberta Brewery, Ltd., Edmonton
Molson's Western Breweries (1976), Ltd., Calgary
Sicks' Lethbridge Brewery, Ltd., Lethbridge (Molson)
Uncle Ben's Breweries of Alberta, Ltd., Red Deer

BRITISH COLUMBIA
Carling O'Keefe Breweries of Canada, Ltd., Vancouver
Columbia Brewing Company, Ltd., Creston (Labatt's)
Labatt Breweries of B.C., Ltd., New Westminster, Victoria
Molson Brewery B.C., Ltd. Vancouver
Uncle Ben's Tartan Breweries (B.C.), Ltd., Prince George*
*Presently inoperative; company headquarters are at Richmond, B.C.

Carling O'Keefe, Ltd.

The business of the Carling end of this Canadian brewing giant began in 1840 when Thomas Carling opened a brewery in London, Ontario. He was succeeded by his sons Sir John and William, who continued the business in their names until 1876, when the firm was named Carling & Company. In 1879 a fire destroyed most of the plant, including buildings only recently erected. The plant was rebuilt and in 1883 a stock company, Carling Brewing and Malting Company, Ltd., was formed. The head of the company at that time was Sir John Carling, who represented London, Ontario, in the Canadian Parliament and was one of the best known public figures in the Dominion.

At the same time that Thomas Carling was beginning that side of the house, Charles Hanneth formed Hanneth & Hart, a brewing firm in Toronto. In 1862 Eugene O'Keefe took over this business in partnership with George M. Hawke. O'Keefe was one of the first in Canada to recognize the potential for the new lager beer and in 1879 erected a plant devoted entirely to its manufacture. Sales of the new beer immediately justified the soundness of the idea; by 1892 O'Keefe's ale plant had been torn down to double the capacity for producing lager. In 1891 a stock company was formed, known as the O'Keefe Brewery Company of Toronto, Ltd.

Today Carling O'Keefe is one of the three giants of the Canadian brewing industry, with nine plants and coast-to-cast coverage (like the motto of Canada—Ad Mare Usque ad Mare [from sea to sea]). Some thirty brands are produced, mostly within the province in which they are marketed. This is in additicn to the brands produced in the U.S. by Carling O'Keefe's subsidiary, the Carling National Brewing Co. Included in the list of Canadian products is Carlsberg Lager Beer, brewed by Carling O'Keefe under the supervision of Carlsberg of Copenhagen.

The Carling O'Keefe brands by *province* and *plant* are (including alcohol percentage by volume if other than five percent):

BRITISH COLUMBIA, VANCOUVER
Black Label Beer*
Carlsberg Beer*
Colt .45 Beer
Extra Old Stock Malt Liquor (6.2%)
4X Cream Stout (4.8%)
Heidelberg Beer*
Kronenbrau 1308 Beer
Old Vienna Beer
Pilsener Beer*
Toby Beer
Old Country Malt Liquor (6%)
*Also distributed in the Yukon Territory.

ALBERTA, CALGARY
Alta 3.9 Beer (3.9%)*
Black Label Beer*
Calgary Export Lager Beer*
Carlsberg Beer*
Extra Old Stock Malt Liquor (6.2%)*
Heidelberg Beer*
Old Vienna Beer*
*Also distributed in the Northwest Territories.

SASKATCHEWAN, REGINA
Calgary Export Lager Beer
Carlsberg Beer
Heidelberg Beer

SASKATCHEWAN, SASKATOON
Black Label Beer
Calgary Export Lager Beer
Cascade Beer
O'Keefe Ale
Old Vienna Beer
Pilsener Beer
Red Cap Ale

MANITOBA, WINNIPEG
Black Label Beer
Calgary Export Lager Beer

Carlsberg Beer
Cascade Pilsener Beer (3.9%)
Extra Old Stock Malt Liquor (6.2%)
Heidelberg Beer
Old Vienna Beer
Pilsener Beer
Standard Lager Beer

ONTARIO, TORONTO
Black HOrse Ale*
Black Label Beer#
Blended Ale#
Brading Ale#
Calgary Export Ale
Carlsberg Beer
Dow Ale#
Dow Porter (4.9%)
Heidelberg Ale (termed beer on label)#
Highlite Beer (68 Cal., 2.5%)
Holiday Beer#
Kingsbeer Beer#
O'Keefe Ale*#
Old Vienna Beer*#
Red Cap Ale#
Toby Ale*#
Calgary Export Lager Beer**
Cinci Beer#**
*Also exported to the U.S.
#Also produced at Waterloo, Ont.
**Produced at Toronto only for export to the U.S.

QUEBEC, MONTREAL
Black Label Beer*
Carlsberg Beer
Champlain Porter (4.8%)
Dow Ale
Heidelberg Ale (termed beer on label)*
Kronenbrau 1308 Beer
O'Keefe Ale*
Red Cap Ale
Old Vienna Beer**
*Also distributed in the Maritimes.
**Only distributed in the Maritimes.

NEWFOUNDLAND, ST. JOHN'S
Black Horse Beer
Dominion Ale
Extra Old Stock Malt Liquor (6.2%)
Haig Light Beer (2.2%)

BENNETT'S DOMINION ALE—tawny gold color, light malty yeasty aroma, malty yeasty taste dominated by hops, lightly flavored in a bitter style; very much a regional taste and definitely in the style preferred by the English peoples, who make up the vast majority of Newfoundland's population. Made by Carling O'Keefe for the Bennett Brewing Co., Ltd. The first brewery in Newfoundland was founded in St. John's by C. F. Bennett, about 1850.

O'KEEFE ALE—gold color, clouded, clean malty nose, malty flavor that trails off to nothing toward the finish. Made by La Brasserie O'Keefe, Ltd., Montreal. This is the Canadian domestic version, from the Maritimes.

O'KEEFE ALE—gold color, clean faint malty aroma, light malty ale taste, highly carbonated, good finish, and lingering pleasant aftertaste. This is the version exported to the U.S., made in Toronto.

BLACK HORSE BEER PREMIUM STOCK—off, definitely repelling aroma, bitter flavor, very unlikable. All samples found to be the same, but may have been from a mishandled batch. Made for Bennett Brewing Co., Ltd.

O'KEEFE'S OLD VIENNA LAGER BEER—cloudy with particulate matter in solution, taste was pleasant enough but not very interesting. This is the export version made in Toronto.

TOBY ALE—no aroma, sweet ale flavor, unpleasant unbalanced finish. The product is brewed under licence from Bass Charrington, Ltd., of England. This is the export version made in Toronto.

CINCI LAGER BEER—slightly skunky aroma, flavor almost only bitterness, overdone with the hops. Very unusual for a Canadian beer, and especially for an export beer. It says something for the Canadian beer drinker when you remember that this beer is made for export only. And says much about the Canadian's view of the American's beer taste.

HEIDELBERG BEER—faint hydrogen sulfide (rotten eggs) nose, sour taste, unappetizing. Made by La Brasserie O'Keefe, Ltd., Montreal, for the Maritimes market (at least this sample was).

CALGARY EXPORT LAGER BEER—spring-water aroma, dull soapy taste. "Brewed from the heart of Alberta's world famous Conquest barley, malt, and other grains. Have a good old barley sandwich." This can was made in Toronto for export.

DOW BLACK HORSE ALE—Spring-water aroma, spring-water flavor; unpleasant metal background to the taste, as if it came from the spring in a very rusty pipe; very unusual finish, like dried apricots. Not greatly different in early impressions from the Calgary Export above. The Dow label goes way back in the history of Montreal brewing, with William Dow & Co. starting in 1809.

Doran's Northern Ontario Breweries, Ltd.

Back in 1907 hotel keeper and amateur boxer J. J. Doran got together with two partners and bought the Sudbury Brewing and Malting Co. A few years later they bought out the Soo Falls Brewing Co. and the Kakabeka Brewing Co., both of Sault Ste. Marie. In 1928, J. J. built Doran's Brewing Ltd. in Timmins, and by 1948 had added the Port Arthur Beverage Co., Ltd.

The five companies were merged in 1960 to form Doran's Northern Ontario Breweries. When J. J. Doran's son William retired in 1971, the business was purchased by Canadian Breweries, Ltd. (now Carling O'Keefe). J. M. Coulter was an accountant with Doran for years and served as president of the soft-drink side of the firm, and when the firm failed to make a profit for Canadian Breweries, he was concerned that, with its reputation for buying and closing, it might shut down the five plants and throw 225 Doran employees out of work. When Carling O'Keefe stopped making the traditional Doran labels, Coulter began to round up

pledges from employees to purchase the company. With some support from the Bank of Montreal, Coulter and 170 Doran employees bought the company back for about $4 million in 1977.

Now president of Doran's, Coulter believes it can get along for a while on the profitable Doran soft-drink franchised bottling business while the firm ponders marketing and sales plans to generate renewed interest in the traditional Doran brands that hadn't been produced since 1974. Northern Ontario beer drinkers can once again enjoy Doran's Lager, Northern Ale, 55 Lager, Edelbrau, Encore Ale, Silver Spray, Doran's Cream Porter and Kakabeka Cream being made at Thunder Bay, Timmins, Sault Ste. Marie and Sudbury. All four plants produce draught beer for their individual markets, but only Sudbury and Sault Ste. Marie have bottling lines. No Doran products are canned.

Henninger Brewery (Ontario), Ltd.

Henninger is Canada's youngest brewing firm, starting operations in June 1973 in the refurbished Peller's Brewery in Hamilton, Ontario. The company was put together when E. M. "Ted" Dunal came in as a consultant to a holder of a brewery franchise from Henninger Brau of Frankfurt, West Germany. Mr. Dunal, now president of Henninger (Ontario), was previously vice president of sales for Canada with Carling O'Keefe.

With a production capacity of 150,000 barrels, Henninger is Canada's smallest brewer, and its sales account for only about one percent of that in its marketing area. It was Mr. Dunal's personal conviction that the Canadian beer drinker was becoming increasingly sophisticated and that these more cosmopolitan consumers in urban central Canada would be willing to pay a few cents more for German-style beer with more body and more hop character. It was deemed a worthy thought by Henninger Brau KgA, which supplied malt, hops, yeast, money, and a license to produce the fine beers.

The company is yet to turn a profit, but the losses have been decreasing (two principal creditors are their advertising agency and Henninger International royalty payments)

and the management is optimistic. The company is now financed primarily by Canadian interests and the stock is listed on the Toronto exchange.

The product line consists of two German-type beers (Henninger Export Bier and Henninger Meister Pils). Under separate franchise with Brauerei A. Hurlimann A. G. Zurich (Switzerland), the firm produces nonalcoholic (less than one-half of one percent) Birell, an internationally known delicatessen beer. They also handle a Henninger import, a five-liter-draught can sold only in Quebec. The Henninger beers are all malt beers, using only German hops, are doubly fermented and naturally carbonated. It is the formula for excellent beer and if Ted Dunal can catch the attention of Ontario beer drinkers, success should follow.

Labatt's Breweries of Canada, Ltd.

The original Simcoe Street brewery of Labatt's was built in London, Canada West (now Ontario), by John Balkwell in 1828. It was burned and rebuilt and sold in 1847 to John K. Labatt and Samuel Eccles, an experienced brewer. Eccles retired in 1853 and Labatt operated the brewery as sole owner until 1866 when he died. He was succeeded by his son, also named John. Once more, the brewery burned down and was rebuilt (in 1874). Another fresh start was needed in 1899 when, you guessed it, the brewery again burned to the ground.

With the fire problem apparently under control, Labatt's Brewery was incorporated in 1911 and the name changed to John Labatt, Ltd. That year Labatt first began to brew lager beer.

Labatt's began "exporting" beer as early as 1853 with shipments to Hamilton, Toronto, and Montreal. In 1878 Labatt's set up a distribution agency in Montreal. For the next fifty years gold medals were accumulated by the dozens at international competitions.

Prohibition came to Ontario in 1916 and lasted for eleven years. During that stretch of time all but fifteen of the

This composite of early Labatt photos was long displayed in the company's head office in London, Ontario.

province's sixty-four breweries were wiped out. Only Labatt's opened with the same management.

Labatt's went public in 1945 and soon after began one of the most remarkable growth sequences in Canadian industry. First Labatt's bought the Copland Brewing Co. of Toronto, a firm dating to 1830. In 1953, it bought Shea's Winnipeg Brewery, Ltd., and a controlling interest in Kiewel's and Pelissier's breweries. The corporate structure was decentralized in 1956 with the head office maintained in London and operating divisions in Quebec, Ontario, and Manitoba, the new Montreal brewery being opened in June of that year. The Labatt labels were introduced in Manitoba, marking the beginning of a national label in Canada. In 1958 Labatt's acquired Lucky Lager Breweries, Ltd., in British Columbia and an interest in the Lucky Lager Brewing Co. in the U.S. At that time Labatt's also formed a research alliance with Ind Coope, Ltd., of England and Lucky Lager.

Harpo Marx Advertising Campaign 1958.

Saskatchewan joined the fold in 1960 with the acquisition of the Saskatoon Brewing Co. (founded in 1906) and Labatt labels were immediately marketed in that province. In 1961 Labatt's diversified, established a special products division, and soon was deeply involved in international pharmaceuticals and chemicals.

Newfoundland was reached in 1962 with the purchase of Bavarian Brewing, Ltd., in St. John's. In 1964, an offer was made by the Joseph Schlitz Brewing Co. of Milwaukee to purchase thirty-nine percent of Labatt stock. The offer was accepted by the Labatt family, but the U.S. Justice Dept. ordered Schlitz to divest itself of the Labatt holdings and Schlitz sold the stock to three Canadian investment organizations in 1967. Meanwhile, the company had again reorganized with John Labatt, Ltd., surrendering its brewing license to a new company, Labatt Breweries of Canada,

Ltd., and construction began on a new brewhouse for the London plant, the largest in the world.

SKOL International, Ltd., was formed in 1964 by Labatt's, Allied Breweries of Great Britain, Pripps of Sweden, and Unibra of Belgium to brew and market SKOL beer throughout the world. Later that year a brewery was opened in Edmonton, General Brewing Co. of San Francisco began to brew Labatt brands, and Labatt's entered the Canadian food industry through Maple Leaf Mills, Ltd.

Wines were added in 1965 when control of Parkdale Wines, Ltd. of Toronto was gained. Grimsby Wines, Ltd., of Ontario, Normandie Wines, Ltd., of New Brunswick, and the well-known Chateau-Gai Wines, Ltd., were added subsequently. Another major development in 1965 was formation of Guiness Canada, Ltd., with Labatt licensed to produce Guiness Stout in Canada.

In 1968 Labatt's began construction on a new brewery

Labatt products of the 1950s. Bottles of this shape are no longer in use in the Canadian domestic market.

in Toronto, acquired the Ogilvie Flour Mills Co., and obtained a controlling interest in the Oakland Seals of the National Hockey League (which it later sold when a transfer of the franchise to Vancouver could not be arranged). Expansion into nonbrewing activites continued at an increasing rate throughout the 1968–77 period as Labatt's grew into a giant well-diversified corporation. It makes interesting reading, but I'll leave that to someone who wants to write the history of Labatt's. Labatt's even obtained a forty-five percent interest in the Toronto Blue Jays of the American (baseball) League.

Nova Scotia and New Brunswick joined Labatt's in 1971 when the Halifax and St. John breweries of Oland and Son, Ltd., were obtained. These facilities were renamed Oland's Breweries (1971), Ltd., and became the Maritimes Region of Labatt Breweries of Canada, Ltd. The Oland family remained as directors of the new company. Later, the Alexander Keith Nova Scotia Brewery was acquired and

COURTESY LABATT BREWERIES OF CANADA LTD.

Labatt domestic bottles. Note the squat shape common to all Canadian domestic bottlings.

closed, the manufacture of the Keith label being resumed at Oland's.

The Stephenville, Newfoundland, brewery of the Bison Brewing Co. was acquired and reopened in 1974, giving Labatt's the western Newfoundland market, and the Columbia Brewing Co. of Creston, British Columbia, was obtained in 1976.

As you can see, Labatt's Breweries is now a giant chain of regional breweries stretching from coast to coast, with an annual production over 6.6 million barrels. Three of the Labatt national labels (50 Ale, Blue, and Special Lite, a low-calorie beer) are available in the U.S. in bottles and (in selected areas) on draft. Labatt's 50 Ale is now the largest selling ale in Canada and Labatt's Blue is the third largest selling beer. Labatt also produces India Pale Ale, John Labatt's Extra Stock Ale, Cool Spring, Gold Keg, Crystal Lager, and Velvet Cream Stout. In Newfoundland it produces Blue Star, Jockey Club, and Black Label. In Nova Scotia the brands made are Keith's IPA and the Oland line. In Manitoba the brands produced are Manitoba 200 Malt Liquor, Manitoba's Select, White Seal, Club, and Country Club Stout. The labels produced by Labatt's in British Columbia are Kokanee, Kootenay Ale, Columbia, Silver Spring, and names familiar in the States: Rainier and Lucky Lager Beer.

LABATT'S 50 ALE—pale color, pleasant malty aroma and flavor with good hop balance, good but very average brew. The Molson ale is more complex. The 50 was introduced in 1950 to commemorate fifty years of service by John (the Third) and Hugh Labatt, grandsons of the founder.

LABATT'S PILSENER BLUE—pale color, slightly tawny, faint sour malt aroma, light bitter-sour taste, lightly carbonated. This brand was introduced in 1951.

LABATT'S PILSENER DRAFT—served at the Boston Garden for hockey games; medium gold color, clear and bright, light-flavored good malt taste with the right touch of hops for a well-balanced brew; clean and refreshing, little aftertaste.

JOCKEY CLUB BEER—tawny gold color, particulate matter in solution, smells like a rubber boot, bitter overly hopped flavor. Label says five percent, original Bavarian style, uncomplicated brew. Made in and for Newfoundland.

BLUE STAR—tawny gold color, starts out sweet, quickly turns bitter with the bitterness increasing toward the finish. Brewed in and for Newfoundland, this beer is very popular with the English of eastern Newfoundland and there is some resemblance to the "bitter" of England, except that this is an unbalanced example of that type of brew.

246

Oland's Breweries, Ltd.

Oland's produces most of the Maritime (Atlantic) Provinces' favorite beers (exclusive of the large national brands). All were found to be worthy efforts. Oland's was founded in 1867 by Susannah Culverwell Oland, great-grandmother of the present Oland family member serving on the board of directors.

OLAND EXPORT ALE—pale color, pleasant malty aroma, good clean taste, medium to light body, good balance, a little zest, no offensive features, no apparent faults, good clean aftertaste. Nothing super about it, but nothing wrong either.

OLAND'S OLD SCOTIA ALE—yellow gold with tawny-brown hues, pleasant malty aroma, medium body, good flavor but little character, inoffensive, very brief finish. Another pleasant brew.

OLAND'S SCHOONER BEER—pale color; very clean, slightly malty nose; light and pleasant but with no character and too much carbonation. Great for people who don't want their beer to taste too much like beer. A big seller in eastern Canada today.

OLAND EXTRA STOUT—dark brown color, light molasses aroma, light body, medium sweetness, good balance, overall impression is very good for a stout of a light style.

Alexander Keith's Nova Scotia Brewery, Ltd.

This brewery, founded in 1830 by Alexander Keith, was the oldest in existence in Nova Scotia when obtained by Labatt's. In continuous operation since, its one very fine product, Keith's India Pale Ale, is now produced in Halifax at the Oland's plant.

ALEXANDER KEITH'S INDIA PALE ALE—slightly tawny gold color, fine malty aroma with good hop character, pleasant malty flavor with some hop bitterness in the background, reasonably well balanced, a good brew. Has plenty of character without being overdone.

Molson Breweries of Canada, Ltd.

Molson is the oldest brewery in continuous operation in Canada (and in North America), having been founded in Montreal by John Molson in 1786. It is now one of Canada's big three with ten plants operating from Vancouver,

British Columbia, to St. John's, Newfoundland. In 1972 the then nine Molson plants produced over two million barrels of their fine beers. In 1977 the Formosa Spring Brewery of Barrie, Ontario, was added as the tenth Molson facility.

Molson beers are equally popular in the U.S. and Canada. In the U.S. they are handled by the Martlet Importing Co., Inc., of Great Neck, New York, a firm established by Molson in 1971. Martlet expects to distribute twelve million imperial gallons in eighteen states during 1978, making molson the No. 2 import of all the brands shipped into the United States from all the countries of the world. Molson products are available in sixteen northeastern states and in Florida and California.

I have tasted Molson's beers and ales in both Canada and the U.S. and, although similar, that tasted in Canada seemed better than the U.S. import. Both versions were submitted to a tasting panel several times with the same opinion resulting.

Martlet (speaking for Molson) disagrees with that opinion, declaring that the brews are identical. It suggests that any difference is the result of receiving an overage product from the local retailer. This is probably the case, but perhaps more consideration should be given to assuring that the stock in stores is fresh, lest the reputation of the product should suffer unnecessarily. All of the U.S. samples tried came from large stores with heavy turnover. If I can regularly obtain overage Molsons in my stores, so can others in my area and elsewhere.

Just to make sure of the opinion on the Molson exports to the U.S., as compared with the Molson products prepared for the Canadian market, samples of Molson Ale, Golden Ale, and Canadian were picked up in Montreal, while still fresh, newly arrived Molson equivalents were obtained in New Jersey; each sample was at its very best when submitted to a taste panel.

Only one of the samples was skunky and it was a Molson Ale export to the U.S. None of the Canadian domestic products showed so much as a trace of skunkiness, nor did the fresh Golden Ale or Canadian Lager obtained in the U.S.

All of the beers obtained in Montreal were canned and

Labatt Streamliner – in use until 1950.

all of the items obtained in the U.S. were in bottles. The Martlet statement was borne out in that the taste of the beers in fresh condition was identical. The tasters preferred the samples obtained in the U.S. because the domestic Canadian samples were much more carbonated, even to the point of being gassy. I did not find them to be gassy; in fact, the carbonation was in the nature of being a small bubble or a naturallike carbonation, but the Canadian samples were more carbonated than the U.S. imports.

A listing of the Molson brands by plant is as follows (all brands are five percent alcohol, except for Brador Malt liquor, 6.2 percent, and Crown Lager, 3.9 percent)

MOLSON NEWFOUNDLAND BREWERY, LTD.

(*St. John's*
India Beer
India Pale Ale Malt Liquor
Molson Canadian Lager
Molson Export Ale

251

Labatt's Anniversary Bridge – Korea 1952 complete with bullet holes.

MOLSON'S BREWERY QUEBEC, LTD.
(*Montreal*)
Molson Export Ale
Molson Golden Ale
Molson Canadian Lager
Molson Cream Porter
Brador Premium Ale (ML)
Laurentide Ale

MOLSON'S BREWERY (ONTARIO), LTD.
(*Toronto*)
Molson Canadian Lager
Molson Oktoberfest Lager
Molson Diamond Lager
Molson Golden Ale
Molson Stock Ale
Molson Export Ale
Molson Porter
Molson Club Ale

MOLSON'S BARRIE BREWERY, LTD.
Molson Canadian Lager
Molson Export Ale
Molson Golden Ale
Keg Ale
Molson Cream Porter
Molson Club Ale
Molson Stock Ale

MOLSON ALBERTA BREWERY, LTD.
(*Edmonton*)
Molson Export Ale
Edmonton Export Beer
Molson Canadian Lager
Molson Golden Lager
Lethbridge Pilsner
Crown Lager

SICKS LETHBRIDGE BREWERY, LTD.
(*Lethbridge, Alta.*)
Molson Canadian Lager
Lethbridge Beer
Lethbridge Pilsner
Lethbridge Royal Stout

MOLSON BREWERY B.C., LTD.
(*Vancouver*)
Old Style Lager
Molson Export Ale
Molson Canadian Lager
Ryder

MOLSON BREWERY MANITOBA, LTD.
(*Winnipeg*)
Frontier Beer
Frontier Stout
Molson Canadian Lager
Molson Export Ale
Crown Lager

MOLSON SASKATCHEWAN BREWERY, LTD
(*Prince Albert*)
Bohemian Lager
Pilsner Beer
Molson Canadian Lager
Molson Golden Lager
Molson Imperial Stout
Crown Lager

MOLSON SASKATCHEWAN BREWERY, LTD
(*Regina*)
Pilsner Beer
Bohemian Lager
Molson Export Ale
Molson Canadian Lager
Molson Golden Lager
Crown Lager

The combined capacity of the Molson plants is just under eight million barrels, with the Montreal and Toronto breweries each contributing 2.5 million of that total.

MOLSON'S CANADIAN LAGER BEER—big clean malty aroma with some hops in support, good body, finely balanced, good yeasty malty flavor with just a touch of hops. A fine light flavorful lager with no apparent faults. This particular sample was a canned domestic version, made in Montreal. Exports to the U.S. are bottled.

MOLSON EXPORT ALE—deep gold with a brown cast, clean grain nose with distinctive hop character, good malty flavor with hops finely balanced in (called by many as being typical of "canadian sparkling ale"), good tasting throughout with a long and pleasant aftertaste. The ale shipped to

254

...ts in New Brunswick – Moosehead Ale and Alpine Beer

...etitiveness and property disputes between Philip
...er, George, and his uncle, Sidney, leader of the
... of the family. Since then the two sides of the
...gone separate (although similar) ways. The rift
...971 when the Halifax Olands sold out to La-
...land is determined to maintain the indepen-
...sehead, and his two sons, who share his dislike
...anada corporate mentality, intend to preserve
... and its regional brews. With sales close to a
...s annually, they are still well in the fight for
...n the Maritime market.
...heir sales are still in their good-tasting zesty
... lager is gaining popularity. Moosehead also
...esting stout. All Moosehead brands are made
... Canadian barley and U.S. grown, Canadian
...d U.S., Yugoslavian, and domestic hops. A...
... percent alcohol.

the U.S. is called Molson Ale; in Canada it is called Molson Export.

MOLSON GOLDEN ALE—Golden is an ale similar to Export but is paler in color, lighter in aroma, and lighter and sweeter in taste. It is not bad at all, but the Export is better.

Over the last two years I have been unab[le to find]
this ale in the U.S. that did not have a[n overpower]ing skunky aroma. I had heard this co[mplaint before,]
so I asked several Canadians in the U[.S. if this phe]nomenon had been encountered in Ca[nada. I learned]
occasionally a skunky batch of Mols[on escaped in]
Canada but that it was more commo[n when Ca]nadians bring their Molsons in fro[m the U.S. who]
buy them here.

Moosehead Breweries, Ltd.

The president of Moosehead i[s Derek Oland. If you]
feel that Oland might be a familia[r name in Canadian brew]ing, you are correct. Susannah [Oland, who]
founded the Halifax (Nova Scoti[a) brewery in]
1867, was greatgrandmother to [Derek Oland]
and the Olands of St. John, New[foundland. Be]tween the two sides of the family[...]

Mural in the Moosehead Bre[wery]

Familiar sigh[t ...]
trucks

to the comp[any ...]
Oland's fath[er ...]
Halifax side [...]
family have [...]
widened in 1[...]
batt's.

Philip O[land ...]
dence of Moo[sehead ...]
of the mid-C[...]
this company[...]
million barrel[s ...]
preeminence i[n ...]

Most of t[he ...]
ales, but their[...]
makes an inter[...]
from western [...]
milled corn, an[d ...]
are rated at five[...]

Bière

Moosehead

Pale Ale

Moosehead Breweries Ltd. Saint John, N.B. Dartmouth, N.S.
UNION MADE/FABRICATION SYNDICALE

Bière

TEN-PENNY

Old Stock Ale

MOOSEHEAD BREWERIES LTD. DARTMOUTH, N.S. SAINT JOHN, N.B.

NET CONTENTS 341 ML. 12 OZ. CONTENU NET · 5% ALC. VOL.

MOOSEHEAD

London

STOUT

MOOSEHEAD BREWERIES LTD. SAINT JOHN, N.B. DARTMOUTH, N.S.
UNION MADE/FABRICATION SYNDICALE

BIÈRE

Alpine

LAGER

BEER

MOOSEHEAD PALE ALE—pale gold color, malty yeasty nose, flavor on the bitter side with some hops coming through in the finish. An average light or pale ale, not quite in the English style, but similar.

TEN-PENNY ALE—almost exactly the same as Moosehead but with a little more flavor. I prefer this ale to Moosehead by a wide margin because it has a lot of the zest that Moosehead lacks.

ALPINE LAGER BEER (Alpine Breweries, Ltd.)—pale color, sweet vegetal aroma, malty grainy taste; for some reason, very filling even though the body doesn't seem to be great.

MOOSEHEAD LONDON STOUT—very deep brown, opaque; malt, molasses, licorice aroma and flavor, like a molasses malted milk shake; creamy texture. This one has to be called a dessert beer; it is unique in that respect.

Uncle Ben's Industries Ltd.
(Vancouver/Richmond, B.C.)

Uncle Ben's comprises three brewing plants: Uncle Ben's Breweries (Manitoba), Ltd., Transcona, Manitoba; Uncle Ben's Breweries of Alberta, Ltd., Red Deer, Alberta; Uncle Ben's Tartan Breweries (B.C.), Ltd., Prince George, British Columbia (presently not operating).

The company continues to brew its regular product line even though it is in the hands of a trustee in bankruptcy proceedings.

The Uncle Ben's beers are Uncle Ben's Beer and Malt Liquor, Gentle Ben Beer, Old Blue Pilsener Beer, and Tartan Pilsener Beer.

UNCLE BEN'S MALT LIQUOR—medium yellow, cloudy, foamy with a big head, sour malt aroma, some yeast present in the nose, cereal flavor; high carbonation gives most of the palate sensation.

China, Hong Kong, Taiwan

Since this book is on beer, I shall take the very apolitical course of lumping these three together. If I had samples of the fine beers of Singapore, I would include them here as well.

The most familiar of the three products listed is the Mon-Lei, which apparently is no longer imported. Beer brewing on Taiwan and the Chinese mainland has only recently developed to any great extent.

The products reported below have all been found in Chinese restaurants, and occasionally elsewhere. None has been found to be worth a second try.

Tsing-Tao Brewery
(Tsing-Tao, China)

TSING-TAP—murky yellow color, faint malty aroma, sour-salty taste, sour aftertaste. Not unpleasant, but nothing to attract a retry.

Taiwan Tobacco & Wine Monopoly Bureau
(Taiwan)

TAIWAN BEER—very yeasty aroma, with a background of cardboard and vegetable soup (really); malty cardboard taste.

Hong Kong Brewery, Ltd.
(Hong Kong)

MON-LEI BEER—pale yellow, very bright appearance, sour malt aroma, slightly sour flavor, finishes poorly with sour metallic aftertaste. May have been a little elderly. I can recall others that performed similarly except that the ending was sour malt without the unpleasantness. The name *Mon-Lei* means 10,000 miles, infinity, or the Great Wall. The implication is that it is "the infinitely better beer."

Examining kegs of aging beer at Urquell Brewery in Pilsen, Czechoslovakia

Czechoslovakia

No work on beer could ever be complete without paying homage to Bohemia and the role it has long played in the development and history of beer. It was the ancient center of brewing in Europe, and noted for the brews of Wenzel

II in Pilsen in 1292. Franciscan monks brewed their fine brews there for centuries. Pilsen has always been associated with only the highest-quality beers. The Saaz hops of Bohemia have long been regarded as the finest in the world, and demand for them has always exceeded their availability.

When bottom-fermentation came along in the mid-1840s, the success of the method in Bohemia was such that the beer became known as pilsener, the model for all lager beers to follow.

Czechoslovakia still holds a position of high regard today; its Pilsener Urquell is famous and sought after the world over. It is probably the main reason that the Czechs are the most prodigious quaffers of brew in the world (forty-plus gallons of beer per person each year).

The Urquell brewery of today is the result of an 1842 consolidation of small firms in that city, then called Burgerliches Brauhaus Urquell. The beer was sufficiently popular that it was exported in 1856 and seen in American by 1873. Urquell disappeared from the American market for almost forty years after World War I, but there was no loss of its popularity on world markets. Today it is still recognized as one of the world's great beers.

Brewery Pilsener Urquell
(Pilsen)

PILSENER URQUELL—deep yellow color, huge malty hop aroma, heavy body, marvelous malt-hop flavor with an attractive sour dryness, excellent balance between hops and malt. A fine beer, worthy of its reputation.

Denmark

According to the early Norse writings, ale, or oel, was the chief national drink of ancient Scandinavians. At their three great winter festivals, it was an effective means of lightening the gloom that came with winter nights, that lasted for the greater portion of each day.

The ale was drunk very young and each feast was preceded by a great brewing. A special brewer was often en-

gaged for a private entertainment. The feast usually lasted until the ale was gone and then the guests went home. Even to recent times it was a custom of Norwegian peasants to brew a strong ale for Christmas and entertain neighbors until it was consumed.

At present there are five major breweries in Denmark. The most famous of these are Tuborg and Carlsberg. It can be said that these two names are synonymous with Danish beer. Once independent firms, they were merged in 1969 but remain competitive in the international marketplace. Tuborg is now made by Carling in the United States, so that fine import is now no more.

Albani Breweries, Ltd.
(Odense)

One of Denmark's smaller breweries, Albani produces some fine brews, one of them excellent.

ALBANI BEER FOR EXPORT—yellow-gold color, slightly malty nose with some hops in back, very pleasant flavor with good balance of hops and malt; unfortunately, the finish is too sour in the throat and mars the aftertaste.

ALBANI PILSENER—medium hoppy nose, good flavor characteristic of a European pils, good balance, pleasant but not complex, short pleasant finish.

ALBANI PORTER—deep molasses-brown color, smooth light malty aroma, big rich sourish taste, pineapple background, long rich finish, complex, balanced and smooth; an absolute delight. I have found this only in Boston at the bargain price of 45¢ per bottle. One of the most enjoyable dark brews I have every tasted.

The United Breweries, Ltd. (Carlsberg)
(Copenhagen)

The Carlsberg history begins before 1835, for at that time a small brewery passed into the hands of Jacob C. Jacobsen from his father, Christian. Young Jacobsen paid several visits to the famous Sedlmayr (Zum Spaten) Brewery in Munich where the practicality of the "Bavarian system" (bottom-fermentation beer making) was being demonstrated

with great success. He secured two pots of yeast from Sedl-mayr and carried them by coach from Munich to Copenhagen, stopping at every resting place on the route to throw water on the yeast to cool it and keep it alive. This was in 1845. Jacobsen built in a Copenhagen suburb a new brewery which he named Carlsberg, in honor of his infant son Carl, and brew No. 1 appeared on November 10, 1847. In the first year, the production of beer at Carlsberg was just under 100,000 gallons, now the daily production figure at Carlsberg.

A second and third brewery followed and Carlsberg became world famous. At the turn of the twentieth century Carlsberg was deemed a model brewing facility. In *One Hundred Years of Brewing*, the definitive work on the subject at the time, Carlsberg was selected for the chapter describing a modern brewing plant. Today the plant covers approximately eighty-five acres.

On October 1, 1969, the Carlsberg Breweries and the United Breweries Co., Ltd (Tuborg and the Royal Breweries), were amalgamated, the merger being a natural conclusion to the close cooperation entered into by agreement between the breweries in 1903.

CARLSBERG BEER—deep golden color; light, clean malty aroma with some hops in back; light and dry but with a slight lack of flavor; finishes mostly on the bitter side. A very good beer by American standards but not up to the taste of many other European beers.

CARLSBERG ELEPHANT MALT LIQUOR—dark color, fruitlike aroma and flavor, sweet and perfumy, ends very unbalanced. A clumsy brew.

CARLSBERG DARK—dark copper color, light malt aroma, weak body, very light flavor, weak and watery. Disappointing.

Ceres Breweries, Ltd.
(Aarhus)

CERES BEER—faint apple nose, light taste with slight sweetness, bitter and short finish.

Thor Breweries
(Randers)

Established 1856.

THOR BEER—light, faintly sweet nose, small bubble carbonation, sour and bitter taste, long but poor finish.

Wiibroes Brewery
(Elsinore)

This brewery dates back to 1840.

IMPERIAL STOUT—almost opaque black, rich complex stout aroma hiding all kinds of good things, rich luxurious malty flavor, and a long, long finish; fairly dry for type and might well please many American palates; quite good.

England, Scotland, Ireland

England has long been a source of great beer for the world, and aside from Germany, no other country has a greater reputation for the quality of its malt beverages. When it comes to ales, there is absolutely no competitor worth naming, for the pale ales of Burton and the nut-brown ales of Scotland have known no peer since inception.

For the most part, the enjoyment of malt beverages in Britain takes place in the pub. Rather than being places of escape, as are the bars of America, they are social gathering places, friendly and warm. It is almost impossible to be alone in an English pub. They are places to meet the locals, learn their customs, and drink their favorite brews. Any foreign visitor should hie off to the nearest pub soon after arrival lest he miss an opportunity to take part in British life.

British pubs come in two styles: "tied," whose complete line is that of a single brewery or brewing conglomerate; and those that are free to serve a selection of their choosing. It takes a lot of pub visits to sample all of England's beers, and most locals never stray beyond their nearest favorites.

Home consumption of beer in England is still a small percentage of the total consumed, and most beer in Britain is top-fermented. For a number of years, I have heard that lager is gaining a following in the United Kingdom, but even yet it accounts for no more than five percent of British production. There is a trend toward paler beers, but they are more alelike than lager, in the American sense.

Allied Breweries (UK) Ltd.
(Burton-on-Trent, England)

The name of Allsopp is inseparably linked to the brewing trade of Great Britain and to the famous ales of Burton-on-Trent. The area is first mentioned in history as being connected with brewing in the year 1295. By the time of King Richard and the Crusades, the monks had discovered the fine qualities of Burton ales and were commencing to add to their fame. Hugh de Allsopp, who won his spurs with Richard in the Holy Land, was founder of the honorable Derbyshire family, which was to become prominent in the brewing trade and closely attached to royalty. According to Samuel Pepys diary, an Allsopp was appointed as king's brewer to Charles II. The Allsopps were not to become involved with Burton brewing until 1805.

Meanwhile, the Burton ales were becoming famous. They were known throughout England and in Russia, where they were great favorites, particularly with Peter the Great and Empress Catherine.

One of the leading brewers of this (mid-eighteenth-century) period was Benjamin Wilson. It was his firm that in 1805 was to be headed by Samuel Allsopp, descendant of the ancient family of Derbyshire, and eventually to become Samuel Allsop & Sons, Ltd.

Samuel Allsopp is credited with being the force behind the development of what was to become India Pale Ale, the actual work having been done by Allsopp's maltster, Job Goodhead. This ale was the forerunner of the Double Diamond, Britain's top-selling ale.

Allsopp prospered throughout the years, finally merging in 1934 with another famous Burton brewery, Ind Coope, Ltd., a company with roots reaching to 1799 and a high reputation in southern England. More firms, including Benskins and Taylor-Walker, were acquired in the 1950s, and in 1961 Ind Coope merged with Tetley Walker of Leeds and with Warrington & Ansells of Birmingham to form Allied Breweries, Ltd.

IND COOPE DOUBLE DIAMOND BURTON PALE ALE—tawny deep gold, aroma like dry coffee or coffee beans, bitter roast-coffee flavor with sourness in the back, flavor actually quite light, finish dry and brief. Somewhat disappointing for Britain's top-selling ale.

Alpine Ayingerbrau (U.K.), Ltd.
(Tadcaster, Yorkshire, England)

ALPINE AYINGERBRAU LAGER—Sour aroma, sour taste, sour aftertaste. Can says it's brewed in the U.K. under license, but doesn't say whose.

Bass Productions, Ltd.
(Burton-on-Trent, England)

William Bass erected the first Bass brewery in 1777. He was succeeded by son Michael and grandson Michael Thomas, who built additional breweries in 1853 and 1864. When great-grandson Michael Arthur took over in 1884, the brewery was entirely rebuilt. Michael Thomas Bass began the Bass political tradition, representing Derby in the British Parliament for thirty-three years, and Michael Arthur Bass, his eldest son, was made a peer, under title of Lord Burton.

The pale ales of Bass & Co. became famous the world over. By 1900 the Bass, Ratcliff & Gretton plant had extended to over seven hundred fifty acres; despite the firm's efforts to brew the ales elsewhere, as in London, those ales were never the equal of the ales brewed at Burton.

The brewery of William Worthington actually dates back to 1744, and Worthington & Co. of Burton-on-Trent quickly entered the export trade to St. Petersburg, Russia, a trade of considerable magnitude at the time. Over the next century, Worthington & Co. was to absorb three neighboring Burton breweries. By 1900 it was by reputation the larg-

est brewery in the U.K. in the hands of one family. Worthington & Co. merged with Bass, Ratcliff & Gretton in 1926.

In 1961 Bass Worthington merged with Mitchells and Butlers to form Bass, Mitchells & Butlers, and in 1967 a further merger with Charrington United Breweries created the huge Bass Charrington Group. The Charrington name, popular in London and vicinity, is another old firm dating back to 1766 and John Charrington.

Wine buyers will recognize the Bass Charrington name as readily as beer drinkers in the United States. In recent years some heavy Bass Charrington investments in bad vintages have cost the firm dearly; consequently, it has dumped enormous quantities of its better wines on the market at a severe loss to stabilize its cash position. Most of the Charrington wines carried the Alexis Lichine label.

BASS PALE ALE (imported by Guiness-Harp Corp.)—pleasant malty aroma, medium body, good malty flavor, not heavy handed, excellent balance, long finish, a beautiful ale. (*Note*: The Bass symbol, a red triangle, is the oldest registered trademark in the world. It supposedly stands for a divinity of the pyramid builders called Tammuz, or Bassareus the Fortifier, who was son of the goddess Ops. His symbol was a cross [X], and he was honored by the Egyptians with libations of wine and malt. Through the centuries, Tammuz became Thomas, Bassareus became Bass, X became XXX, and you can just guess what Ops became. Perhaps Tammuz' father was the god Ogwash.)

Courage Ltd.
(London)

The roots of this firm run deep in the London brewing trade, resting with Courage & Co. and the firm of Barclay, Perkins & Co. The Barclay side has the most interesting history; its original Anchor Brewery was erected on the site of the old Globe theater in the Southwark district of London, made famous by Shakespeare's plays. Although the Anchor Brewery was not established until the seventeenth century, the ales of Southwark were remarked by Chaucer. In the latter half of the eighteenth century, the brewery was owned by the Thrales, who were fine intellectual people and friends of Samuel Johnson, who was a constant visitor to the brewery. The Barclays purchased the brewery upon the death of Mr. Thrale.

The most famous product of Courage, Ltd., is Russian Imperial Stout, which came to the firm via Barclay Perkins. This strong brew is so named because it was the choice of Catherine the Great in 1795. The highly reputed brew is aged for two months in cask and matured for at least one year in bottle. It is the only beer believed to be "vintaged," that is, labeled with the year of brewing. Like rare vintage port, vintages of Russian Stout are discussed and compared by aficianados; they are in fact corked and "laid down," like port. If you get the opportunity to sample the stout, please do.

Visitors to the London area can't miss the brews of this firm, for they are found almost everywhere. Each bears the rooster trademark and the exhortation to "take courage."

COURAGE LAGER EXPORT BEER—cloudy yellow gold, heavily carbonated, hops dominate the nose and palate, sour aftertaste.

JOHN COURAGE EXPORT—tawny color, foamy, sweet malt aroma, unbalanced, bitterness dominates the flavor throughout, shallow.

St. James' Gate Brewery,
Arthur Guinness Son & Company, Ltd.
(Dublin)

Porter was introduced in 1722, and there were as many as thirty small breweries in Dublin making brown ales in 1735. But excellence was not achieved until 1759, when St. James' Gate Brewery came to the forefront of the industry.

Founded by Arthur Guinness in that year (1759), the brewery began with a porter that was quickly recognized as being the best. By 1825 Guinness porter was famous abroad. In 1856, 62,000 barrels were exported, and by 1881 annual production of Guinness products had passed one million barrels.

Today Guinness sells eighty-five percent of its output in Ireland and the United Kingdom, but its market includes 147 countries. The product line is extremely popular in Africa and Guinness breweries stand in Nigeria, Ghana, and Cameroon. There are also plants in Malaysia and Jamaica. Guinness supervises the brewing of its beers in all its breweries worldwide.

Guinness uses only barley grown in Ireland and England (even exporting them for beers brewed overseas) without any adjuncts or artificial ingredients. The flavor and color are entirely natural. Only the recipe is changed to suit the tastes of the various markets. Brews packaged for the Irish and English market are unpasteurized and not refrigerated. The bottled export variety is pasteurized, a completely different brew with higher alcoholic content and added hops. The export version is also shipped unpasteurized in kegs. It is far superior to the bottled variety.

GUINNESS EXTRA STOUT—opaque red-brown color with a creamy, tawny head; very full-bodied, dense, and thick; a complex spicy Worcestershire sauce aroma; dry coffee-toffee flavor with a chocolatelike finish (but still dry). Good stuff if you like it; may be a bit overpowering for the uninitiated. Try it, and if it is too much for you to enjoy "neat," try it mixed with a lager.

HARP LAGER (Harp Lager Brewery)—deep gold color, pungent hop aroma, flavor very bitter, carries right through to the end. Bitterness probably too much for most American palates, but for those who prefer a well-hopped brew, try this one, by all means.

The Old Brewery
(Tadcaster, York, England)

SAMUEL SMITH'S OLD BREWERY GOLDEN BROWN ALE—copperish color, burnt malt aroma of medium intensity, sudsy texture, smooth and mellow on the tongue, well balanced, pleasant appetizing finish. A good-tasting brew. In scarce supply in the U.S., which is a shame because it is of more interest than just an unusual can for collectors. Labeled "strong brown ale" on the can with a "golden brown ale" sticker attached, this brew comes from a firm claiming establishment in 1758.

G. Ruddle & Co.
(Oakham, Rutland, England)

RUDDLE'S COUNTRY ALE—medium tawny brown color, pungent malty nose, sour taste with a bitter finish. Not one of the winners.

Scottish and Newcastle Breweries, Ltd.
(Edinburgh)

William MacEwan started this firm in Edinburgh in 1856. He was convinced that there were both a home and an export market for high-quality Scottish ale. By 1900 MacEwan was producing nearly ninety percent of all the beer consumed in northeast England and had a rapidly growing export trade.

Today, MacEwan's Brewery, still located on the original site, produces over a million barrels annually. MacEwan's is now joined in the Scottish and Newcastle Breweries, Ltd., by Wm. Younger & Co., Ltd., and the Newcastle Breweries, Ltd.

The product line includes some of the finest brown ales found in the world; fortunately, they are readily available in the U.S. and Canada.

Father MacEwan, mainstay of the MacEwan labels with his traditional Scot's garb and tartan background, is being replaced by a cavalier motif and less colorful label on the Scotch Ale and Strong Ale (formerly called Tartan Ale) packages. MacEwan's Extra Stout is no longer in production.

MacEWAN'S SCOTCH ALE—deep-hued amber; creamy texture with a good foamy appearance without being highly

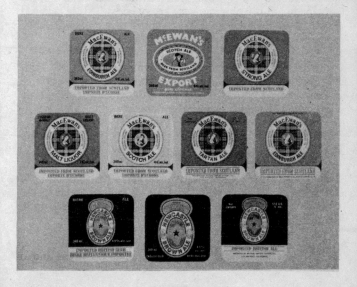

carbonated; heavy malty aroma with some piquancy; big-bodied; distinctive mealy malty taste, with some bitterness for zest; a solid big-flavored beer with a good finish and lingering aftertaste. An excellent brew.

MacEWAN'S TARTAN ALE—dark brown with red hues, again creamy textured but with less foam and head, some family resemblance to Scotch Ale except that the flavor has more sweetness and more intensity, yet not cloying. It finishes well and has an even longer-lasting aftertaste. The balance on some samples has been questionable, but it is another excellent brew done in a slightly different style.

MacEWAN'S EDINBURGH ALE—deep brown color, creamy texture, only medium to light head, faint but richly endowed malt aroma that is unusually complex, beautiful roast-bacon flavor with a smoky aftertaste; an absolute delight that I found to be the perfect balance between the two ales reported above.

MacEWAN'S STRONG ALE—deep copper and gold color, clean delicate malty nose, rich full-flavored taste on the sweet side but not cloying, very heavy body. This is believed to be the same brew as Tartan, but with a different label, perhaps one meant for markets outside the U.S.

MacEWAN'S MALT LIQUOR—label says 7.8 percent alcohol; extremely dark brown color, almost opaque; light toffee aroma; heavy body; rich very sweet flavor, like Tartan only more so; bitter finish; toffee aftertaste.

NEWCASTLE BROWN ALE—medium brown with tawny hues, or dark amber; equipped with a good head but not as creamy textured as the MacEwan's; nutty aroma; smooth and mellow with a good malty taste; just a touch of bitter in the finish; a long-pleasant aftertaste. Wonderful beer in the can or bottle, extraordinary on draft—but you have to go to Scotland or England for that treat.

Tennent Caledonian Breweries, Ltd.
(Glasgow)

The history of J. and R. Tennent, Ltd., goes back to 1556. The Tennent name has been linked to many of the happenings in the Glasgow area since then. By the late eighteenth century the firm of Tennents, headed by John and Robert Tennent, was well established.

In 1963 Tennents joined the Charrington United Breweries Group with the original company of J. and R. Tennent, to become part of Tennent Caledonian Breweries Ltd., the Scottish unit of the Group. Since then Tennent has become part of Bass Charrington, the largest brewery organization with over 12,000 tied public houses.

TENNENT'S LAGER BEER—tawny golden color, creamy texture, clean malty aroma and flavor, taste very slightly soapy, clean fresh finish; a very pleasant and fresh-tasting brew that most beer drinkers should favor. An excellent import, seen quite frequently in cans featuring Penny, a scantily clad voluptuous blonde.

PIPER EXPORT ALE—dark amber color, aroma of roasted mash, burnt toffee-apple flavor, sourness in the back of the palate, assertive at first with too much of the burnt flavor, mars the pleasant aspects.

T. & R. Theakston
(Maksham, England)

THEAKSTON OLD PECULIAR YORKSHIRE ALE—brown color; aroma of canned brown bread, dry molasses taste; fast fading at the finish, leaving little aftertaste. Canned in little seven-ounce tins, this, we understand, is one of the "new-wave" beers made in the style of the traditional old (rather, ancient) English brews. Can't say I favor this one.

Watney-Mann, Ltd.
(London)

Watney's began in London in 1837, when James Watney was admitted to the Stag Brewery at Pimlico as a partner. The brewery remained in the possession of his relatives

until 1884, when it was transformed into a private limited company with Vernon J. Watney as chairman. In 1900 Watney merged with Reid's Brewery and Combe & Co. (a firm dating to 1740) to form Watney, Combe, Reid & Co. of London. Subsequent consolidation has resulted in the current Watney firm name.

WATNEY'S RED BARREL BEER (brewed and bottled for Watney's, Mortlake Brewery, London)—copper gold, toasted-malt aroma, flavor starts out strongly malty but finishes sour, long aftertaste on the sour side. A much better product on draft.

MANN'S THE ORIGINAL BROWN ALE—(brewed for Watney-Mann, Mortlake Brewery)—nut-brown color, good rich coffee aroma with burnt charcoal in back, lightly carbonated with very small bubbles, full-flavored with all-malt taste, no hops noticeable, smooth and mellow, good balance, slightly sweet finish. A delight, excellent of type, much like the "mild" of the British pubs.

Whitbread & Co., Ltd.
(London)

Whitbread & Co. was founded in 1742 and ranked second in London as early as 1760. Like the Bass family, the Whitbreads were active in politics. At the turn of the century (1900), Whitbread was adjudged one of England's top half-dozen breweries and had a capitalization in excess of two million pounds sterling. Whitbread beers reached America as early as 1759, and have been more or less regularly available here since. All Whitbread products are made from pure British malt—without adjuncts—from British, German, Yugoslav, and Czech hops, and from the firm's own strain of cultivated yeast.

WHITBREAD TANKARD LONDON ALE—tawny brown coloring, nose of caramel and yeast, fair to good balance, good malty flavor, short finish. A good, better-than-average ale that lets down only at the very end.

WHITBREAD PALE ALE—deep tawny brown color, beautiful smooth rich caramel aroma, taste decidedly caramel, very pleasant and appetizing, finely balanced, long finish and aftertaste. Smooth and mellow.

WHITBREAD BREWMASTER—brown gold, highly carbonated, malty aroma and flavor, neutral finish, lacks balance.

MACKESON STOUT—extremely deep brown color, almost opaque; rich malty aroma; heavy body, syrupy; rich malty flavor, like a coffee beer, and a thick one at that. An excellent stout; Guinness's greatest rival, and the preference of many. If you like stout, you must try this one.

GOLD LABEL No. 1 SPARKLING BARLEY WINE—orange rose color, sweet candy-apple nose, assertive aroma and flavor, taste like a powerful sweet cough medicine, "puckery" on sides and back of tongue, bitter aftertaste. This demands an acquired taste.

Finland

The climate of Finland, like that of Sweden, is not conducive to growing barley because of the severe night frosts. Nevertheless, a small brewing industry thrives, producing at least one very fine product that is exported widely.

Osakeyhtio Mallasjuoma, Inc.
(Lahti)

FINLANDIA GOLD FINEST FINNISH EXPORT BEER—lovely malty aroma; pleasant malty taste; excellent balance; plenty of hop character without being bitter; good, long aftertaste with only the slightest hint of bitterness. An excellent brew. A pleasure to sip for its complexity of flavor.

France

France commenced brewing malt beverages very early. In the days of Julius Caesar the ancient Gauls brewed a beverage similar to the white beers that afterward were made from wheat and oats. In the eighth and ninth centuries the subject of brewing received royal notice. Charlemagne and his son, Louis de Debonnaire, enforced regulations regarding the monastic beers, fixing, in some cases, the amount of grain to be used, and encouraging the making of malt liquors in moderate quantities because of the high price of wine.

Hops were cultivated in France even in the time of Pepin the Short, father of Charles the Great; a certain paper referred to the transfer of a field of hops to the Abbey of St. Denis in 768. Hops, however, were not with certainty known to be in use in French malted liquors until the thirteenth or fourteenth century. At that time the brews were called *Godale*, or *Goudale*, or *Servoise*. The word *biere* does not appear until near to the middle of the fifteenth century. The brewing industry is believed to have spread from the Low Countries to France via Normandy and thence to Paris about the eleventh or twelfth century.

Alsace-Lorraine constitutes historic ground in French brewing with important breweries founded as early as 1259. Much of the beer exported from France to the U.S. today is brewed in that region.

Brasseries Kronenburg SA
(Strasbourg)

This firm dates back to 1664, according to its label. The beer is widely available in the U.S. and Canada.

KRONENBURG 1664 IMPORTED BEER—medium gold color; light malty aroma; strange, almost fruity, vinous flavor; light hops in the finish.

Brasserie Meteor
(Hochfelden) (Haag-Metzger & Cie., S.A.)

METEOR PILS BIER DE LUXE—cloudy pale yellow, faint pilsener nose, small bubble carbonation, hops dominate the flavor, clean finish. Seen only in Cambridge, Massachusetts, at Cave Atlantique; may be a unique import by that firm.

Brasserie du Pecheur
(Schiltigheim) (Brasserie Mattiere du Pecheur, S.A.)

FISCHER GOLD LA BIERE AMOUREUSE—sweet fruity aroma; fairly intense, sweet vinous malty flavor; long malt finish; a fairly good beer of the winy type.

FISCHER PILS FRENCH BEER—light vegetal aroma; pale color; rusty metal (ferruginous) and vegetable taste with excessive bitterness, especially toward the finish.

FISCHER LA BELLE STRASBOURGEOISE—malty grainy aroma; not pleasant at the first sip, but improved as it slid across the tongue; metallic finish. Overall effect under-average. Pretty label and seen only in large-size bottles.

Brasseries Pelican
(Lille) (Brasseries Pelforth, S.A.)

PELFORTH PALE BEER—LA BIERE BLONDE DE FRANCE—deep gold, good malty nose, very nice malty hop flavor with excellent balance, sweet malt finish that is pleasant but would be better if drier. Seen only in small seven-ounce bottles, this is the best of the French beers.

Union de Brasseries
(Paris)

SLAVIA—amber color, aroma of vegetable and meat extract (like Bovril), taste reflects the nose. A strange beer.

Germany

The history and the art of beer making in Germany are the history and the art of beer making in the world. Without question, Germany is the beer capital of the world and has been so for centuries. Even where competitors rose to challenge German leadership in the trade, it was usually transplanted Germans who did so. As a race, the Germans are hard-working perfectionists who preserve quality at all costs. This is evident in their beer, concerning which strict laws regulating production are continually enforced, to assure that the highest standards are maintained. The fact that a beer is German-made is a considerable guarantee that it is a quality product.

The German government's laws regulating beer making were laid down in 1516 by Duke William IV of Bavaria. The laws forbade using any ingredient other than barley malt, hops, yeast, and water. These laws are regarded as the standard of excellence in brewing throughout most of the world, and in a great many countries they are observed by choice, if not by law.

Beer is a household word in Germany. Hundreds of songs Hail that great traditional food and one such song proclaims that there is no beer in heaven, so you had better get all you can while here. Frankly, if there is no beer in heaven, then it is a poor place to send a German when he dies. He might well consider the offerings of the other place.

The local beers of Germany are a delight to sample. Distinctive regional tastes vary from town to town, each town better than the preceding (you see, the best beer in Germany is the one in front of you). As towns are only about twenty kilometers apart and most of them have their own breweries (there are still over fifteen hundred breweries in Germany), one could devote a lifetime to tasting the local brews of Deutschland.

Beer is served at all restaurants and hotels, even at those establishments that are not permitted to serve (or choose not to serve) wine or hard liquors. Everyone drinks beer with lunch or dinner. The main meal of the day is served at noon, when a two-hour lunch break takes place. Dining is leisurely and the two-hour period is devoted solely to that function. No one hurries about running lunchtime errands for none of the stores or businesses is open then. The owners and clerks are at lunch.

Supper is a light meal, usually some bread and wurst

washed down casually with beer. This meal is even more casual than lunch, for even more time is available to devote to it. In each establishment there is a large table traditionally reserved for the "regulars," who, in a small town with only one Gasthaus restaurant, probably include the mayor and the rest of the city fathers; they will hold a leisurely court over Krugs of the fine local beer and discuss matters of state.

This is not to say that there is no drunkenness in Germany, for when the Germans have their festivals, they eat, drink and frolic with the same passion and energy that they apply to their industry.

Each September the rites of beer reach a peak with the annual Volksfests, the most famous of them being the Munich Oktoberfest. At a Volkfest huge tents are erected by the local breweries and outfitted with long tables and benches; a bandstand is in the center. Beginning at about seven o'clock each evening of the Fest, everybody gathers for a time of wurst, chicken, camaraderie, laughter, song, and enormous quantities of beer made especially for the occasion. For four hours—it rarely goes past 11 P.M. on a weekday—all the old songs are sung, all the old toasts remembered and repeated, new toasts made, jokes and stories told and retold, and friendships made and remembered. Consequently, a little part of every non-German will forever be German.

The German attitude to beer is best summed up by the beer code of Heidelberg University, beginning at paragraph eleven: "Keep on drinking." The university's students had societies of drinkers and meted out punishment to offenders against the beer laws. More serious offenses were punished with beer excommunication, which deprived the offender of beer and the good fellowship that attended drinking. Such a disability could be relieved only by a drinking contest, whereat four tankards of beer must be emptied in succession (with five-minute intervals). Drinking alone was strictly forbidden. Even a solitary sip could bring beer punishment. Challenges of up to eight tankards of beer were not uncommon, and drinking duels continued far into the night, every night.

The excessive use of alcohol as a social norm and form of entertainment was not greatly different from the practices of some groups in today's society, but for sheer quantity the German student of the nineteenth century (and well into the twentieth) is nonpareil. For all his excesses, he was at least civilized enough not to talk shop while drinking, a barbarian custom all too frequently encountered in our society.

Drinking in Germany, as in England and other parts of the world lacking the sorry effects of stigmatism, is done for enjoyment of the taste and the occasion, and not to escape the troubles of life. The least desired state is to be drunk, for you will miss the fun.

Augustiner Brauerei A.G.
(Munich, West Germany)

The origins of this brewery go back to 1328 and to a cloister brewhouse of the Augustine monks. It passed out of their hands in 1803 and into the possession of the Wagner family in 1829.

According to a Connecticut distributor, the beer is not pasteurized and must be kept refrigerated. We can doubt the economics of such a venture but it is agreed that all too many bottles of this beer taste as though they were mishandled. It is a good beer, however, but only when fresh. It is popular in those German restaurants outside Bavaria that wish to add a prestigious Munich beer to their list.

AUGUSTINERBRAU MUNICH EXPORT LIGHT BEER—a beautiful bright beer, very attractive in appearance, clean but very light aroma, malty taste on the sweet side with only a delicate hop flavoring, clean and light finish. Considerably lighter in flavor than most quality German imports.

AUGUSTINERBRAU MUNICH MAXIMATOR DARK EXPORT BEER—pale brown with copper tones, strong malty hop nose, rich complex malty flavor with plenty of zest and character, slightly bitter finish. A powerful full-flavored brew. Extremely good of type, one of Germany's best, but not one of the mellow Bavarian darks. This one has gusto.

Brauerei Beck & Co.
(Bremen, West Germany)

Beck & Co. enjoys the unique distinction of being the largest-selling beer in Germany. The quality of the beer is such that it comes as no surprise to those who enjoy it regularly. The light beers of Bremen are very similar to the light beers of Munich and several of them provide as much competition to Munich as does Dortmund.

BECK'S BEER—pale gold color, mild malty nose, light-bodied, light-flavored, pleasant, finely balanced, lightly hopped, faint on finish and with little aftertaste. Almost identical to St. Pauli Girl Light, another Bremen beer.

BECK'S DARK BIER—medium dark color, hoppy aroma, big flavor but too harsh and the harshness follows through to a bitter aftertaste.

Dinkelacker Wulle A.G.
(Stuttgart, West Germany)

The Dinkelacker family and beer go back to about 1600. The present house was established in Stuttgart in 1888 and is today one of the largest breweries in Germany. Each day almost fifty-thousand cases leave the brewery for markets at home and abroad, including some five thousand restaurants and hotels.

Dinkelacker produces a light, a dark, and a bock for export, and a pilsener, a lager, and a diet-pils (eighty percent lower in calories). A Weiss beer (Weizenkrone) is produced for both markets.

DINKELACKER LIGHT EXTRA C.D.—gold; complex malty hop aroma; great heft and plenty of zest; a beer with flavor, body, character, and reasonably good balance.

DINKELACKER BLACK FOREST LIGHT BEER—cloudy; blueberry pulp nose; sweet slightly off taste; dank finish. Only poor Dinkelacker found. Also the only one found without the usual Dinkelacker label or brewery identification.

DINKELACKER BOCK C.D. EXTRA—dark and cloudy, big malty aroma and taste, heavy body, extremely rich and long aftertaste. A very, very good beer for those who like their Germans rich, full, heavy, and zesty.

DINKELACKER DARK C.D. EXTRA—brown color, big malty nose, bit yeasty flavor, slightly sour taste with a medicinal nature; good nonetheless, but not as good as the Bock, which was super.

DINKELACKER DARK IMPORT PRIVAT—the new label of Dark C.D. Extra, which was tasted just to check on the recipe; unfortunately, it was a bad bottle, with a brown-orange color, slightly skunky aroma, and a sour metallic taste and finish.

Dortmunder Actien Brauerei/
Dortmunder Hansa Brauerei
(Dortmund, West Germany)

The older of these two firms was formed in 1860 and transformed into a stock company known as Dortmunder Aktien-Brauerei in 1872. The Hansa brewery was founded in 1901. In 1971 the two companies merged but separate facilities have been maintained.

The Hansa beers reported below are made with very nearly identical recipes and from the same ingredients. Barley malt is obtained from German, Belgian, and French suppliers and the hops are the German strains, Hallertau-Nordbrauer, Hallertau-Goldbrauer and Tettnang. Neither one showed very well.

"DAB" Meister Pils is available in cans and bottles. It has been reviewed quite well at each appearance in taste trials.

DORTMUNDER HANSA IMPORTED GERMAN BEER—vegetable aroma, sour malt flavor, bitter finish. Not a good beer.

ALT SEIDELBRAU (Dortmunder Hansa)—deep gold color; hoppy nose with sour malt in back; bitterness dominates throughout the taste; an unpleasant, unlikable harsh beer.

DAB MEISTER PILS (Dortmunder Actien)—initial aroma of rubber, which cleaned itself after being open a few moments; eventually the aroma became clean and malty; fresh hop-malt flavor with a lot of character and zest, good tasting despite a poor start on the aroma and some indications of imbalance. This one seems to be highly variable from batch to batch, which may be a result of mishandling or "too long to market."

Dortmunder Union–Brauerei A.G.
(Dortmund)

Combined with Schultheiss, Berlin since 1972, Dortmunder Union–Schultheiss is Germany's largest brewery combine. Dortmunder Union itself was formed in 1873 as an amalgamation of several small breweries, the business formerly being conducted by W. Struck & Co. Schultheiss

Brauerei, A.G., of Berlin was the largest brewery in Germany at the turn of the century.

Dortmunder Union exports two of its excellent brews to America and Schultheiss provides its famous Berliner Weiss.

DORTMUNDER UNION SIEGEL PILS—pale yellow gold, clouds when too cold, good sour malt aroma with some hops in back, fine malt-hop flavor; very much like Urquell in style; a good European Pilsener. Has plenty of character.

BERLINER WEISS SCHULTHEISS—pale cloudy white, foamy, typical yeasty aroma and taste, traditionally served with a syrup (preferably raspberry schnapps to my taste). This famous brew is by itself strictly a matter of taste. With the Himbeergeist, or at least some fruit syrup, it is somewhat like a liqueur.

DORTMUNDER UNION SPECIAL—pale gold, intense malty aroma, good malt flavor strongly accented with hops, good balance, straightforward, good throughout; especially favored by those who like a hoppier brew. A highly rated light beer with strong flavor and a great deal of zest.

Dortmunder Ritterbrauerei A.G.
(Dortmund)

Since a letter forwarding labels from Dortmunder Union contained samples of labels from Ritterbrauerei, I assume that this brewery is now part of the massive firm of Dortmunder Union–Schultheiss.

DORTMUNDER RITTER BRAU LIGHT BEER—deep yellow color, big hop-malt aroma, huge hop flavor, a hearty brew, pungent at the end. A good, well-hopped beer, robust for those who like their beer extra zesty.

DORTMUNDER RITTER PILS—particulate matter in solution, sharp hop aroma, sour hop flavor, heavy vegetal malt background, finishes softly without bitterness. Reasonably good in a Czechoslovakian style.

DORTMUNDER RITTER DARK—heavy malty aroma, some hops noticeable in the flavor but the sour malt taste dominates to the detriment of the overall effect. Not a bad beer, but there are too many others that are better.

DORTMUNDER WESTFALIA SPECIAL—faint malty hop aroma with metallic overtones, sour metallic taste, iodine finish.

DORTMUNDER WESTFALIA EXPORT BEER—bright pale gold, light nose with medium hops, sweet in the middle of the palate after a neutral start, bitter finish and aftertaste.

Dressler Brauerei GMBH
(Bremen)

DRESSLER EXPORT BEER—yellow gold, slightly clouded, skunky aroma, sour taste. Continued to search for one sample in better condition. Best that could be found was not too good, being bitter in the front and salty sour in back. Not very likable even at its best.

Furstlich Furstenbergische Brauerei K.G.
(Donaueschingen, West Germany)

FURSTENBERG PILSENER—aroma mainly malt, but with some hops in the back; flavor almost entirely hops, but still not overly bitter; lacks complexity and interest, a monolithic beer; lightly hopped in the finish.

(Brewery name not given on label)
(Hamburg, West Germany)

EXTRACTO de MALTA HAMBURG MALT BEVERAGE—claims (but not on label) to be thirteen percent alcohol; deep brown with very small bubble carbonation, heavy, even viscous; malty cereal aroma; stoutlike; molasses flavor, sweet but not cloying; some bitterness seeps through in the finish. Interesting.

Hacker-Pschorr Brauerei A.G.
(Munich)

Hackerbrau originated with a brewery established on the site of an old brewing operation that dated back to the fifteenth century. Simon Hacker bought the plant in 1783 and in 1793 the Hacker firm was bought by Joseph Pschorr, the same year that he married Maria Theresia Hacker, Simon's daughter. In 1865 a large brewery was built by Matthias Pschorr and this plant was remodeled in 1881 when the stock company was organized.

The same Joseph Pschorr established the nucleus of the Pschorr Brauerei in 1820 and was succeeded in this venture by his sons and grandsons. Throughout the nineteenth century, the widely exported Pschorrbrau was famous not only in Germany but throughout the world. That fame continues today.

Joseph Pschorr was Germany's most famous brewer in his time. He received many honors and was the only brewer to be elected to the (Bavarian) Hall of Fame in Munich, where his bust presides over the site of the Munich Oktoberfest. Well ahead of his time in the brewing industry, he created huge underground storage facilities, popularly known as "The Beer Fortress," which made it possible for beer to be brewed year round. On his deathbed, he called upon his two sons to choose, by lottery, who would run either of the two breweries, in order to divide the inheritance into equal shares. Matthias became owner of Hacker and Georg became owner of Pschorr and they shared the Beer Fortress equally between them.

In post-World War II Munich, Hacker and Pschorr were two of the less famous breweries, but their products were well appreciated locally. As a tourist visiting the Oktoberfests of the early 1960s, I was pleased to find that their offerings were as satisfying as those provided by the more famous (and more crowded) Lowenbrau festhalle. In my opinion, Pschorrbrau was slightly better than Hackerbrau and was my frequent companion at mealtime. It is still a good friend, for the current line of Hacker-Pschorr products available in most American markets is excellent and worthy of consideration. All the brews performed extremely well in the taste trials.

Given the common origin of the firms of Hacker and Pschorr, their 1972 merger came as no surprise. It is a fitting combination in many ways.

HACKER EDELHELL EXPORT—medium hop aroma, good hoppy flavor with a sweet malty background, excellent balance, good body, a fine brew with lots of character and a long aftertaste. Very satisfying. One of the best beers I have ever tasted from a can.

HACKER-PSCHORR ORIGINAL OKTOBERFEST BIER BRAUROSL-MARZEN—deep amber color, big hop nose with plenty of malt, big flavor to match the aroma, chewy, a beer of substance; big in all its features from aroma to aftertaste, yet magnificently balanced; closest thing to a real Oktoberfest beer found in a bottle outside Germany. Excellent in all respects, for those who dote on German beer. Don't miss it.

HACKER-PSCHORR LIGHT BEER—pale gold, beautiful clean malt-hop aroma, big malt-hop flavor, very good balance, clean finish with some hops adding to but not marring the finish. Another excellent beer. One of the best light German beers ever tasted in this country.

HACKER-PSCHORR DARK BEER—medium dark brown color, malt-hop aroma with molasses in the background, malt flavor but not heavy, finish sweet and a bit dull. Good, but not up to the excellence of most other Hacker-Pschorr brews.

Henninger Brauerei KGuA
(Frankfurt, West Germany)

Business began in 1869 and the plant was completed in 1875. In 1880 it was formed into a stock company known as Heinrich Henninger & Sohne.

HENNINGER INTERNATIONAL—faint sweet aroma; highly carbonated unlike most German imports; dull malty flavor; too much on the sweet side and with insufficient hops. This sample could have been bad but the faults seemed not like those of mishandling.

Brauerei Herrenhausen
(Hanover, West Germany)

This brewery was founded in Hanover in 1868.

HERRENHAUSEN EXPORT LAGER BEER—nicknamed Horsy, this beer is medium gold in color, has a sharp malty nose, and a mild malty flavor with a bitter finish. Not well balanced; the components have their strengths in the wrong places.

Hofbrauhaus Munich
(Munich)

HOFBRAU LIGHT RESERVE—tawny, big malty-hop aroma and flavor; hops seem a bit overdone; the whole effect comes off a bit clumsily—too much of everything except balance and finesse, which are missing.

HOFBRAU OKTOBERFEST BEER—amber color, big hop nose with plenty of malt, big chewy taste; a beer with heft and substance. Not a bad effort but the lowest rated of the four Oktoberfest beers available.

HOFBRAU BAVARIA DARK RESERVE—deep brownish orange, light malty aroma, strong malty taste, finish better than the start. An average beer; not up to expected standards for a German import.

Holsten Brauerei
(Hamburg)

HOLSTEN LAGER—yellow gold, aroma mostly of hops with a little malt peeping through, flavor too dominated by hops, even for those whose tastes run to German beers.

HOLSTEN CERVEZA TIGRE—light gold color, malty aroma, sour-bitter taste, sour finish, badly balanced. Seen only in Hispanic neighborhoods; probably aimed at that market.

Isenbeck Brewery
(Hamm, West Germany) (Brauerei Isenbeck A.G.)

This brewery claims its origin to date back to 1645.

ISENBECK EXPORT DELUXE—pleasant sweet aroma, sweet-bitter flavor, all bitter aftertaste.

ISENBECK EXTRA DRY—very mild smoky aroma, hops dominate the taste with a pulpwood-cardboard background, metallic finish.

Konigsbacher Brauerei A.G.
(Koblenz, West Germany)

This brewery uses interesting winelike labels on its products—for example, "feinste bierqualitat" and "origina-labfullung."

KONIGSBACHER PILS—big malty aroma with vegetal backtones, semisweet vegetal malt flavor, long-pleasant aftertaste. A decent brew but too common for import prices.

Lindener Gilde-Brau A.G.
(Hannover)

This firm gives 1546 as its birthdate.

GILDA RATSKELLER PILS-BEER—bright gold color, well-hoped nose, hops dominant flavor throughout, sweet malt comes through in the finish, dry aftertaste, lacks balance. Recently arrived in the U.S.

Lowenbrau
(Munich)

Odd bottles of this fine beer can still be found in America. They are being supplanted by the domestic Lowenbrau. Instead of having an excellent import and a good domestic brew, we are to have only the domestic. A poor bargain for those of us who appreciated the Munich Lowenbrau, one of the world's finest brews (see discussion under Miller Brewing Co.).

Lowenbrau goes back to the year 1383, to a little brewhouse in Munich, supposedly producing beer by that name. It is known for certain that there was a brewery on the site producing Lowenbrau in 1818. It became a stock company in 1872, after many ownership changes. By the turn of the century, Lowenbrau was one of Germany's largest breweries with an export business as large as its domestic sales.

Lowenbrau was the largest-selling German beer in the United States until removed by corporate decision.

LOWNBRAU MUNICH LIGHT SPECIAL—golden color, lovely hoppy aroma, enormous chewy beer with tremendous body and marvelous flavor, extremely well balanced, deserving of fine reputation.

LOWENBRAU MUNICH DARK SPECIAL—deep brown with reddish orange hues, very clean malt aroma with some hops, strongly flavored with the malt intense up front, bitter finish, sour aftertaste. Good start, poor finish.

Monschshof Brauerei
(Kulmbach, West Germany)

Kulmbach has had for many years a great reputation for the quality of its export beers. As early as 1831 Kulmbach beer was well known outside Bavaria. Kulmbach beer also was famous for its very high alcohol content. (The beer reputed to have the greatest alcoholic content [over thirteen percent] is EKU Kulminator Urtyp Hell from Kulmbach.) I doubt that the Kulmbacher exports to the U.S. are high in alcohol; for one thing, they are called beer, which limits them to five percent in this country. The brewery producing these two beers was founded in 1349.

KULMBACHER MONKSHOF AMBER LIGHT BEER— aroma started skunky, but eventually cleared and the nose remained clean and malty; good flavor, balanced well between the hops and the malt. Good but no cigar.

KULMBACHER MONKSHOF DRY LIGHT BEER—tart hop aroma, big hop taste, bitterness sustains throughout the taste, slight metallic background to the flavor that comes through stronger in the finish.

Paderborner Brauerei GMBH
(Paderborn, West Germany)

PADERBORNER LIGHT BEER (PB)—although not clear from the label, the general impression given is that this may be a low-calorie beer that is less filling. It has a light malty nose, small bubbly carbonation, a poor sour metallic taste and finish.

Paulaner Salvator Thomasbrau A.G.
(Munich)

Atkien-Gesellschaft Paulanerbrau Zum Salvatorkeller was founded about the year 1600 upon an old cloister brewery. In 1806, when the property of the religious orders had passed to the state, the ancient brewhouse was leased out. In 1849 it came into the hands of the Schmeder family, whose descendants have since operated it. It became a stock company in 1886.

It recently merged with Thomasbrau, one of the fine old smaller Bavarian breweries, whose products were previously marketed mostly in the area of Bavaria, south of Munich.

PAULANER SALVATOR—gold color, toasted malt aroma, bitter toffee taste, faintly bitter finish, very short aftertaste.

PAULANER HELL URTYP EXPORT—rich malty aroma; strong hop flavor; sour finish that clashes with the bitterness of the hops, but pretty good even with that defect.

Spaten Franziskaner–Brau KGaA
(Munich)

This firm dates back to 1391, but it did not come into the possession of the Spaeth families until the early seventeenth century. From then "Spaethbrau" became a famous name in German brewing. In 1807 the brewery was bought by Gabriel Sedlmayr and has continued in that family since; it has been called the Brauerei zum Spaten since 1874. Spaten beers are now the largest-selling original Munich beers in America. The site of the present brewery dates back only to 1851.

SPATEN MUNICH LIGHT—light malt aroma, big hoppy taste with good balance, flattens out somewhat near the end and finishes faintly bitter. A good beer overall, excellent except at the very end.

SPATEN OPTIMATOR (DOPPELSPATEN)—very dark brown color with reddish hues, neutral faintly malty aroma, heavy sweet molasses-malt flavor, sour malty finish and aftertaste. Really good when you are in the mood for it. Be careful not to overchill it, though; it tastes best closer to 50°F. than to 40°F.

SPATEN GOLD—deep golden appearance, malty toffee aroma, heavy body, big bitter and malty flavor, a hearty brew with a long, long finish. May be overdone for some tastes, but perfect for those who like a heavy-handed bright hop character.

SPATEN URMARZEN OKTOBERFEST—gold-brown color, big malty-toffee nose but slightly skunky, lightly flavored on the neutral side, a very dull brew. The samples at the one source found must have been mishandled because I cannot believe that anyone would go to the trouble of importing this unpleasant smelling, dull tasting beer.

St. Pauli Brewery
(Bremen)

This brewery exports a pair of beers that many Americans will find equal to or better than Beck's. The light was almost identical to Beck's and actually outscored it in comparisons, and the dark was far superior.

ST. PAULI GIRL BEER—pale color, faint malty-hop aroma, mild pleasant flavor with good hop-malt balance, slightly hopped finish.

ST. PAULI GIRL DARK BEER—deep brown; hops dominate the malty aroma, but the taste is heavy with malt, which comes as a sort of surprise after the hoppy aroma; good balance, and a very appetizing finish and aftertaste. One of the most appetizing dark beers tasted; a nice compromise between the mellow types and the zesty well-hopped versions.

Warsteiner Brauerei GEBR
(Warstein, West Germany)

This firm dates back to 1753. The label also contains the name of Cramer K. G. of Warstein, which may be an owner or a distributor.

WARSTEIN PREMIUM VERUM—faint sour malty aroma, sour salty taste, fairly poor among German beers tasted.

Wurzburger Hofbrau A.G.
(Wurzburg, West Germany)

The origins of Wurzburg lie with a seventh-century settlement chosen by Irish monks (St. Kilian et al. in 689) for the center of Bavarian missionary work. About 740 Wurzburg was elevated to a bishopric by Boniface. Over the next nine hundred years secular power increasingly came to repose with the bishops of Wurzburg. One of them, Prince-

302

Bishop Johann Philipp von Schonborn, erected a brewery in 1643 to supply his court and the local citizenry with beer. As late as 1736 a prince of this same Schonborn family was conducting the business. Under Napoleonic occupation, the breweries were secularized and subsequently attached by the royal Bavarian government when they assumed political power following Napoleon's removal. The brewery did not long remain the property of the Bavarian kings, for in 1863 it passed into private hands. In 1884 a private stock company was formed and the business merged with that of another (Bauch) brewery.

Like all German brews, Wurzburger is made only from pure barley malt (no adjuncts), and fermentation proceeds for several months. The brews of this fine old firm have been exported to the U.S. since 1882 and have always enjoyed a well-deserved popularity here.

WURZBURGER LIGHT BEER—golden color, marvelous malty hop aroma (better than the aroma of Munich Lowenbrau), very Germanic malty sour taste with a lingering finish and a very satisfying aftertaste. An excellent brew, finely balanced.

WURZBURGER DARK BEER—deep amber brown, heavy malty nose, hearty rich malty flavor, mellow more than zesty, sour malty finish, very much in character for a dark Bavarian brew. Good stuff in the bottle, fantastic on draft.

WURZBURGER OKTOBERFEST BEER—medium amber-brown color; faint hops in the aroma but more hops than malt; a soft and mellow brew beautifully balanced with the proper amount of hops; rich and lingering aftertaste. An excellent brew that could please both German and American tastes by striking a fine balance between the differences.

WURZBURGER BOCK BEER—very deep dark color, subdued burnt malt nose, hops noticeable in the aroma, roasted malt flavor dominates, very distinctive, lots of character but the roasted quality is overdone.

Greece

Beer is neither traditional nor popular to any great degree in Greece. Greece produces mostly the traditional pine-flavored Retsina (which accounts for over eighty percent of the alcoholic-beverage consumption in the country) and *ouzo*, the spiritous traditional liquor.

In Greece only Fix Beer is available and found everywhere. Two other labels are exported to America; it is understood that these are products of the same brewery that makes Fix, but only for export.

Karolos Fix, S.A.
(Athens)

This brewery was established in 1864. Its beers have since won thirty-six gold medals in international competition.

FIX BEER—aroma of bubble gum reflected in the taste; very poor on the tip of the tongue but flavor improves in the middle; the finish is again poor and the aftertaste decidedly unpleasant.

ATHENIAN GREEK BEER (Athenian Brewery, S.A.)—cloudy yellow, creamy head, light pilsener nose, slightly bitter flavor, not really pleasant tasting, no aftertaste to speak of.

MARATHON GREEK BEER (Athenian Brewery, S.A.)—cloudy yellow, faint malt nose, slightly bitter flavor, all features quite light, virtually no aftertaste.

Holland

Beer dates back to early times in Holland. In the thirteenth century Dutch scholars Isaac and John Hollandus wrote learned dissertations on the subjects of fermenting and brewing. Delft became as famous for its beers as for its ceramics, and for many years beer was the great staple of that port. In the nineteenth century Gouda was a brewing center and as well know for its beers as for its cheese.

Beer has always been produced in great quantity in Holland to meet the high per capita consumption. But before the late 1800s the major business interest in alcoholic beverages lay with distilled spirits, especially the world-famous Holland gin. In 1842 the Dutch Temperance League was formed to suppress strong drinks and to promote malt liquors instead. Success was achieved in 1881 when the Dutch government voted to regulate spirits, but not malt liquors, wine, and cider.

Temperance advocates then gave their encouragement to the manufacture of malt liquors, offering premiums and prizes for superior beers. Many of their number entered the brewing trade themselves. Indeed, the beer halls of the temperance societies at the 1886 Colonial Exposition of Amsterdam did the most thriving business. Since then, fine beer has been a Dutch tradition.

Heineken is the largest brewery in Holland today, accounting for nearly forty percent of all the beer consumed in the country. Heineken also exports to more than a hundred countries.

Heineken Brouwerjen
(Amsterdam, Rotterdam, Hertogenbosch)

Heineken operates three breweries today. The Amsterdam brewery is the oldest, dating back to 1433, and produces Heineken's dark beers and stout. Hertogenbosch supplies the local market. Export lager is brewed at the Rotterdam brewery, built in 1874. The firm was founded in 1864 when twenty-two-year old Gerard Adriaan Heineken purchased the old De Hooiberg (Haystack) brewery in Amsterdam.

The Heineken yeast culture dates from 1886 and was once widely sold to other brewers, but that practice ended with World War I. Heineken Lager is the leading imported beer in America. It is widely available and can be found on draft even in the most unlikely neighborhoods. It appeared in the U.S. first in 1933 when twenty-four quarter barrels

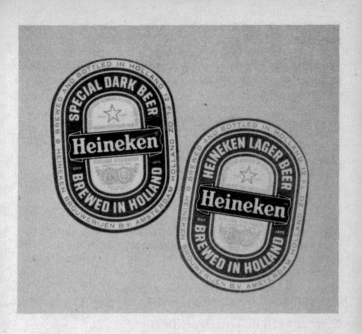

and fifty cases of bottles were unloaded, the first shipment of beer from abroad following Repeal. Heineken Dark is an exceptional brew made from roasted caramelized malts and a high level of malt extract, resulting in a full rich flavor. Heineken also produces Amstel, but it has not been seen in the U.S. in the past two years following a period of regular availability. It is also an excellent product, apparently produced in the Netherlands Antilles.

HEINEKEN LAGER BEER—medium gold color, smooth bouquet of hops and malt, dry, well-hopped but not overpowering, finely balanced with a good dry and slightly salty finish. A good beer in bottle, excellent on draft. This is the No. 1 choice of a vast number of Americans who regularly drink beer.

HEINEKEN LAGER BEER (draft)—medium gold, good head, medium-strength hoppy nose, good hop flavor, big body, smooth finish with hops present only faintly in the aftertaste.

HEINEKEN SPECIAL DARK BEER—light copper gold, pleasant rich malty aroma and taste, fine balance, long-pleasing aftertaste. One of the best dark beers available in the world.

Bavaria Breweries
(Lieshout)

This firm was founded in 1719.

BAVARIA LAGER—pale yellow color, slightly cloudy appearance, lettuce-leaf aroma, unbalanced with most of the flavor in the throat and on the far back of the tongue, lingering bitter aftertaste.

Birebrowerij de Drie Hoefijzers
(Breda)

This "Three Horseshoes" brewery dates back to 1628.

BREDA ROYAL HOLLAND BEER—strong hop nose, dull taste, neutral.

ROYAL DUTCH (N.V. de Posthoorn, Breda)—medium hop nose, dull taste consisting only of hops, very bitter finish and aftertaste.

Grolsche Bierbrowerij
(Enschede)

GROLSCH NATURAL HOLLAND BEER—amber color, tart aroma, sour malty flavor with good hops, richly flavored but strange and unbalanced.

International Beer Export, Ltd.
(Amsterdam)

THREE HORSES BRAND PILSENER LAGER BEER—
sharp pilsener aroma, sour flavor with a bitter background,
bitterness strong in the finish and aftertaste.

Oranjeboom Breweries
(Rotterdam)

*ORANJEBOOM HOLLAND PILSENER DELUXE—*yellow-gold color slightly cloudy, strong vegetal aroma (somewhat decayed), tart flavor with slightly sour background,
weak in the middle of the palate but finishes well. Lots of
character.

Skol Associates in Holland
(under license from Skol Int'l, Ltd.)

*SKOL LAGER BEER—*tawny gold color, fairly brown for a
light lager, small bubble carbonation, malty hop nose, taste
little more than just hops.

United Dutch Breweries
(Rotterdam)

*JAEGER BEER—*strong aroma of apples and hops, complex flavor but no harmony of tastes, hard bitter finish.

(Brewery not identified on the label)

*PETER'S BRAND HOLLAND PILSENER BEER—*pale
yellow, slightly cloudy; skunky aroma with light malty typical European pils flavor in back; the skunkiness stayed only
a short time; the skunky hop flavor soon developed into a
good light hop flavor with some character. Once the skunk
left, it wasn't bad at all; pretty good in fact. Seen only in San
Francisco.

India and Pakistan

The British established breweries in India as early as 1834 to satisfy the demands of empire troops stationed there. Beer was not generally in use by the natives before or during that time. It is said that the British troops in India preferred the locally produced (by British brewers, of course) beer to that imported from England, but economics may have colored that choice.

In 1900 the largest brewing establishment in India was the Murree Brewery Company, Ltd., located at Gora Gully, near Murree, in the Punjab. Its four breweries produced more than a million gallons of beer. Murree was established in 1861.

Murree Brewing Co.
(Rawalpindi, Pakistan)

MURREE EXPORT LAGER—pale cloudy yellow, dry sour taste, quite astringent, awful.

Mohan Meakin Breweries, Ltd.
(Ghaziabad, India) (Mohan Nagar Brewery)

GOLDEN EAGLE LAGER BEER—deep color, slightly cloudy, pleasant semi-sweet malty aroma (described by one taster as being like some brand of floorwax), unique smoky-salty flavor.

Israel

The brewing industry of Israel is necessarily a young one. The first signs of an ongoing brewing trade appeared in the 1970s with the importation of the two beers reported below. As with the Israeli wine exports, a good measure of loyalty to the ideals of the state of Israel is required for continued support of the beers.

Cabeer Breweries, Ltd.
(Bat Yam)

BEERSHEBA PREMIUM—slightly skunky aroma, astrinently sour taste, highly carbonated, very lightly finished, almost no aftertaste.

National Breweries, Ltd.
(Tel Aviv)

MACCABEE PREMIUM BEER—pale color; creamy head; dull sweet apple aroma with a trace of wood pulp or cardboard; sweet candy-apple flavor, but not so sweet as to be cloying; sweet aftertaste mostly in the throat; not unpleasant for a sweet beer, but not dry enough for most beer palates.

Italy

With good inexpensive wine available in profusion, a beer industry in Italy has never gained nationwide momentum, but the northern Italians have a taste for German and Swiss beers.

Up to the twentieth century, the thirst of the Italian beer drinker was satisfied largely by imports from Germany and Austria. Since then, production of beer in Italy has slowly risen nearly to match consumption.

The brewing industry in Italy had its beginnings when portions of Italy were included in the Austro-Hungarian Empire; the famous Austrian name of Dreher still appears on a fine Italian beer exported to America. In fact, the three Italian beers exported to North America are of excellent quality.

Dreher S.P.A.
(Pedavena)

DREHER FORTE EXPORT LAGER BEER—dark yellow-brown color, dank sour aroma, sweet taste up front that is

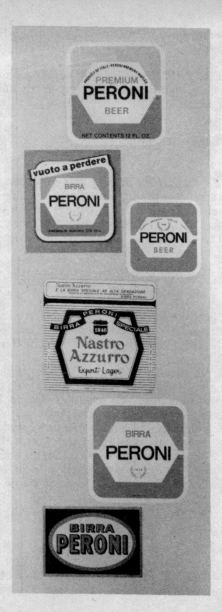

sour-bitter to the back of the palate, good balance, pleasantly finished, overall effect is very good.

Peroni Breweries
(Naples)

PERONI PREMIUM BEER—light brown, great zest and character, hops dominate nose and taste, strong-flavored.

Birra Wührer SPA
(Brescia)

CRYSTALL WUHRER BEER—medium yellow brown, nicely balanced malty hop aroma, bitter hop taste with a soapy background, relatively clean finish. Good, but the Dreher was better.

Japan

It is said that sake has been in general use in Japan for over two thousand years. It is an alcoholic beverage brewed from rice, and probably is still rightfully called Japan's national drink. If it is, however, it is not very far ahead of beer, for that beverage has been gaining steadily since its introduction shortly before the end of the nineteenth century.

Although a brewery had been built in Yokohama about 1870, the first event of national significance to the Japanese brewing trade took place in 1873, when a young man named Nakawara was sent by the Japanese government to Germany to learn the art of brewing and all of its branches. He remained in Germany for three years and then returned home to head a brewery built by the government at Tokyo.

Before 1887, however, domestic production was still quite small and most of the beer consumed in Japan was imported from Germany, but by 1899 production had risen so sharply that Japan began to export beer to Siberia, the Philippines, Hawaii, and Chinese ports.

With the Japanese inclination to Western ways, the consumption of beer increases each year and is approaching

ten gallons per capita. The beer brewed is very pale, with rice used as an adjunct. The style of Japanese beer today, say some, is influenced more by Nordic beers (especially Finnish) than by German types.

Asahi Breweries
(Tokyo)

ASAHI LAGER BEER—very pale, almost water color; clean, fresh spring-water aroma; a unique flavor, mostly like spring water with a ferruginous character. Light, inoffensive beer. Not too exciting for a real beer drinker.

Kirin Brewery Co., Ltd.
(Kyobashi, Tokyo)

It has been reported that the first brewery in Japan, the one which is mentioned above and which was founded by Americans Weigand and Copeland in Yokohama about 1870, was the foundation upon which the Kirin Brewery originated. That may be partly so. The Japan Brewery Company, Ltd., is believed to have first marketed a brew called Kirin Beer in Yokohama about 1888. This firm was founded by an English corporation and may have been set up on the Wiegand business base. In any event, the Kirin (a mythical beast, combining a horse and a dragon) dominates the domestic Japanese brewing scene, commanding over sixty percent of domestic beer sales. In 1974 Kirin opened its twelfth brewery. It is the best of the Japanese beers tasted.

KIRIN BEER—pale cloudy yellow, complex aroma, good smoky malt flavor, very refreshing, some metallic taste in the background but not obtrusive, soapy finish. Kirin is brewed from Japanese barley, rice, cornstarch, and corn grits. It is fermented eight days and stored two months before being filtered and pasteurized.

Orion Breweries Ltd.
(Nago, Okinawa)

ORION LAGER BEER—deep yellow with brown tinge, malt aroma with a touch of the "grape," unappealing tart and sour taste.

Sapporo Breweries Ltd.
(Tokyo)

The Sapporo brewery was founded in 1876 at Sapporo by the colonial government of Hokkaido to provide a market for barley grown in the vicinity. In 1886 the business passed into private hands and two years later incorporated as the Sapporo Brewing Co., Ltd.

SAPPORO LAGER BEER—deep brownish yellow color, sweet malty nose, bittersweet fruitlike flavor with a cardboard and wood-pulp background.

Korea

The beer of Korea has never developed any appreciable reputation. Soldiers returning from Korea were never heard to generate any enthusiasm for Korean brews; in fact, comments were usually quite to the contrary. Nevertheless, a Korean beer is exported to the U.S. regularly, and somewhere there may be some beer drinkers who found the brew of their choice in a little pub in Seoul.

Oriental Brewery Co., Ltd.
(Seoul)

ORIENTAL OB LAGER BEER—pale color, some samples clouded, light apple-peel aroma, light sweet cardboard and apple taste.

Luxembourg

This tiny country has only one brewery but produces some of Europe's finest brews. Diekirch Pils is the largest-selling foreign beer in Germany, which is quite a claim. As in Germany, the beers of Luxembourg can contain only barley, hops, yeast, and water.

The Diekirch Brewery, founded in 1871, produces its own malt, a brewing rarity in these days.

Brasserie Diekirch Brauerei
(Luxembourg)

DIEKIRCH PILS—good malty aroma, typical sour vegetable pils flavor, tart hop finish. A very good, well-balanced brew. No wonder it sells so well in Germany, it's one of Europe's finest beers.

DIEKIRCH MALT LIQUOR—sweet malty aroma, a taste like a Spruce beer, pleasant malty finish marred by bitterness in the aftertaste. Different but fairly likable.

DIEKIRCH MALT LIQUOR EXCLUSIVE—cloudy pale yellow, aroma of apples with a background of decaying vegetation, sour and sharp flavor, sour finish.

Mexico

Beer is a relative newcomer to Mexico. Until the last half of the nineteenth century, only the native drinks mescal, tequila, and pulque were in regular use. Even now, some hundred years later, these beverages are more popular than beer probably because they are cheap and easy to make.

Pulque, the juice of the *maguey* or agave cactus, is fermented for twenty-four hours, and then must be consumed immediately as it soon becomes unfit to drink. Tequila and mescal are liquors distilled from the same plant. Tequila enjoys considerable popularity above the border as well, particularly among the under-forty group. It is sipped with salt, a practice that originated in the area of Mexico subject to high temperatures, which cause men to develop a salt hunger to replace body losses.

The earliest Mexican brewers made a brown beer from malt which, after having been spread on the roof of the brewery, was toasted by the sun. Later, but before 1900, a beer called sencilla was popular. It was brewed somewhat like a lager, but with less extract. It was cold-stored for several weeks in the better breweries, but some smaller brewers casked the beer directly after fermentation, often for drinking that same day.

Top-fermentation breweries existed in Mexico City as early as 1845. They used a malt of sun-dried Mexican barley mixed with a brown sugar, *pilancillo*. The beer so made was inferior, but these breweries survived until a good lager produced in Toluca appeared on the scene. In the 1860s the base of the present Mexican brewing industry was established with the arrival of the Swiss, Bavarian, and Alsatian immigrants. Lager beer made its appearance in Mexico about 1891.

Cerveceria Cuahtemoc
(Monterrey, N.L.; Culiacán, Sin.; Toluca, Mex.; Guadalajara, Jal.)

This firm was the third lager brewery founded in Mexico. It was established in 1891. Its Carta Blanca brand was once the most famous and largest-selling beer of Mexico.

BOHEMIA ALE—pale yellow, faint malt aroma, very slightly vegetal malt flavor with very little hop character, not alelike, average inoffensive beer.

TECATE CERVEZA (Tecate Brewery, Toluca)—pale gold color, nice malty hop aroma but very light, pleasant malty hop dry flavor, nicely balanced but overall everything is just too lightly done. Tecate is popular in Mexico drunk straight from the can with salt crusted around the rim, softened with lemon or lime juice. It is at least an interesting taste.

CERVEZA CARTA BLANCA—pale color, dank offensive aroma; inoffensive flavor, almost nothing at all on the palate until the finish, which is faintly bitter. Seems much more ordinary than it was twenty years ago.

Cerveceria Moctezuma S.A.
(Orizaba, Ver.; Guadalajara, Jal.; Mexico City; Monterrey, N.L.)

This brewing firm was established in 1894. Its Superior brand became Mexico's largest-selling label as the national tastes tended to favor lighter beers. The recently introduced Tres Equis is even paler and doubtless aimed at satisfying a continuation of that trend. Dos Equis has its largest following in the United States, although it was Moctezuma's leading brand in 1960.

SUPERIOR LIGHT BEER—pale color, light malt aroma, light body, yeasty flavor with only a trace of hops. Although Moctezuma says only natural carbonation is used, the strong carbonation and foamy head indicate the use of injection and foaming agents. There was a problem in obtaining a good bottle of this beer in the eastern U.S., and then it was disappointing.

DOS EQUIS XX BEER—brown color of medium saturation, clean sweet malty nose, big malty flavor like molasses with a fine hop finish. Warning: There is a wide variation from batch to batch as obtained in the U.S. Most of it is very good, but occasionally you will get some that is just plain dull, like caramel-colored water with a faint "fake" malty background.

TRES EQUIS XXX LIGHT BEER (Cerveza Clara)—very pale color; light malty aroma; fruity, sour, cardboard taste; wood-pulp finish and aftertaste; too mild. This sample was obtained on the West Coast of the U.S. and is attributed specifically to the Orizaba brewery.

New Guinea

The island of New Guinea has several breweries, including one that produces San Miguel, but the most famous of New Guinea beers is South Pacific, or more simply, SP.

SP Brewery, Ltd.
(Papua)

SOUTH PACIFIC SP GOLD MEDAL DRAUGHT LAGER—medicinal aroma; flavor that lies somewhere in a mix of anise, cardboard, and the old bandaids you might recall from your youth.

New Zealand

The climate of New Zealand is materially different from that of its (distant) neighbor Australia, and is more suitable to the making of beer. New Zealand brews its beverages very much on the English style, supposedly even more so than do the Australians.

New Zealand Breweries, Ltd.
(Auckland)

STEINLAGER LAGER BEER—skunky malt aroma, highly carbonated, dull flavor and finish.

LEOPARD LAGER—pineapple aroma, with a gradual development of hops; sweet and fruitlike rather than malt; a finish of fizz and hops.

Norway

Barley has been cultivated in Norway for hundreds of years, but a malt beverage industry could not develop until late in the nineteenth century because of a general preference for distilled spirits. In all of Scandinavia, however, the valleys of Norway offered the best climatic conditions for the cultivation of barley, with some locations capable of yielding two crops in each summer.

By 1900 forty-four Norwegian breweries were annually producing about four hundred thousand barrels, mostly for local consumption on draft. Today, fine Norwegian brews are exported about the world, including the standard-bearer of Frydenlund's, which had a fine reputation in the world over seventy-five years ago, the well-known and highly appreciated Ringnes line of beers, and the very excellent brews from the Hansa brewery in Bergen.

Frydenlund Bryggeri
(Oslo)

Established in 1859 in Christiana, Frydenlund's was the largest brewery in Norway at the turn of the century.

FRYDENLUND'S EXPORT III PILSENER BEER—hop aroma, bitter hop taste throughout with a sweet background at the beginning and a salty background at the finish.

Hansa Bryggeri
(Bergen)

HANSA FJORD NORWEGIAN PILSENER BEER—pale cloudy yellow-green appearance; beautiful malty hop aroma; semisweet malty flavor with excellent hop balance; a luscious full-flavored and full-bodied brew with all kinds of character; complex yet refreshing. I have found nothing in the U.S. to compare with this brew. It is difficult to find, but if you happen to spot it, buy enough to last a drought.

Ringnes Brewery
(Oslo)

In the 1860s, brothers Amund and Ellef Ringnes moved to Christiana (now Oslo) and established a small brewery in partnership with Consul Heiberg. The name Ringnes & Co. was registered in 1877 with Amund brewing and Ellef selling their beer. In 1899 the business was incorporated. Last year the brewery produced 370,000 barrels.

Ringnes has a history of supporting cultural projects and humanitarian goals. The name Ringnes is especially connected to Norwegian polar expeditions and to Fridtjof Nansen, Roald Amundsen, and Otto Sverdrup and their

famous polar ship *Fram*. It was the Ringnes support that made these explorations possible and islands in the polar regions of Canada still bear the names of the Ringnes brothers and Consul Heiberg.

RINGNES SPECIAL BEER—deep color, strong hoppy nose and flavor but lacking complexity and character, all hops, worsens toward the finish.

RINGNES MALT LIQUOR—sweet malt nose, very sweet and very malty taste and aftertaste, sudden bitterness at the end.

RINGNES EXPORT—aroma of hops and caramel; starts out tasting very good but sags a bit in the middle, showing poor balance; a very poor finish of sour celery. Several of these were tried with similar results. I believe these all to be old or mishandled stock; it should be retried after the bad stock has cleared the shelves.

RINGNES SPECIAL BOCK BEER—very dark color, strong malty aroma, big body, heavy and thick, very light carbonation, good flavor throughout with an excellent finish. A good brew, certainly the best from Ringnes.

Philippines

Since it was founded in 1890 as the first brewery in Southeast Asia, the San Miguel brewery of Manila has been one of the most famous names across the Pacific. Rarely seen in the U.S. before World War II, San Miguel has long been a favorite with U.S. military personnel in the Pacific and Hawaii.

I have heard stories about how prime space aboard U.S. Navy vessels was reserved for San Miguel and have no doubt that priority was given to that great morale booster. Stories concerning San Miguel and World War II are popular in the South Pacific. One story allows how bombers on missions over Manila had specific instructions not to hit the brewery, reportedly a firm in which Douglas MacArthur held a substantial interest.

Regardless of the truth of any of the stories, no intelligent bombardier would try to hit what would eventually be the source of some really fine beers for the liberating forces. In the Pacific it was always San Miguel, of course.

San Miguel operates three breweries in the Philippines, three in Spain, and one each in Hong Kong, Guam, and Papua. The brews are tailored to their markets. For instance, the local Manila brew is more bitter than the export version because that's the way the Filipinos like it.

Crew members of the Polish full-rigged ship "Dar Pomorza" enjoy their native Krakus in New York at Op Sail '76.

San Miguel Brewery
(Manila)

SAN MIGUEL BEER—cloudy, pale yellow; strongly hopped and complex malt aroma; creamy, fresh tasting; excellent middle flavor and a very refreshing finish. One of the world's best beers.

SAN MIGUEL DARK BEER—extremely dark color, faint but rich malty aroma, a subtle complex well-balanced malt-hop blend with a fine refreshing aftertaste. A marvelous brew. Of its style none other is better.

Poland

The history of Polish breweries traces in part to the time of the Austro-Hungarian Empire. For example, there was a brewing firm of substantial size in Okocim, Galicia, in 1900 by the name of J. Edler v. Goetz. Without visiting the brewery in person, one would be hard put to track down the pedigree of this or any other brewery in Poland because of the turbulent history of the area in the past seventy-five years. The Okocim Brewery says its origins reach to 1845; if so, it seems highly likely that the Edler firm formed at least the foundation of the present Okocim Brewery.

Okocim Brewery

OKOCIM FULL LIGHT O.K. BEER—pungent soapy aroma, soapy metallic taste, metallic finish. Not as bad as it sounds but nothing much to look forward to at the end of a hard day.

OKOCIM PORTER—dark brown color, malty burnt caramel taste, ponderous, sweet and heavy, overdone.

Zyweic Brewery

KRAKUS LIGHT BEER—faint sweet malt nose, creamy texture, strong yeasty barley malt flavor. Not bad for its type; best of the Polish imports.

ZYWIEC FULL LIGHT—dark color, malty soapy nose, sour-sweet mealy flavor.

ZYWIEC FULL LIGHT PIAST—very faint aroma, too faint to identify; sour malt taste; sour malt finish. Too sour to be interesting.

Portugal

The brewing industry in Portugal suffers from competition with the Portuguese preference for wine. As in Spain, wine is good and it is also inexpensive. The larger of the two brewing companies in Portugal is the Sociedade Central de Cervejas, which has about seventy percent of the Portuguese market.

Sociedade Central de Cervejas
(Lisbon)

This firm was created in 1934 by the merger of four of Portugal's largest breweries. Two plants are operated, at Vialonga and Coimbra.

CERVEJA SAGRES—pale yellow; slightly clouded; skunky vegetal aroma; wood-pulp and cardboard flavor, with excessive bitterness especially toward the finish.

SAGRES DARK BEER—very dark brown color, strong malt nose, too heavy and filling, bitter molasses taste with a sweet molasses finish and aftertaste.

South Africa

Brewing in South Africa began in the latter half of the nineteenth century and was greatly disturbed during the Boer War when many of the major breweries were being built or remodeled. At the turn of the century, South African Breweries, Ltd., was the leading South African brewer. It was a firm with its headquarters in London and a brewery of American design. Both beers reported below are products of this company, the Castle brand going back almost one hundred years with the Castle Brewery of Johannesburg.

South African Breweries, Ltd.
(Johannesburg)

ROGUE LONG BREW BEER—faint applesauce nose, highly carbonated, very little flavor, slight bitterness in the finish.

CASTLE LAGER GREAT SOUTH AFRICAN BEER—(Ohlsson's Cape Breweries, Ltd., subsidiary of South African Breweries, Ltd.)—malty apple-cider nose, sweet grainy flavor, cardboard finish.

328

South America, Central America, and the Caribbean Islands

When the conquistadores arrived, the highly civilized Peruvians had developed agriculture to a high level, and were making the fermented beverage chicha from maize. Another fermented liquor, also made from corn, was sora. Sora was of such strength that the common people were forbidden to use it. The Incas, like the Aztecs of Mexico, also made pulque, but chicha was the national beverage. At the coronation of the last of the Incas, who received his crown from Pizarro, it is recorded that "the Inca pledged the Spanish commander in a golden goblet of the sparkling chicha."

As in Mexico, the beginnings of today's brewing trade in South America came with the arrival of Euoprean immigrants, among whom were experienced brewmasters, and may generally be dated 1860–90. The first brewery in Columbia was established in 1889; Bieckert was Argentina's first, in 1860; Brazil had one in 1870; Bolivia in 1882, and Ecuador got its first brewery in 1876.

Because of the high average temperatures, some of the early brews were pretty strange stuff. When the daily ambient temperature is over 85°F. and there are no refrigeration facilities, the brew will likely be a desperate concoction. And so it was in South America. When modern refrigeration came along, (about the turn of the twentieth century in Latin America), the beers became more like their counterparts in cooler North America, and in recent years the lighter-flavored and very pale pilseners have become the most favored.

Although every major city has a number of breweries, few Latin American beers ever find their way to North America. Most of them are rarely seen outside their city of manufacture.

ARGENTINA

Compania Cerveceria Bieckert Industria Argentina
(Buenos Aires)

Bieckert is the pioneer brewery of Argentina, having been founded by a man of that name in 1860. In 1889 the plant passed into the hands of an English syndicate, but is now believed to have been "nationalized."

BIECKERT ETIQUETA AZUL PILSEN ESPECIAL CERVEZA BLANCA GENUINA—yellow-gold color with greenish cast, sour malty aroma, heavy body, heavy cardboard taste with the sense of licorice in the background. Interesting but not too enjoyable.

BRAZIL

Companhia Cervejaria Brahma
(Rio de Janeiro)

The Brahma brewery was founded in the late nineteenth century by a German named George Maschke and was originally operated by George Maschke & Co. By the turn of the century it was one of South America's largest breweries.

BRAHMA CHOPP EXPORT BEER—cloudy greenish yellow color, vanilla-malt cookie-dough aroma and taste, not complex, sour malt finish, not really likable.

Cervejarias Reunidas Skol Caracu Industria Brasileira

Skol is the largest-selling international lager beer, being brewed or sold in fifty-five countries throughout the world, and especially popular in England and several European countries. I have never found it to be anything more than average-quality lager beer. Reported below is the Brazilian version.

SKOL LAGER BEER—cloudy yellow, small bubble natural carbonation, faint sweet malt aroma, clean grainy flavor, clean but austere finish, very little aftertaste.

COLOMBIA

Bavaria Brewery

(Bogota) (Bavaria S.A.)

This brewery was established in 1889 by a member of the house of Jacob Kopp & Sons of Frankfurt am Main, Germany. In 1897 it was sold to the German-Colombian Brewing Co. of Hamburg, with the original owners retaining half the stock and the general management. The present company structure is not known.

CLUB COLOMBIA PILSENER-TYPE BEER—pale cloudy yellow with a greenish cast, malty pineapple aroma, malty taste that is too sweet at the start and too bitter in the finish, bitterness dominates the aftertaste, poorly balanced.

DOMINICAN REPUBLIC

Cerveceria Nacional
Dominicana
(Santo Domingo)

Although not found everywhere, this beer seems to sell quite well in Hispanic neighborhoods in major East Coast and southern U.S. cities.

PRESIDENTE PILSENER TYPE BEER—deep yellow, very pleasant malty aroma with good intensity, disappointing metallic flavor that intensifies toward the finish, sour metal aftertaste.

JAMAICA

Desnoes & Geddes, Ltd.
(Kingston)

RED STRIPE LAGER BEER—slightly skunky aroma that fades with time, highly carbonated, slightly sweet spring-water taste but most of the palate sensation is the carbonation.

PERU

Cerveceria Backus y Johnston
(Lima)

CRISTAL—only the faintest of malt aroma, mostly like the smell of cardboard, a weird sour malt taste, more like a cross between beer and Champale, poorly balanced, a very strange brew.

PUERTO RICO

Cerveceria Corona
(San Juan and Santurce)

CORONA PILSENER TYPE BEER—pale golden yellow, austere wood-pulp aroma, light slightly malty taste, not much of anything. This beer was made around 1960 in New York City by the Five Star Brewing Co. as Corona Cerveza Banda Blanca.

Cerveceria India, Inc.
(Mayaguez)

INDIA BEER—pale yellow; fresh malty aroma; clean taste but unbalanced; dull, uninteresting finish and aftertaste.

VENEZUELA

Cerveceria Polar
(Caracas)

POLAR CERVEZA TIPO PILSEN—faint malt aroma, smooth, well balanced, a good-flavored blend of hops and malt. The best Latin American beer that was found in the U.S. over a long period of time.

Spain

Spain is not noted for its beers or its breweries, mostly because inexpensive wine abounds. Spain's vineyards are copious and legendary, making it difficult to produce a beer competitive in price. Notwithstanding, reputable breweries do exist in Spain, several of which export their products to America.

Cervejeria San Martin
(Orense)

SAN MARTIN CERVEJA ESPECIAL—pale slightly cloudy yellow, faint malty aroma, salty sour taste, metallic aftertaste (not as in an old can; this was bottled beer).

Sociedad Anonima Damm
(city not given)

ESTRELLA DORADA CERVEZA ESPECIAL PILSEN CLASE EXTRA—pale cloudy yellow; sweet cardboard, wood-pulp taste; virtually no aroma; a paper-flavor finish.

San Miguel Fabrica de Cerveja y Malta S.A.
(Lerida, Malaga, Burgos)

SAN MIGUEL LAGER BEER—cloudy yellow with some particulate matter in a recently imported batch; sour malty aroma; sour vegetal taste; same label as the Philippine product, but a very different brew.

Sweden

Until the nineteenth century, the production and consumption of distilled spirits were of such importance that malted liquors were hardly mentioned. Only in Sweden did the manufacture of malt beverages outside of home brew exist. Late in that century the Swedish people began to drink less spirituous liquors and more malt beverages. By 1901 there were 520 breweries in Sweden producing over two million barrels of beer annually.

The climate is not suited to growing barley; severe night frosts during much of the year are destructive to young crops.

The Swedish government continues to be concerned with excessive alcoholism. Since 1955 the tax structure on alcohol has been designed to encourage the consumption of beer rather than distilled spirits and wine.

Falcon Brewery
(Falkenberg)

The Falcon Brewery of Sweden dates back to 1896.

FALCON EXPORT III BEER—4.5 percent alcohol according to label; light malty aroma; bitter flavor; light cardboardlike finish and aftertaste. Found in a sixteen-ounce, very attractively designed can. A must for collectors.

Pripp Bryggerie
(Stockholm)

PRIPPS EXPORT SWEDISH BEER—deep yellow-brown color, hops dominate the nose and taste, much like some English beers (bitters), great character and full flavor. An excellent beer worth trying. It has all the gusto many others beers brag about but lack.

Switzerland

The beers of Switzerland are made according to the standards in Germany; that is, made with only water, malt, hops, and yeast. No additives are permitted. Brewing in Switzerland is recorded as early as A.D. 620, when a brewhouse was erected as part of the monastery at St. Gall. At the turn of the twentieth century there were 367 breweries in Switzerland. Today there are fourteen.

Cardinal Brewery truck, a 1913 Saurer

Cardinal S.A.; Feldschlossen S.A.
(Fribourg, Sibra, Frankendorf, Rheinfelden, Waedenswil)

The beer industry in Fribourg commenced in 1788 when Francois Piller set up a brewery. In 1802 the brewery passed into the hands of Andre Keller, a master cooper. After several more changes of ownership, a watch manufacturer, Paul-Alcide Blancpain, obtained the brewery in 1877 and reorganized and modernized the company. In 1890 Cardinal's Beer was introduced in honor of the elevation of Msgr. Mermillod, bishop of Fribourg, to the cardinalate.

In 1901 Blancpain's sons, Achille, Paul, and Georges, took over the company and continued the firm's growth. Cardinal was joined by Feldschlossen in 1881, and both enhance the firm's economic position in the highly competitive European beer market.

Cardinal Beer is an all-barley malt beer made according to Bavarian beer laws and is aged a full eight weeks. The Cardinal line includes Pale Lager (a light beer), Pale Special (a bit stronger—this version Cardinal is exported to the world as Cardinal Beer) Dark Special, Top (a rich malt

335

The cart is modern but the method is traditional. Hürlimann beer on its way from the brewery to Zurich

beer), High Life (a light and sparkling luxury beer with a refined bitter taste), and Moussy, a nonalcoholic beer exported to the U.S.

CARDINAL LAGER BEER—tawny gold, smooth aroma with hops evident, finely balanced flavor with good hops and malt, great character and finesse. One of the finest beers tasted. Cardinal is produced at all five breweries; the export version is produced at Fribourg.

FELDSCHLOSSEN BIER SPECIAL (Spezial Hell)—dark tawny brown, but not a dark beer; malty Bavarian-style aroma; good malty, well-hopped flavor; excellent balance between malt and hops; long malt finish; fairly strong-flavored. Widely available in the U.S.

336

Brauerei A. Hurlimann A.G.
(Zurich)

This fine old firm was established in 1836 by Heinrich Hurlimann in Feldbach on Lake Zurich. The firm never did achieve notable success until son Albert set up the industrial enterprise that has grown to the large company we see today, which includes the former brewing firm of Uetilberg, Ltd.

HURLIMANN SPEZIAL BIER—medium yellow-brown color, big hoppy nose, enormous hop flavor, assertive. Perhaps too assertive for most American tastes.

BIRELL MALT BEVERAGE—this famous international near-beer contains less than one percent alcohol; extremely pale colored, almost none at all; no noticeable body; a malty aroma, but weak and watery on the palate.

Lowenbrau Brauerei
(Zurich)

This firm dates back to 1898 as the Aktienbrauerei Zurich. In the economic turmoils of the early twentieth century, it was involved in a series of amalgamations resulting, in 1925, in the present firm of Lowenbrau Zurich. Most of their export market today is in Italy and the United States. The primary product of this firm is reported below. I understand that it is one of the few unpasteurized bottled beers. Because of a special (and secret) filtration process, the beer is guaranteed to keep for a period of six months after bottling.

LOWENBRAU SWISS BEER SPECIAL EXPORT LIGHT (Zurich)—very dark tawny brown color, dark for a light beer, intense malty aroma, strong malty flavor, lacks balance; seems more on the style of an English product than a German type.

Yugoslavia

The Balkan countries have slowly begun to establish a reputation for beer making, following the lead of the famous brews of nearby Czechoslovakia. Beer has been made in these countries for hundreds of years, but almost solely for local markets. Two Yugoslavian beers are now exported to the United States. In addition, I have included a report on Union Svetlo Pivo, which was hand-carried into the U.S. by a Yugoslav tourist.

338

Niksicko Pivovare
(Niksic)

NIKSICKO PIVO—celery aroma, sour and bitter celery taste, salty molasses finish, malt aftertaste.

Union Pivovare
(Triglav, Ljubljana)

This firm dates back to 1864.

UNION SVETLO PIVO—label says twelve percent alcohol, which may well be true since many of the local beers are long brewed for a high alcohol content; vegetal, wood-pulp, cardboard aroma, hops dominate taste. German in style; not bad, but not great.

Zagrebacke Pivovare
(Karlovac)

This firm was established in 1854.

ZAGREBACKE KARLOVACKO SVIJETLO PIVO LIGHT BEER—pale yellow color; particulate matter in suspension; sour pilsener, vegetal aroma; sour-bitter flavor and aftertaste.

Prior Double Dark from Schmidt's of Philadelphia – judged to be No. 1 dark beer brewed in America.

6. The Finals

After the taste trials the beers with the highest scores were entered into a double-elimination competition to determine the best in a number of categories by a tasting panel. After about three sessions of the taste trials, an arbitrary cutoff value of fifty for domestic brews and sixty for imports was selected. The numbers were chosen so as to limit the number of "finalists" to about two dozen each of domestic and foreign. At that time the estimated maximum number of available brands in the country was woefully inaccurate and the finals ended up with thirty-two domestic beers and fifty-one imports.

The finalists were compared in pairs, matching type and style as closely as possible. Entrants had to be defeated by two competing brands before they were eliminated from further consideration. Pourings were made "double-blind" so that no taster knew which beer was in a given glass and only one person would know what beers were being compared. This was carefully done because it was established early in the taste trials that advertising does have its effect (both positive and negative) and it is difficult to avoid prejudice if you know what you are tasting.

The finals were a pleasureful, but difficult, chore. Since all the beers now involved were already established as superior, it was no longer a case of separating the best from the mass. Here we were dealing with degrees of excellence and subtle nuances of difference, and comparing fine points of style. In many cases, judgment had to be made on balance only; that is, the harmony among the flavors. Everything else was the same. Those beers that had made the finals more by chance than by merit were quickly eliminated. Others, thought to be accidents, showed that they were indeed flawless, had a fine balance of qualities, and were worthy entries.

Oland's Export emerged as the top-rated imported light ale because of its outstanding balance. It prevailed over the excellent Bass Pale and Whitbread Pale simply because it did not contain some unpleasant background flavors as did they, even though Oland's Export Ale had considerably less character than those two fine British ales. Hull's Export, Krueger Beer, and Krueger Light/Pils continued on into the latter stages of the finals even though they lacked greatly in character and style. They are pleasant-tasting, refreshing, lightly flavored, and reasonably faultless brews with a fine balance. But to a beer drinker who looks beyond those qualities, Perfection, Augsburger, Michelob, and Maximus Super are preferable, though he could find Hull's et al. more than acceptable, and certainly preferable to some of the nationally advertised brands like Pabst and Miller.

The pairings were made at random, but where styles were greatly different in the random draw (particularly where there was an extreme color difference), a redrawing was made. The results of the individual comparisons are listed below. The order of the comparisons is not represented by the order of this list. The complete list of finalists and a tabulation of the resulting winners follow this list of comparisons.

Carling Red Cap over McSorley
Perfection over Schmidt's
Carling Black Label over Budweiser
Yuengling over Reading
Black Horse over Ballantine IPA

Krueger over Prior
Tuborg over Knickerbocker
Hull over Michelob
Max Super over Andeker
National Boh over Piels
Prior Double Dark over Old Chicago Dark
Prior Double Dark over Genessee Bock
Michelob over Wiedemann
Yuengling over Budweiser
Heineken over Feldschlossen
Lowenbrau over Gold Fassl
Gold Fassl over Cardinal
Gold Fassl over St. Pauli Girl
Gold Fassl over Wurzburger
Gold Fassl over Lowenbrau
Tuborg over Prior
Hansa Fjord over Gold Fassl
Beck's over Finlandia
Heineken over Peroni
Oland's Export over Bass
Oland's Export over Whitbread Pale
MacEwan's Edinburgh over Newcastle Brown
MacEwan's Edinburgh over Scotch
Newcastle over MacEwan's Tartan
Wurzburger over Feldschlossen
San Miguel Dark over Heineken Dark
Augustiner Dark over Dinkelacker Dark
Albani Porter over Guinness
Tennent's over San Miguel
Cardinal over Kirin
Hull over Yuengling
Augsburger over Perfection
Dos Equis over Peroni
Mackeson over Tooth Sheaf
Hacker-Pschorr Oktoberfest over Dortmunder Union Special
Dierkirch Pils over Molson CDN
Hacker-Pschorr Light over Cardinal
San Miguel Dark over Augustiner Dark
Molson Export over Whitbread Pale
Hacker-Pschorr Light over Hacker-Pschorr Edelhell

MacEwan's Edinburgh over Tartan
Hansa Fjord over Diekirch Pils
Dortmunder Union Special over Hacker-Pschorr Edelhell
Albani Porter over Newcastle Brown
Black Horse over Carling Red Cap
Heineken Dark over Wurzburger Oktoberfest
Augsburger over Tuborg
Augsburger over Krueger
Michelob over Augsburger
Max Super over National Boh
Diekirch Pils over Dortmunder Siegel
Dos Equis over Hacker—Pschorr Light
Urquell over Dortmunder Siegel
Heineken Dark over Dinkelacker Dark
San Miguel Dark over Augustiner Dark
Hacker Oktoberfest over Dinkelacker Bock
Whitbread Pale over Castlemaine
Molson Export over Castlemaine
Mackeson over Imperial Stout
Dortmunder Siegel over Dinkelacker
Hacker-Pschorr Light over St. Pauli Girl
Hacker-Pschorr Oktoberfest over Pripps
Black Horse over Carling Red Cap
National Boh over Reading
Michelob over Yuengling
Hull over Coors
Tuborg over Ft. Schuyler
Kruger over Carling Black Label
Perfection over Tuborg Gold
Mickey over Mustang (to determine top U.S. malt liquor)
Prior Double Dark over Old Chicago Dark (repeat to determine top U.S. dark)
Max Super over Schmidts
Krueger Pils/Light over Wiedemann
Wurzburger Oktoberfest over San Miguel Dark
Tooth Sheaf Stout over Mackeson
Hansa Fjord over Urquell
Hacker-Pschorr Oktoberfest over Wurzburger Oktoberfest
Dortmunder Siegel over DAB
Oland's Export over Molson Export
Whitbread Pale over Bass Pale

Lowenbrau over Dortmunder Union Special
Dortmunder Union Special over Heineken
Heineken Dark over St. Pauli Girl Dark
Augustiner Dark over St. Pauli Girl Dark
Molson CDN over Tennent's
Wurzburger over Beck's
Peroni over Finlandia
Fassl Gold over Tennent's
Finlandia over Dinkelacker Bock
Dos Equis over Molson CDN
Lowenbrau over Kirin
St. Pauli Girl over Wurzburger
Max Super over Krueger Pils/Light
Hansa Fjord over Lowenbrau
Fassl Gold over Heineken
Lowenbrau (U.S.) over Tuborg
Krueger over Lowenbrau (U.S.)
Lowenbrau (U.S.) over Michelob
Hull over National Boh
San Miguel Dark over Heineken Dark
Mackeson over Tooth Sheaf
Hacker-Pschorr Oktoberfest over Dos Equis
Hacker-Pschorr Light over Diekirch Pils
Krueger over Hull
Perfection over Lowenbrau (U.S.)
Krueger Light/Pils over Krueger
Perfection over Max Super
Lowenbrau over Hacker-Pschorr Light
Perfection over Augsburger
Perfection over Black Horse
Oland's Export over Molson Export
San Miguel Dark over Dos Equis
Hacker-Pschorr Light over Dortmunder Ritter Light
Dortmunder Ritter Light over Wurzburger Light
Lowenbrau over Dortmunder Ritter Light
Augsburger over Max Super
Augsburger over Krueger Pils/Light
San Miguel Dark over Hacker-Pschorr Oktoberfest
San Miguel over Mackeson
MacEwan's Edinburgh over Albani Porter
San Miguel Dark over Albani Porter

San Miguel Dark over MacEwan's Edinburgh
San Miguel Dark over Prior Double Dark
Perfection over Hull
Black Horse over McSorley
Reading over Mickey
Tuborg Gold over Piels
Ft. Schuyler over Carling Black Label
Hull over Knickerbocker
Coors over Ft. Schuyler
Krueger Pils over Andeker
Carling Red Cap over Ballantine IPA
Perfection over Mickey
National Boh over Tuborg Gold
Krueger over Coors
Old Chicago Dark over Genesee Bock
Krueger Pils over Mustang
Schmidt's over Mustang
Diekirch Pils over DAB·
Molson CDN over Pripps
Cardinal over Dinkelacker
Peroni over Beck's
MacEwan's Tartan over Scotch
Bass Pale over Whitbread Tankard
Makeson over Cooper Stout
Albani Porter over Imperial Stout
Tooth Sheaf over Guinness
Molson Export over Whitbread Tankard
Tooth Sheaf over Cooper Stout
DAB over Urquell
Hansa Fjord over San Miguel
Hansa Fjord over Oland's Export
Black Horse over Oland's Export
(Note: Samuel Smith Brown Ale never was entered into finals competition because a second sample was never located.)

Domestic Beers Honor Roll

The following domestic brews, in alphabetical order, were determined by a taste panel to be superior in quality and were entered into a final series of comparisons to decide the best domestic beer in each category of beer type:

Andeker
Augsburger
Ballantine IPA
Black Horse Ale
Budweiser
Carling Black Label
Carling Red Cap
Coors Banquet
Ft. Schuyler
Gennesee Bock
Hull's Export
Knickerbocker
Krueger
Krueger Light/Pils
Lowenbrau Light
McSorley's Ale

Maximus Super
Michelob
Mickey ML
Mustang ML
National Bohemian
Old Chicago Dark
Perfection
Piels
Prior
Prior Double Dark
Reading
Schmidt's
Tuborg Gold
Widemann
Yuengling

Honorable Mention

The following beers (again in alphabetical order) performed well but did not compare favorably with those listed above:

Ballantine
Foxhead 400
Frankenmuth Light
Gablinger Extra Light
Genesee
Genesee Ale
Haffenreffer
Kaier's

Lowenbrau Dark
Rolling Rock
Schaefer
Schlitz ML
Schmidt's Oktoberfest
Seven Springs
Stag

Imported Beers Honor Roll

The following imported beers (in alphabetical order) were determined by the taste panel to be the best available non-U.S. malt beverages and were entered into a final series of comparisons to decide the best in each category of beer type:

Albani Porter
Augustiner Dark
Bass Pale Ale
Cardinal
Castlemaine XXXX Ale
Cooper Stout
Diekirch Pils
Dinkelacker Bock
Dinkelacker Dark
Dinkelacker Light
Dortmunder Actien (DAB)
Dortmunder Ritter Light
Dortmunder Siegel Pils
Dortmunder Union Special
Dos Equis
Feldschlossen
Finlandia Gold
Gold Fassl
Guinness
Hacker-Pschorr Edelhell
Hacker-Pschorr Light
Hacker-Pschorr Oktober
Hansa Fjord
Heineken Dark
Heineken Light

Imperial Stout
Kirin
Lowenbrau
MacEwan's Edinburgh
MacEwan's Scotch
MacEwan's Tartan
Mackeson
Molson Canadian
Molson Export
Newcastle Brown
Oland's Export
Peroni
Pripps
St. Pauli Girl
St. Pauli Girl Dark
Samuel Smith Brown Ale
San Miguel
San Miguel Dark
Tennent's Lager
Tooth Sheaf Stout
Urquell
Whitbread Pale
Whitbread Tankard
Wurzburger
Wurzburger Oktoberfest

Honorable Mention

Augustiner Light
Carlsberg
Cascade SPA
Crystall Wuhrer
Dortmunder Ritter Pils

Oland's Extra Stout
Oland's Old Scotia
Paulaner
Paulaner Salvator
Pelforth

Dreher Forte
Keith's IPA
Labatt's 50
Mann's Brown Ale
O'Keefe Old Vienna

Ringnes Bock
Swan Lager
Tecate
Wurzburger Dark

The Winners

When the dust (or suds) had settled, a winner for each meaningful category of beer type decided. The results are:

DOMESTIC
Lager—Augsburger (Jos. Huber, Monroe, Wisc.)
Dark—Prior Double Dark (Schmidt's, Philadelphia, Pa.)
Ale—Black Horse (Black Horse Brewery, Trenton, N.J.)*
Bock—Genesee (Genesee, Rochester, N.Y.)
ML—Mickey (G. Heileman, LaCrosse, Wis. et al.)
IMPORTED
Lager—Hansa Fjord (Norway)*
Dark Lager—San Miguel (Philippines)
Light Ale—Oland's Export (Canada)
Dark Ale—MacEwan's Edinburgh (Scotland)
Oktober/Bock—Hacker-Pschorr Oktoberfest (West Germany)*
Porter—Albani (Denmark
Stout—Mackeson (Scotland)
Dark (all categories)—San Miguel (Philippines)*
*Winners of domestic vs. imported in category.
The products listed below scored extremely well throughout the trials and the final comparisons. Within their type or category they are very nearly as good as the winner. With a different set of raters under different circumstances, some of them might very well be adjudged better beers.

Honorable Mentions

Gold Fassl—Austria
Augsburger—U.S.
Hull's Export—U.S.
Cardinal—Switzerland
Krueger—U.S.
Dos Equis—Mexico
Krueger Pils—U.S.
Heineken Light—Holland
Heineken Dark—Holland
Maximus Super—U.S.
Tooth Shea—Australia
Lowenbrau Light—West Germany
Hacker-Pschorr Light—West Germany
Augustiner Dark—West Germany

7. The Bottom of the Barrel

After all the suds had blown away, all the data gathered and analyzed, all the glasses washed, and all the cans handed over to grateful collectors, it was time to review what had been learned (besides finding out what were the best beers). Some of the information that follows was learned directly by intentional investigation and experimentation. Some of it was discovered by accident, in passing, or by examining the results.

Labels

Beer labels the world over have one feature in common. With few exceptions they guarantee nothing more than that there is some form of alcoholic malt beverage within. About the only label information required for beer in any country is alcohol percentage—and the U.S. is not one of those requiring such data. Nowhere do the legal requirements for labeling beer measure those regulating the identification of wine.

351

In the United States labeling practices are particularly atrocious. Terms like *ale* and *premium* are regularly misused. That a label identifies its product as an ale is no guarantee that it is a bottom-fermented brew; just about everything is called premium, export quality, or special. In most cases these are just buzz words. Even import labels are deficient in usable information.

One of the few times the U.S. government got involved in beer labeling was in the case of Gablinger (see Rheingold), in which the brewer was actually prohibited from including consumer information on the label. There is now a growing practice of including nutritional data on beer packages, especially when the product is aimed at the calorie-conscious market. Since all do not do it, the practice is assumed not to be obligatory.

Age

Wine has often been described as a "living thing." In its youth, it is sharp and vigorous. With time, it matures and becomes mellow and rich. With more time, age takes its toll and the features fade; the wine becomes more fragile and eventually passes into the past tense.

Without the poetry, beer too is a living thing. It is rough and unbalanced in its brief "green" stage, at its best when matured, takes on some unpleasant characteristics with advanced age, and eventually will become too old and will die. Age and handling (as a function of style) are perhaps the two greatest factors bearing on the pleasure that can be derived from a beer.

The important question concerns the beer's being too old for its style. Can you judge if a beer is likely to be stale with age without actually having to buy and try it to find out if it is? A number of experiments were conducted to determine how old a beer can grow before losing quality. Beers were held for varying amounts of time at a cool constant temperature (to minimize any handling damage) and in refrigeration. These were injected into the taste trials at random intervals and subjected to the criticism of the taster panel. The following results indicated no simple or single answer (just as with so many other facets of life);

a. Pasteurized beer has a greater life expectancy than unpasteurized beer.
b. Dark beer has a greater life expectancy than light beer.
c. Among light beers, life expectancy decreases with lightness. The paler the beer, the more fragile the constitution.
d. Beers with a high alcoholic content live longer than low alcohol beer. Low-calorie beers are at their best for a very short time.
e. Heavily hopped beers are longer-lived than lightly hopped beers. They are, however, subject to a flaw that results in skunkiness.
f. Beers with a high percentage of barley malt live longer than beers with a lesser amount. In its simplest form, that could be construed as a restatement of "c" above, but here I intend it to refer to heavier light beers and to dark beers. Some very dark, 100 percent roasted-barley malt ales have an extremely long life expectancy, like a wine.
g. A beer constantly (and consistently) refrigerated is more likely to survive a given time period than one kept at room temperature.

Note: The rules that apply to life expectancy directly apply to the fragility of a malt beverage, its susceptibility to harm from mishandling.

Some examples of these rules: Perfection, the highly hopped richly malted beer from Horlacher, known to have been produced before Christmas 1976, is showing no signs of wear in mid-1978. However, a sample of Coors about five months old showed considerable loss of character. India Pale Ale, highly hopped and with a relatively high level of malt and alcohol, was devised to be a viable beverage after months of ocean transport in conditions that would severely test any beer.

Translating the findings into practice yields the following guidelines:

a. Before purchasing an unpasteurized beer (and the only one I know for certain to be unpasteurized is Coors), check the date (Mr. Coors thoughtfully dates his cartons). If it is more than three months old, you run the risk of getting something less than what you paid for. Since there is no real reason to fear getting a beer that is too young, where there is a choice, get the youngest available. If unpasteurized beer is stored in a refrigerated facility (as it should be), you have only the concern that it is too old or that it might have spent some time out of refrigeration when you weren't looking. If unpasteurized beer is stored in an unrefrigerated area, even for a matter of hours, buy it elsewhere. I have heard that the Augustiner beers from Munich are not pasteurized (though I doubt it), some care should be exercised in buying those products. So-called canned or bottled draft beer is pasteurized, to my knowledge. Supposedly it is "draft" style, but that may mean little more than that it is highly carbonated.

b. In dealing with pasteurized beer, you usually have nothing to go on beyond observable conditions at the retail outlet. Some have massive walk-in refrigerators and all beer is stored in and sold from that facility. This affords you the best chance of purchasing fresh beer. Most have some form of refrigeration, but unless turnover is high, the back stock is subject to the effects of aging from exposure to temperature extremes. This could be called premature aging. With separate facilities for beer "up front" and "in back," there is always the risk of improper stock rotation. Where there is no refrigeration, you are advised to buy only popular items. In these last two cases the object is simply to try to get the youngest, freshest package possible. Unless there is personal knowledge of a new supply, trust in the retailer, or other clues (like a change in package design), choice is by guess and by golly. If your store seems frequently to have stale beer in stock, buy it elsewhere.

Foreign vs. Domestic

Most beer drinkers will freely admit that (in general) foreign beers are better than domestic beers. It is true of many commodities that the imports are equal to or better than the best comparable domestic product. Mostly this is because a country normally exports only its best efforts. Foreign beers may be better for the additional reason that their manufacture is strictly regulated by law as to ingredients and purity of process. There is no comparable domestic regulation.

The scores resulting from the tastings indicate that the best imports are better than the best domestic brews. The best domestic brews, however, fared much better than the average import. This is mostly because there was a large percentage of imported beers that ranked very low.

The distribution of scores for domestic beers was much as would be expected for the quality of any commercially produced item. Most beers scored in a cluster near to the center of the possible scoring range, with a scattering of values at the high and low ends. The distribution of scores for the imported beers differed. The distribution lacked the clustering effect expected for the center of the distribution. No area of the distribution resembled the expected bell shape. Most natural distributions follow some predictable shape that is or can be associated with "normal" or classical mathematical distributions. In general, the shape of the curve of distribution of values resembles a bell, with a great many values lumped somewhere on the curve (usually somewhere near the midrange point) and the rest scattered throughout the range decreasing in quantity toward the extremes. The curve may be skewed toward one end or the other, but the bell shape generally obtains. When it does not, there usually is the effect of some outside "agent".

There is no certain way to explain the departure of the import distribution curve from that expected, but it may be the result of getting a relatively large number of samples from abroad that were in an overage or mishandled condition. If it is assumed that the import beers would have had a distribution much like the domestic brews and that a significant number of samples tried had been so damaged, the distribution of scores would have turned out to be like that experienced in the tastings. The good products, with a large following and a high turnover rate, would be obtained fresh and would perform as well as they could under ideal conditions. Average, middle grade, or unfamiliar (new) imports, with little or no following, might have sat on a shelf for some time, and could have been too old to perform up to their potential.

Accepting this explanation, which appears to be reasonable, one concludes that obscure or less popular imported beers should be bought with care. Newly marketed brews may be fresh on first appearance, but if they don't sell at a high rate, it may take a long time to deplete that initial shipment, and the stock on shelves and in warehouses may become stale.

Effects of Beer on the Palate

The effects of food on palate sensitivity were discovered early in the taste trials and have been discussed at length in chapter four, "The Great Experiment" (see under "Foods at Tastings"). But what about the effect of the beer itself on the palate? Surely, the ability of a human being to make valid judgments on the characteristics and value of a given beer will be reduced with an increasing number of samples, if for no reason other than the alcohol in his bloodstream. The limitations of tasters were tested by requiring them to taste different quantities of beers at each tasting and retrying the items tasted at later times of the experiment.

It was found that people have greatly varying tolerance and palate ability with regard to beer. Some were able to judge relatively fine points of difference among brews after tasting over thirty samples. Others had judgment problems after a dozen or so. Since the portions of each sample were small and the time taken for a tasting was on the order of three hours, it is believed that innate palate sensitivity was more of a factor than the effects of the alcohol. Those oriented to tasting (anything) could discriminate between more beers in an evening than those who were not. One taster who does not normally drink beer but who is highly experienced in wine and food tasting was able to perform like the most experienced beer connoisseur on the panel, once he had been thoroughly briefed on the criteria.

Another effect noted was that the tasting ability of an individual varies. On a given night, a person's taste buds might be off right from the start or after only a few samples. At those times his reaction to a brand might be at odds with the reactions of other tasters.

Since all the beers were being tasted in pairs, there was some concern about the effects of the pairings. Would a beer be unfairly rated because it had the misfortune to be sampled along with something very good or very bad? To see if there was any cause for worry, several dozen beers that had already been sampled by the panel were included in tastings again but paired differently. The second set of scores was virtually the same, well within the variance that would be expected from a subjective examination (within ten percent).

An American Taste

Is it possible to identify and describe a typical American taste for beer? Could it be done with any other national group?

The large beer companies seem to think so. They have computer programs that have taste preference worked in as a parameter, but at the same time new beers are subjected to trial marketing—so they aren't all that certain. There is certainly such a thing in America as regional taste. But like the chicken and the egg, which came first? Did the beer satisfy the market for that regional taste or did the taste become inured to the beer available? Belgium is a classic example of regional tastes, yet sales of the Artois and Loburg beers, both very different from any of the unique regional types, indicate that they are at least candidates for a Belgian national palate preference.

In the taste trials and experiments there was no method for quantifying an American national taste preference, but there were data on the opinions of a random sampling of American beer drinkers from widely diverse backgrounds over a wide geographical area. With over three dozen tasters and over five hundred beers, some observations can be made.

Collectively they preferred beer that was zesty but not highly hopped, beer that was naturally and lightly carbonated, beer that was richly flavored with a high percentage of barley malt, and, above all, beer that was balanced. Perhaps it is more revealing to identify what they didn't favor: very pale, very light, or low-calorie beers; soda-pop, winy, and highly carbonated beer; highly hopped beer and ale like those so popular in Great Britain (Harp, Double Diamond, etc.); and so-called house flavors. Although their collective preference takes a middle-of-the-road taste, it was surprisingly cosmopolitan. They liked well-made beers from all over the world. They did not approve the vast majority of American beers that have arrived on the market in the past half decade, which may indicate a difference in opinion with the computer. Miller's domestic Lowenbrau Light is one of the few recent additions that met with the approval of the taste panel.

Individual Preference

"Before we could go out to the cabin we'd pick up a case of Genesee. It's my favorite. I can pick it out of a crowd anytime."

"Budweiser's my brew. They tested me in a bar once. Three times I picked my Bud out of a group of four beers."

"That Blatz is real horse——."

"I had my brother-in-law haul in a case of Coors from Boulder last summer. It's the one thing I really miss since I moved east."

The Genesee fan couldn't tell his beer without being shown the label in his "day in court." The Bud lover couldn't successfully pick his beer out of a pair. The Blatz hater gave it the highest score of the evening. The Coors "importer" picked Schmidt's when he didn't know which was which, and in a second try, selected Old Frothingslosh.

In dozens of tests, long-time beer drinkers failed to recognize their beer in blind trials. Not only could they not pick their long-time preference from a group of two, *most of* the time they failed to select their avowed favorite as their choice. Only once did a taster recognize his favorite, the distinctive Maximus Super. Another time he failed to recognize it, but did give it the higher score.

In short, beer drinkers are hard pressed to identify their favorite brew unless they know it is being served to them. Random guessing would have produced better results for picking out a favorite than the results obtained in the tastings.

On the other hand, tasters could reliably predict their preference as to style or type of beer. If a taster stated that he preferred German beer, he invariably scored German or German-type beer higher. If ales were the avowed preference, the taster could be depended upon to score ales higher than lagers.

The effect of advertising on preference should not be underestimated. Tasters' descriptions of beers served "open" closely matched the qualities promised by advertisements. This effect has long been noted in the wine trade, where the reputed qualities of a famous wine are likely to be observed by tasters more when they can see the label than when they cannot. Descriptions from "blind" trials are usually different and much more critical of the product.

No wonder that many of the top brewers in the country spend more money on advertising than on the product.

Beers of Mystique

When I was twenty-five years younger, the mystique belonged to Michelob. "Everybody" knew it was the best beer you could get. It was rarely found in those days in the East, and was available only in draft. That last part guaranteed that it was great stuff. We would thumb down to Framingham, to the only place for miles that had it, and sip the nectar in a dingy smelly bar. When Michelob was packaged and readily available, the mystique left, and we drank it less than when it was hard to get.

At another time, cases of San Miguel made their way all over the Pacific in U.S. Navy ships to ensure that the best was available to swabbies wherever they served. Knowing the premium at which space on board ship is regarded, you can well imagine how esteemed those goods were. During World War II bomber pilots striking at Manila had strict orders not to damage the holy of holies, the San Miguel brewery. Of course, Douglas MacArthur's supposed financial interest in the brewery had little to do with it.

In our time, the Coors mystique is the big item in beer. Long before I arrived in Colorado, I had been told what I had best drink while there. Dutifully, on arrival, I hied over to the Antlers (Colorado Springs great and, alas, late hot spot) and took a long draft of Coors. It was heavenly, like everything else about Colorado. Thereafter I joined the long list of those who smuggled Coors east. The bloom began to fade from the rose one evening in Cody, Wyoming, when my wife, in her ignorance of the subject, noted that the Olympia she was drinking tasted better than my Coors. To prove her wrong, we did a miniblind tasting of the two. Coors lost. I passed it off as a bad sample and nothing more was thought of it until Schmidt's ran its Coors-Schmidt's test and ad campaign. Much to my surprise, we preferred the Schmidt's. But a mystique dies hard and there had to be an acid test. I rounded up a dozen Coors lovers and had them compare the two. Schmidt's trounced Coors eleven to one, to the amazement of the twelve confirmed believers. A little later in the evening, I suggested we repeat the experiment. This time nine tasters voted 7-2 against Coors, only the opponent was Old Frothingslosh, a frequently derided beer from Pittsburgh which is actually the Christmas package of Iron City Beer.

In all fairness to Coors, the supplies of the beer that are available on the East Coast are usually too old and the beer is particularly sensitive to the effects of age. Also, since Coors is not pasteurized, there is a good chance that supplies on the East Coast have been mishandled. Coors should be regarded for what it is, a very good, well-made, lightly flavored beer that can be enjoyed with food or with friends and that is at its best only when young and properly treated. It can be an extraordinary experience when fresh, and especially so when you are very thirsty. But it doesn't measure up to the demands of "mystique."

I suppose everyone should have his collection of mystique items, including a beer that he knows is better than any other. Our testing indicates that the need could be served equally well by a beer that is inexpensive and readily available, if you wish to go by taste alone. If your beer must be hard to come by and expensive as well, you will find brews costlier and rarer than Coors.

Cans vs. Bottles

It is commonly believed that beer tastes better in bottles than in cans. This belief was common long before the glass industry began promoting the thought on TV. Cans are lighter to carry around, have a reputation for being faster to chill, and don't present the hazard of broken glass. Bottles are usually a few cents cheaper and are easier to drink from. Those features can be traded off easily enough, if only one knows what truth there is in the taste belief.

After 379 beers had been sampled, the record for bottled products was compared with canned beers. An arbitrary score of sixty (two-thirds of the maximum possible points) was selected for imported beers and an arbitrary cutoff value of fifty was selected for domestic beers. These values coincided with the qualifying scores for the final double-elimination competition in the taste trials. The number of canned and bottled beers that equaled or bettered the arbitrary values would be compared to see if there was a difference in quality between bottled and canned beer.

Of the 379 beers involved, 229 were bottles and 150 in cans. The results were:

Total Cans—150   Canned beer scoring above cutoff—
                  18 (12%)
Total bottles—229   Bottled beer scoring above cutoff—
                  58 (25%)

CAN BREAKDOWN:
Foreign—26   Foreign cans above cutoff score—
             5 (19%)
Domestic—124   Domestic cans above cutoff score—
             13 (10%)

BOTTLE BREAKDOWN
Foreign—167   Foreign bottled above cutoff score—
*   42 (25%)*
Domestic—62   Domestic bottled above cutoff score—
*   16 (25%)*

These results show a clear advantage for bottled over canned beer, by a two to one margin. Bottled beer products showed equally well for foreign and domestic brands. Foreign cans also appear to have shown well, but the sample size is too small for a conclusion.

The explanation may be related to environment. Aluminum conducts heat much better than glass. According to the *Handbook of Chemistry and Physics*, the conductivity* of aluminum is 0.504, whereas glass is 0.002.

This means that a canned beer is able to receive heat from the environment at a rate over 250 times greater than would bottled beer in the same circumstances. Actually, since the conductivity is specified for a given thickness of the material, the conductivity of a can would be 250 times greater than that of a bottle having the same thickness as the can. Since bottles are much thicker than cans, the actual difference in conductivity rate is probably more on the order of 1,000 than 250. You can test this for yourself by placing a chilled bottle and can in a room, pouring them into glasses after fifteen to thirty minutes, and measuring their temperature with a thermometer. The fluid from the can will have risen closer to room temperature than the fluid from the bottle.

It would seem that beer packaged in cans face a higher possibility of damage from exposure to extremes of temperature simply because damaging exposure can occur in a shorter period of time. Of course, mistreatment over a long period of time will be equal in cans and bottles. After several hours, the heat transfer will be complete and the contents of can or bottle will rest at the ambient temperature. It is only in short-term exposure that the difference in conductivity between glass and aluminum is notable. A sixpack of bottles left on the hood of a car on a hot day may not be significantly affected in a half-hour, but the same treatment could materially affect a sixpack of cans.

A number of additional experiments were conducted with tastings of pairs of the same beer, tried in can and bottle together. The sample was a bit too small for profound conclusions but the results indicated a slight edge for the product in the bottles. The taste of fresh samples was so close as to indicate no advantage for can or bottle. In thirty-nine comparisons of fresh samples, the taste panels preferred the bottled version twenty times and the canned version nineteen times. With more aged samples, a three to two preference for bottled beer over canned resulted, supporting the thesis offered above.

From all the data, analysis, and experiments, one can conclude that with fresh stock it makes little difference whether you buy your beer in cans or bottles. If, however, there has been exposure to potentially harmful conditions or if you intend to keep the beer a long time before using it, bottled beer is the sounder choice.

*Number of calories per second transmitted through a plate 1 cm. thick across an area of 1 sq. cm. when the temperature difference is 1°C.

Summary

The most important fact learned about beer in this entire exercise is that it is a fragile commodity, just like wine. Handled with care and thought, beer drinking can be a rewarding experience.

The consumer of beer has little protection from mishandled or overage beer beyond his personal limited knowledge and experience. Labels tell almost nothing. With the popularity of "natural" products, and the current policy of major brewers to comply with that trend, the number of brews on the market today containing additives represents a small percentage of the total, and those additives must be approved by the U.S. Food & Drug Administration.

Foreign beers are better from the standpoint of ingredients, since they are strictly regulated in that regard. But there is a greater likelihood that imported beer has been mishandled or is overage.

Taste sensitivity is affected by foods, the number of

beers consumed, and the conditioning effects of advertising. Beer tastes as well from cans as from bottles, when both are fresh. But with age or exposure to extremes of temperature, the bottle is more reliable.

Beer should be enjoyed without stigma. In most of the world it is regarded as a food. It certainly has a long record of success as a means of promoting temperance. In short, make an effort to learn which beers you find most enjoyable and then enjoy them with food and friends. Thereby you will add a measure of satisfaction to your life. Here's looking at you, friend!

Sign Called The (Ale-Stake)

Appendix I

Alphabetical Listing of Beers Tasted

This alphabetical list gives the common form of the brand name, the type of beverage according to label (B—beer, A—ale, P—porter, S—stout, IPA—India pale ale, ML—malt liquor, W—Weiss, ST—steam, BK—bock, LO—low calorie, NB—near-beer), country of origin or company for domestic brews, and panel rating (on a scale of 0–90; see chapter four, "The Great Experiment," under "Rating the Beers").

Domestic

BRAND	TYPE	COMPANY	RATING	PAGE
ABC	B	Eastern	41	94
ABC	A	Eastern	32	95
ALPS BRAU	B	Peter Hand	21	117
ALT DEUTSCH DARK	B	Pittsburgh	37	173
ALTES	B	Carling National	30	82

AMERICAN	B	Pittsburgh	28	170
ANCHOR STEAM	ST	Anchor	45	70
ANCHOR PORTER	P	Anchor	21	70
ANDEKER	B	Pabst	55	159
ANHEUSER LIGHT	LO	Anheuser-Busch	24	76
A-1	B	Carling National	36	81
ARROWHEAD	B	Cold Spring	36	88
AUGSBURGER	B	Huber	55	134
AUGUSTINER	B	Pittsburgh	36	171
BALLANTINE	B	Falstaff	48	106
BALLANTINE ALE	A	Falstaff	23	106
BALLANTINE BOCK	BK	Falstaff	25	106
BALLANTINE DRAFT	B	Falstaff	34	106
BALLANTINE IPA	IPA	Falstaff	70	106
BARTELS	B	Lion	34	144
BAVARIAN CLUB	B	Huber	37	133
BAVARIAN DUQUESNE	B	C. Schmidt	44	195
BAVARIAN'S SELECT	B	Koch	24	138
BAVARIAN TYPE	B	Yuengling	25	
BERGHEIM	B	C. Schmidt	33	195
BIG CAT	ML	Pabst	34	160
BILLY	B	Cold Spring	28	87
BILLY	B	Falls City	26	102
BILLY	B	West End	24	208
BLACK HORSE	A	Champale	65	84
BLANCHARDS	B	Eastern	39	95
BLATZ	B	Heileman	43	119
BLATZ ALE	A	Heileman	26	119
BLITZ-WEINHARD	B	Blitz-Weinhard	36	77
BOH	B	Falstaff	24	108
BOHEMIAN CLUB	B	Huber	29	134
BOSCH	B	Leinenkugel	24	141
BRAUMEISTER	B	Peter Hand	17	115
BREUNIGS	B	Walter	36	204
BREWER'S LAGER	B	Erie	30	100
BREWER'S LAGER	B	Ortlieb	37	156
BREWER'S LAGER	B	Rheingold	35	180
BREW 96	LO	C. Schmidt	9	193
BREW II	B	Horlacher	24	129
BRICKSKELLER	B	Pittsburgh	20	173
BROWN DERBY	B	Pittsburgh	24	171
BUBS	B	Walter	31	204
BUCKHORN	B	Olympia	38	152

BUDWEISER	B	Anheuser-Busch	51	75
BUFFALO	B	Blitz-Weinhard	14	78
BURGEMEISTER	B	Peter Hand	31	116
BURGIE!	B	Pabst	18	161
BURGIE GOLDEN LIGHT	LO	Pabst	20	161
BURGUNDY BRAU	B	Pittsburgh	26	172
BUSCH BAVARIAN	B	Anheuser-Busch	34	76
CANADIAN ACE	B	Eastern	40	95
CANADIAN ACE DRAFT	B	Eastern	31	96
CARLING BLACK LABEL	B	Carling National	59	80
CARLING RED CAP	A	Carling National	53	80
CARLING'S 71	LO	Carling National	20	80
CHAMPAGNE VELVET	B	Pickett	12	166
CHAMPALE	ML	Champale	13	84
CHERRY HILL	B	Champale	28	84
CHESTERFIELD	A	Yuengling	20	209
CHIPPEWA FALLS	B	Leinenkugel	38	139
CHIPPEWA PRIDE	B	Leinenkugel	29	139
CHAULTHEISS	W	Berliner WEiss	00	000
COLD BRAU	B	Cold Spring	40	87
COLD SPRING	B	Cold Spring	31	86
COLT .45	ML	Carling National	28	82
COLUMBIA	B	Carling	33	81
COOKS GOLDBLUME	B	Heileman	33	120
COORS	B	Coors	59	90
COUNTRY CLUB	ML	Pearl	20	163
CROFT	A	Falstaff	33	108
DAITSCH SHOPWELL	B	Eastern	17	97
DAWSON	B	Eastern	35	96
DELIGHT BREW	NB	General	9	111
DREWRY	B	Heileman	30	120
DREWRY DRAFT	B	Heileman	33	120
DRUMMOND BROS.	B	Falls City	39	101
DUBOIS BOCK	BK	Pittsburgh	46	173
DUKE	B	C. Schmidt	41	191
DUNKS	B	Duncan	38	94
EASTSIDE	B	Pabst	35	161
EDELWEISS	B	Pickett	29	166
ENGLISH 800	ML	Blitz-Weinhard	12	77,156
ERIE LIGHT	LO	Erie	23	100

ESQUIRE	B	Jones	30	135
ESSLINGER	B	Rheingold/Lion	41	143,181
FALLS CITY	B	Falls City	38	101
FALSTAFF	B	Falstaff	45	104
FALSTAFF LIGHT	B	Falstaff	27	104
FALSTAFF 96	LO	Falstaff	35	104
FISCHER ALE	A	Duncan	34	94
FISCHER BEER	B	Duncan	39	94
FORT SCHUYLER	B	West End	52	208
FOX DE LUXE	B	Cold Spring	26	86
FOXHEAD 400	B	Eastern	47	96
FOXHEAD 400 DRAFT	B	Eastern	22	96
FRANKENMUTH DARK	B	Geyer	30	113
FRANKENMUTH LIGHT	B	Geyer	48	113
FYFE & DRUM	LO	Genesee	40	112
GABLINGER	LO	Rheingold/C. Schmidt	41	179
GABLINGER EXTRA LIGHT	LO	Rheingold/C. Schmidt	49	179
GAMBRINUS GOLD	B	Pittsburgh	10	170
GAMBRINUS GOLD LABEL	B	Pittsburgh	28	170
GARDEN STATE	B	Eastern	22	95
GEMEINDE BRAU	B	Cold Spring	29	87
GENESEE	B	Genesee	47	112
GENESEE ALE	A	Genesee	49	112
GENESEE BOCK	BK	Genesee	49	112
GENESEE LIGHT	LO	Genesee	26	112
GIANT FOOD	B	Lion	34	143
GIBBON'S	B	Lion	34	141
GIBBON'S ALE	A	Lion	26	142
GIBBON'S PORTER	P	Lion	18	142
GLUEK	B	Cold Spring	26	87
GOEBEL	B	Stroh	44	203
GOLD ANNIVERSARY	B	Fred Koch	20	137
GRAIN BELT	B	Heileman	34	121
GRAIN BELT PREMIUM	B	Heileman	26	121
GUNTHER	B	Schaefer	39	184
HAFFENREFFER	B	Falstaff	47	109
HAFFENREFFER MALT LIQUOR	ML	Falstaff	35	109
HAMM'S	B	Olympia	45	151
HAMM'S DRAFT	B	Olympia	29	151

HAUENSTEIN	B	Heileman	45	120
HEIDELBERG	B	Carling	35	81
HEIDELBRAU	B	Heileman	20	127
HEILEMAN	B	Heileman	38	118
HEILEMAN LIGHT	LO	Heileman	38	118
HEILEMAN OLD STYLE	B	Heileman	18	118
HENRY WEINHARD PRIV. RES.	B	Blitz-Weinhard	25	78
HERITAGE HOUSE	B	Pittsburgh	39	170
HI-BRAU	B	Huber	24	133
HOME PILS	B	Lion	20	143
HORLACHER	B	Horlacher	31	129
HORLACHER DRAFT	B	Horlacher	26	129
HUBER	B	Huber	35	134
HUBER BOCK	BK	Huber	42	134
HUDEPOHL	B	Hudepohl	18	132
HULL'S EXPORT	B	Hull	55	135
IMPERIAL PILS	B	Horlacher	39	129
IRON CITY	B	Pittsburgh	41	169
IRON CITY DRAFT	B	Pittsburgh	41	169
IROQUOIS	B	Koch	33	137
IVY LEAGUE	B	Ortlieb	16	155
JAX	B	Pearl	42	163
KAIERS	B	Ortlieb	49	154
KAPPY'S	B	Easter	39	95
KARLSBRAU	B	Cold Spring	20	87
KEG	B	General	25	110
KEGLE BRAU	B	Cold Spring	28	86
KINGSBURY	B	Heileman	17	122
KINGSBURY BREW	NB	Heileman	15	122
KNICKERBOCKER	B	Rheingold/C. Schmidt	58	182
KOCH'S LIGHT	LO	Koch	26	137
KOEHLER	B	Erie	39	99
KOEHLER LAGER	B	Erie	36	100
KOEHLER PILS	B	Erie	32	100
KRUEGER	B	Falstaff	52	107
KRUEGER ALE	A	Falstaff	27	107
KRUEGER PILS/ LIGHT	B	Falstaff	59	107
LEINENKUGEL'S	B	Leinenkugel	41	139
LIEBOTSCHANER ALE	A	Lion	37	142
LIEBOTSCHANER BOCK	BK	Lion	20	142

LITE	LO	Miller	43	147
LONE STAR	B	Olympia	35	152
LOWENBRAU	B	Miller	54	147
LOWENBRAU DARK	B	Miller	48	147
LUCKY BOCK	BK	Falstaff	40	104
LUCKY BOCK	BK	General	20	110
LUCKY DRAFT	B	General	42	110
LUCKY LAGER	B	Falstaff	44	104
LUCKY 96	LO	General	18	110
McSORLEY	A	Rheingold/Ortlieb	63	180
MAGNA CHARTA	A	Pittsburgh	18	173
MARK V	LO	Pittsburgh	34	171
MASTER BREW	B	Walter	14	204
MASTER'S CHOICE	B	Duncan	35	94
MATT'S PREMIUM	B	West End	10	208
MAXIMUS SUPER	B	West End	57	207
MEISTERBRAU	B	Miller	35	147
MICHELOB	B	Anheuser-Busch	57	76
MICHELOB LIGHT	LO	Anheuser-Busch	47	76
MICKEY	ML	Heileman	61	124
MILLER	B	Miller	45	146
MILWAUKEE	B	Eastern	22	96
MILWAUKEE BOCK	BK	Eastern	18	97
MUNICH	B	Falstaff	45	105
MUSTANG	ML	Pittsburgh	51	171
NARRAGANSETT	B	Falstaff	45	108
NARRAGANSETT 96	LO	Falstaff	40	108
NARRAGANSETT PORTER	P	Falstaff	32	108
NATIONAL BOHEMIAN	B	Carling National	57	82
NATIONAL PREMIUM	B	Carling National	45	82
NEUWEILER	A	Ortlieb	14	156
NORTHERN	B	Cold Spring	31	87
NORTH STAR	B	Cold Spring	29	87
OERTELS 92	B	Peter Hand	36	116
OLD BOHEMIAN	B	Eastern	26	97
OLD BOHEMIAN ALE	A	Eastern	17	97
OLD BOHEMIAN BOCK	BK	Eastern	18	97
OLD BOHEMIAN LIGHT	B	Eastern	39	97

370

OLD CHICAGO	B	Peter Hand	12	115
OLD CHICAGO DARK	B	Peter Hand	60	115
OLD CROWN	B	Peter Hand	26	115
OLD CROWN ALE	A	Peter Hand	32	115
OLD DUTCH	B	Pittsburgh	21	172
OLD EXPORT	B	Pittsburgh	6	171
OLD FROTHING-SLOSH	B	Pittsburgh	42	169
OLD GERMAN	B	Eastern	22	97
OLD GERMAN	B	Peter Hand	21	117
OLD GERMAN	B	Pittsburgh	20	172
OLD GERMAN	B	Yuengling	42	209
OLD HEIDELBRAU	B	Falstaff	26	104
OLD MILWAUKEE	B	Schlitz	25	188
OLD TIMERS	B	Walter	31	205
OLDE PUB	B	Erie	19	100
OLYMPIA	B	Olympia	38	150
OLYMPIA GOLD	LO	Olympia	15	150
102	B	Falstaff	41	104
102	B	General	38	111
ORTLIEB	B	Ortlieb	22	156
ORTLIEB BOCK	BK	Ortlieb	23	156
OYSTER HOUSE	B	Pittsburgh	34	171
PABST BLUE RIB-BON	B	Pabst	45	159
PABST BOCK	BK	Pabst	37	159
PABST EXTRA LIGHT	LO	Pabst	20	160
PADRE	B	General	29	110
PEARL	B	Pearl	41	163
PEARL LIGHT	BO	Pearl	24	163
PEARL LIGHT	LO	Pearl	27	163
PERFECTION	B	Horlacher	50	129
PETER HAND	B	Peter Hand	35	114
PETER HAND EX-TRA LIGHT	LO	Peter Hand	42	115
PFEIFFER	B	Heileman	26	123
PICKWICK	A	Falstaff	35	109
PIELS	B	Schaefer	55	185
PIELS REAL DRAFT	B	Schaefer	29	185
PINK CHAMPALE	ML	Champale	8	84
POC	B	C. Schmidt	36	193
POINT VIEW HOTEL	B	Pittsburgh	28	172
POLAR	B	Eastern	30	97

PRIMO	B	Schlitz	24	188
PRINZ BRAU	B	Prinz	20	174
PRINZ EXTRA	B	Prinz	23	174
PRIOR	B	C. Schmidt	58	194
PRIOR DOUBLE DARK	B	C. Schmidt	87	194
RAINER	B	Heileman/Rainier	27	126
RAINIER ALE	A	Heileman/Rainier	39	126
RAM'S HEAD	A	C. Schmidt	37	194
READING	B	C. Schmidt	50	195
RED, WHITE & BLUE	B	Pabst	42	159
REGAL BRAU	B	Huber	36	133
REIDENBACH	B	General	27	110
RHEINGOLD	B	C. Schmidt/Rhein-gold	37	179
RHEINGOLD EXTRA LIGHT	LO	C. Schmidt/ Rhein-gold	29	179
RHINELANDER	B	Huber	28	134
RHINELANDER BOCK	BK	Huber	68	134
ROBIN HOOD ALE	A	Pittsburgh	40	170
ROLLING ROCK	B	Latrobe	49	138
RUPPERT	B	C. Schmidt/Rhein-gold	32	182
SCHAEFER	B B	Schaefer	48	184
SCHAEFER BOCK	BK	Schaefer	20	184
SCHELL EXPORT II	B	Schell	10	187
SCHELL'S	B	Schell	38	187
SCHLITZ	B	Schlitz	39	188
SCHLITZ LIGHT	LO	Schlitz	25	188
SCHLITZ MALT LI-QUOR	ML	Schlitz	49	188
SCHMIDT	B	Heileman	31	122
SCHMIDT BOCK	BK	C. Schmidt	40	192
SCHMIDT EXTRA	B	Heileman	31	122
SCHMIDT SELECT	NB	Heileman	17	122
SCHMIDT TIGER ALE	A	C. Schmidt	44	191
SCHMIDTS	B	C. Schmidt	66	191
SCHMIDTS BAVAR-IAN	B	C. Schmidt	30	192
SCHMIDTS OKTO-BERFEST	B	C. Schmidt	46	192
SCHOENLING	A	Schoenling	33	197
SEVEN SPRINGS	B	Pittsburgh	48	170

SGA	B	Heileman	42	127
SHOP RITE	B	Horlacher	23	129
SIERRA	B	Pittsburgh	26	173
SIR EDWARD				
STOUT	B	Schoenling	29	197
STAG	B	Carling National	47	80
STEEL VALLEY	B	Pittsburgh	25	172
STEIGMAIER	B	Lion	27	143
STEIGMAIER PORTER	B	Lion	14	144
STEINBRAU	NB	Eastern	4	98
STERLING	B	Heileman	45	123
STITE	ML	Heileman	31	123
STONEY'S	B	Jones	15	135
STRAUB	B	Straub	63	200
STROH	B	Stroh	43	203
STROH BOCK	BK	Stroh	32	203
TECH	B	Pittsburgh	30	171
TEXAS PRIDE	B	Pearl	40	163
TIVOLI	B	Blitz-Weinhard	23	78
TOPPER	B	Eastern	21	98
TUBORG	B	Carling National	53	83
TUBORG GOLD	B	Carling National	56	83
TUDOR	B	C. Schmidt	31	194
TUDOR ALE	A	C. Schmidt	25	195
UTICA CLUB	B	West End	17	207
UTICA CLUB ALE	A	West End	30	207
VALLEY FORGE	B	C. Schmidt	43	193
VAN LAUTER BA-VARIAN	B	Carling National	40	82
VAN MERRITT	B	Peter Hand	15	116
WALTER'S	B	Walter	29	204
WALTER'S	B	Walter (Colo.)	36	204
WEIR RADIO	B	Pittsburgh	35	172
WFBG RADIO	B	Pittsburgh	27	173
WHITE LABEL	B	Cold Spring	23	86
WIEDEMANN'S	B	Heileman	57	119
WISCONSIN CLUB	B	Huber	14	133
WISCONSIN GOLD LABEL	B	Huber	35	134
WISCONSIN HOLIDAY	B	Huber	38	134
WISCONSIN OLD TIMERS	B	Walter	28	205
YUENGLING	B	Yuengling	61	209
YUENGLING POR-TER	P	Yuengling	32	211
ZODIAC	ML	Peter Hand	15	117

Imported

BRAND	TYPE	COUNTRY/COMPANY	RATING	Page
ABBAYE de LEFFE	B	Belgium	29	226
ALBANI	B	Denmark/Albani	41	266
ALBANI PILS	B	Denmark/Albani	41	266
ALBANI PORTER	P	Denmark/Albani	75	266
ALPINE	B	Canada/Moosehead	36	260
ALPINE AYERIN-GERBRAU	B	England	22	271
ALT SEIDEL	B	Germany*/Dort Hansa	13	290
ASAHI	B	Japan	48	314
ATHENIAN	B	Greece	45	305
AUGUSTINER	B	Germany	50	287
AUGUSTINER DARK	B	Germany	72	287
AUSTRIAN GOLD	B	Austria	33	222
BASS PALE	A	England	78	273
BAVARIA	B	Holland	28	308
BECK'S	B	Germany	62	288
BECK'S DARK	B	Germany	28	288
BEERSHEBA	B	Israel	14	311
BENNETT	A	Canada/Carling O'Keefe	47	236
BIECKERT	B	Argentina	12	330
BIERE des TRAPPISTS	B	Belgium	23	224
BIRELL	NB	Switzerland/Hurlimann	42	337
BLACK HORSE	B	Canada/Carling O'Keefe	22	236
BLUE STAR	B	Canada/Labatt's	10	246
BOHEMIA	A	Mexico	45	318
BRAHMA CHOPP	B	Brazil	27	330
BREDA	B	Holland	9	308
BUSH	A	Belgium	0	225
CALGARY EXPORT	B	Canada/Carling O'Keefe	32	237
CARDINAL	B	Switzerland	75	336
CARLSBERG	B	Denmark/Carlsberg	54	268
CARLSBERG DARK	B	Denmark/Carlsberg	12	268
CARLSBERG ELEPHANT	ML	Denmark/Carlsberg	21	268
CARTA BLANCA	B	Mexico	34	318
CASCADE DRAUGHT	B	Australia	5	219

CASCADE SPARKLING PALE ALE	A	Australia	50	219
CASTLE	B	South Africa	30	327
CASTLEMAINE'S BITTER ALE	A	Australia	63	214
CERES	B	Denmark	24	268
CINCI	B	Canada/Carling O'Keefe	47	236
CLUB COLOMBIA	B	Colombia	31	331
COOPER EXTRA STOUT	S	Australia	60	215
COOPER GOLD CROWN	B	Australia	28	215
COOPER SPARKLING ALE	A	Australia	18	215
CORONA	B	Puerto Rico	33	332
COURAGE DRAUGHT	B	Australia	42	216
COURAGE LAGER	B	England	24	274
CREST	B	Australia/Courage	22	216
CRISTAL	B	Peru	14	332
CRYSTALL WUHRER	B	Italy	50	313
CUVEE deL'HERMITAGE	B	Belgium	51	225
DIEKIRCH PILS	B	Luxembourg	61	317
DIEKIRCH MALT LIQUOR	ML	Luxembourg	48	317
DIEKIRCH MALT LIQUOR EX	ML	Luxembourg	26	317
DINKELACKER LIGHT CD	B	Germany	61	288
DINKELACKER DARK CD	B	Germany	61	289
DINKELACKER BOCK CD	BK	Germany	80	289
DINKELACKER BLACK FOREST	B	Germany	45	288
DINKELACKER DARK PRIVAT	B	Germany	31	289
DORTMUNDER ACTIEN (DAB)	B	Germany	76	290
DORTMUNDER HANSA	B	Germany	20	289
DORTMUNDER RITTERSBRAU DARK	B	Germany	45	292

DORTMUNDER RITTERSBRAU LIGHT	B	Germany	64	291
DORTMUNDER RITTERSBRAU PILS	B	Germany	54	291
DORTMUNDER UNION SIEGEL PILS	B	Germany	68	291
DORTMUNDER UNION SPECIAL	B	Germany	72	291
DORTMUNDER WESTFALIA	B	Germany	29	292
EXPORT	B	Germany	26	292
DOS EQUIS	B	Mexico	72	319
DOUBLE DIAMOND	A	England	48	271
DOW BLACK HORSE	A	Canada/Carling O'Keefe	22	237
DREHER FORTE	B	Italy	59	311
DRESSLER	B	Germany	10	292
ESTRELLA DOR-ADA	B	Spain	15	333
EXTRACTO de MALTA	B	Germany	40	292
FALCON EXPORT	B	Sweden	24	334
FASSL GOLD	B	Austria/Harmer	61	221
FELDSCHLOSSEN	B	Switzerland	68	336
FINLANDIA GOLD	B	Finland	74	282
FISCHER BELLE STRASBOUR-GEOISE	B	France	42	284
FISCHER GOLD	B	France	48	284
FISCHER PILS	B	France	4	284
FIX	B	Greece	45	305
FOSTER'S	B	Australia	21	213
FRYDENLUNDS	B	Norway	30	321
FURSTENBERG	B	Germany	44	292
GILDA RATS-KELLER	B	Germany	20	297
GOLDEN EAGLE	B	India	45	310
GOLD LABEL BAR-LEY WINE	A	England/Watney-Mann	18	282
GOSSER	B	Austria	24	221
GOSSER GOLDEN ROCK	B	Austria	20	221

GROLSCH	B	Holland	37	308
GUINNESS	S	Ireland	60	276
HACKER EDEL-HELL	B	Germany	67	294
HACKER-PSCHORR DARK	B	Germany	37	294
HACKER-PSCHORR LIGHT	B	Germany	69	294
HACKER-PSCHORR OKTOBERFEST	B	Germany	61	294
HANSA FJORD	B	Norway	82	321
HARP	B	Ireland/Guiness	37	276
HEIDELBERG	B	Canada/Carling O'Keefe	32	237
HEINEKEN DARK	B	Holland	84	308
HEINEKEN DRAFT	B	Holland	62	307
HEINEKEN LIGHT	B	Holland	65	307
HENNINGER	B	Germany	17	295
HERRENHAUSEN	B	Germany	34	296
HOFBRAU	B	Germany	45	296
HOFBRAU DARK	B	Germany	46	296
HOFBRAU OKTO-BERFEST	B	Germany	48	296
HOLSTEN	B	Germany	30	296
HOLSTEN TIGRE	B	Germany	32	296
HURLIMANN	B	Switzerland	46	337
IMPERIAL STOUT	S	Denmark	60	269
INDIA	B	Puerto Rico	24	332
ISENBECK EXPORT	B	Germany	30	297
ISENBECK EXTRA DRY	B	Germany	37	297
JAEGER	B	Holland	14	309
JOCKEY CLUB	B	Canada/Labatt's	8	246
JOHN COURAGE EXPORT	B	England	28	274
KEITH INDIA PALE ALE	IPA	Canada/Labatt's	54	250
KIRIN	B	Japan	60	315
KONIGSBACHER	B	Germany	44	297
KRAKUS	B	Poland	47	326
KRONENBURG	B	France	34	283
KULMBACHER MONKSHOF AMBER LIGHT	B	Germany	48	298
KULMBACHER MONKSHOF DRY LIGHT	B	Germany	44	299
LABATT'S BLUE (Pilsner)	B	Canada	18	245

LABATT'S 50 ALE	A	Canada	47	245
LABATT'S PILSEN-ER DRAFT (Blue)	B	Canada	55	245
LEOPARD	B	New Zealand	17	320
LOBURG	B	Belgium/Artois	30	227
LONDON STOUT	S	Canada/Moosehead	36	260
LOWENBRAU	B	Switzerland	32	337
LOWENBRAU MU-NICH	B	Germany	82	298
LOWENBRAU MU-NICH DARK	B	Germany	30	298
MACCABEE	B	Israel	35	311
MacEWAN'S EDIN-BURGH	A	Scotland	82	278
MacEWAN'S MALT LIQUOR	ML	Scotland	45	278
MacEWAN'S SCOTCH	A	Scotland	70	278
MacEWAN'S STRONG	A	Scotland	34	278
MacEWAN'S TARTAN	A	Scotland	72	278
MACKESON STOUT	S	Scotland	80	282
MANN'S BROWN ALE	A	England	55	281
MARATHON	B	Greece	45	305
METEOR PILS	B	France	29	283
MOLSON CANADI-AN	B	Canada	68	254
MOLSON EXPORT	A	Canada	62	254
MOLSON GOLDEN	A	Canada	24	255
MON-LEI	B	China (Hong Kong)	22	262
MOOSEHEAD	A	Canada	33	260
MURREE	B	Pakistan	14	310
NEWCASTLE BROWN	A	Scotland	65	278
NICSICKO	B	Yugoslavia	16	339
O'KEEFE'S ALE	A	Canada	39	236
O'KEEFE'S EXPORT ALE	A	Canada	22	236
O'KEEFE'S OLD VI-ENNA	B	Canada	52	236
OKOCIM	B	Poland	42	325
OKOCIM PORTER	P	Poland	32	325
OLAND'S EXPORT	A	Canada/Labatt's	64	247
OLAND'S EXTRA STOUT	S	Canada/Labatt's	58	248

OLAND'S OLD SCOTIA	A	Canada/Labatt's	52	248
OLAND'S SCHOONER	B	Canada/Labatt's	14	248
ORANJEBOOM	B	Holland	40	309
ORIENTAL OB	B	Korea	1	316
ORION	B	Okinawa/Japan	9	315
ORVAL ABBEY	A	Belgium	12	223
PADERBORNER LIGHT	LO	Germany	2	299
PAULANER	B	Germany	52	299
PAULANER SAL-VATOR	B	Germany	58	299
PELFORTH	B	France	54	284
PETERS BRAND	B	Holland	54	309
PICKAXE	B	Australia	22	214
PERONI	B	Italy	74	313
PIPER ALE	A	Scotland/Tennent's	25	279
POLAR	B	Venezuela	46	332
PRESIDENTE	B	Dominican Republic	41	331
PRIPPS	B	Sweden	68	334
PUNTIGAM	B	Austria	25	220
RED STRIPE	B	Jamaica	18	331
RESCH PILSENER	B	Australia/Tooth	13	219
RINGNES BOCK	BK	Norway	54	322
RINGNES EXPORT	B	Norway	30	322
RINGNES MALT LI-QUOR	ML	Norway	18	323
RINGNES SPECIAL	B	Norway	35	322
ROGUE	B	South Africa	31	327
ROYAL DUTCH	B	Holland	12	308
RUDDLES	A	England	24	276
SAGRES	B	Portugal	4	327
SAGRES DARK	B	Portugal	46	327
ST. PAULI GIRL DARK	B	Germany	62	302
ST. PAULI GIRL LIGHT	B	Germany	66	302
SAISON REGAL	B	Belgium	0	225
SAMUEL SMITH BROWN ALE	A	England	65	276
SAN MARTIN	B	Spain	13	333
SAN MIGUEL	B	Philippines	60	324
SAN MIGUEL	B	Spain	22	333
SAN MIGUEL DARK	B	Philippines	69	324
SAPPORO	B	Japan	13	315

SKOL	B	Brazil	34	330
SKOL	B	Holland	12	309
SLAVIA	B	France	7	284
SOUTH PACIFIC	B	New Guinea	6	320
SPATEN GOLD	B	Germany	33	301
SPATEN LIGHT	B	Germany	48	301
SPATEN OPTIMATOR	B	Germany	41	301
SPATEN URMARZEN	B	Germany	13	301
STEFFEL	B	Austria	20	222
STEINLAGER	B	New Zealand	26	320
STELLA ARTOIS	B	Belgium	19	226
SUPERIOR	B	Mexico	32	319
SWAN	B	Australia	58	216
SWAN SPECIAL	B	Australia	38	219
TAIWAN	B	Taiwan	12	262
TECATE	B	Mexico	51	318
TENNENT'S LA-GER	B	Scotland	75	279
TEN PENNY	A	Canada/Moosehead	42	260
THEAKSTON OLD PECULIER	A	England	26	279
THOR	B	Denmark	9	269
THREE HORSES	B	Holland	9	309
TOBY	B	Canada/Carling O'Keefe	24	233
TOOTH KB	B	Australia	25	219
TOOTH SHEAF STOUT	S	Australia	67	219
TRES EQUIS	B	Mexico	42	319
TSING-TAO	B	China	36	262
UNCLE BEN'S MALT LIQUOR	ML	Canada	22	260
UNION	B	Yugoslavia	34	339
URQUELL	B	Czechoslovakia	65	264
VICTORIA BITTER	A	Australia	26	213
WARSTEINER PRE-MIUM VERUM	B	Germany	36	302
WATNEY RED BARREL	B	England	29	281
WHITBREAD BREWMASTER	B	England	30	282
WHITBREAD PALE ALE	A	England	70	282
WHITBREAD TAN-KARD	A	England	62	281

WURZBURGER BOCK	BK	Germany	59	304
WURZBURGER DARK	B	Germany	59	304
WURZBURGER LIGHT	B	Germany	72	304
WURZBURGER OK- TOBERFEST	B	Germany	72	304
ZAGREBACHER	B	Yugoslavia	6	340
ZIPFER UTYRP	B	Austria	45	222
ZYWIEC LIGHT	B	Poland	29	325
ZYWIEC PIAST	B	Poland	31	325

*West Germany throughout appendix, unless otherwise noted.

The reader is advised that quantifying something as subjective as taste preference levels is a risky business at best. The numerical values presented in this appendix cannot be considered as a precise rating of the product, but rather as an indication of the class into which it falls. The list of values was compiled over some forty separate tastings with almost as many different combinations of tasters. With human beings as inconsistent as they are, there can be no presumption regarding relativity among ratings of similar magnitude. A beer that is rated 55 cannot be considered to be better than a beer rated 50 unless it was known that the items were both given their scores at the same tasting. It should only be said that the two beers scored in the 50 range. Where scores are greatly different, however, the reader may feel free to regard that difference as a measure of relative taste value.

381

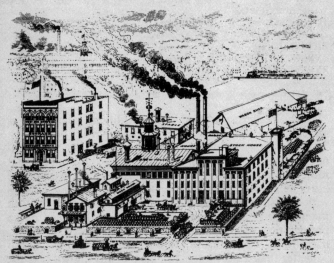

Premises of the West End Brewing Company, Utica, New York (1887)

Appendix II

List of Breweries Authorized to Operate in the United States

Herein is the complete list of breweries authorized to operate in the United States, according to the U.S. Department of the Treasury, Bureau of Alcohol, Tobacco, and Firearms, as of July 1977.

ALASKA
Prinz Brau Alaska, Inc.
Huffman Business Park
Anchorage

ARIZONA
Carling National Breweries, Inc.
150 S. 12 St.
Phoenix

CALIFORNIA
Anchor Brewing Co.
541–8 St.
San Francisco

Anheuser-Busch, Inc.
3101 Magellan Rd.
Fairfield

Anheuser-Busch, Inc.
15800 Roscoe Blvd.
Los Angeles

General Brewing Co.
2601 Newall St.
San Francisco

Miller Brewing Co.
819 N. Vernon Ave.
Azusa

New Albion Brewing Co.
20330–8 St. E.
Sonoma

Pabst Brewing Co.
1910–2026 N. Main St.
Los Angeles

Jos. Schlitz Brewing Co.
7521 Woodman Ave.
Los Angeles (Van Nuys P.O.)

COLORADO
Adolph Coors Co.
Golden

CONNECTICUT
Hull Brewing Co.
820 Congress St.
New Haven

FLORIDA
Anheuser-Busch, Inc.
111 Busch Dr.
Jacksonville

Anheuser-Busch, Inc.
3000 August A. Busch, Jr., Blvd.
Tampa

Duncan Brewing Co., Inc.
202 Gandy Rd.
Auburndale

Jos. Schlitz Brewing Co.
11111–30 St.
Tampa

GEORGIA
Pabst Brewing Co.
Pabst

HAWAII
Hawaii Brewing Co.
98–051 Kamehameha Hwy.
Aiea, Oahu

Honolulu Sake Brewing
& Ice Co., Ltd.
2150 Booth Rd.
Honolulu

ILLINOIS
Carling National Breweries, Inc.
1201 West E St.
Belleville

Miles Laboratories, Inc.
[Experimental Brewery]
4055 W. Peterson Ave.
Chicago

Pabst Brewing Co.
4541 Prospect Rd.
Peoria Heights

Peter Hand Brewing Co.
1000 W. North Ave.
Chicago

Wallerstein Co.
Div. of Travenol Laboratories, Inc.
[Experimental Brewery]
6301 Lincoln Ave.
Morton Grove

INDIANA
Falstaff Brewing Corp.
1019–1051 Grant Ave.
Fort Wayne

G. Heileman Brewing Co., Inc.
1301 W. Pennsylvania St.
Evansville

IOWA
Dubuque Star Brewing Co.
E. 4 St. Extension
Dubuque

Grain Processing Co.
[Experimental Brewery]
1600 Oregon St.
Muscatine

KENTUCKY
Falls City Brewing Co.
3050 W. Broadway
Louisville

Geo. Wiedemann Brewing Co.
Div. of G. Heileman
Brewing Co., Inc.
601 Columbia St.
Newport

LOUISIANA
Dixie Brewing Co., Inc.
2537 Tulane Ave.
New Orleans

Falstaff Brewing Corp.
2600 Gravier St.
New Orleans

MARYLAND
Carling National Breweries, Inc.
Baltimore Beltway at
Hammond's Ferry Rd.
Baltimore

Carling National Breweries, Inc.
3602 O'Donnell St.
Baltimore

The F. & M. Schaefer Brewing Co.
1101 S. Conkling St.
Baltimore

MICHIGAN
Carling National Breweries, Inc.
907 S. Main st.
Frankenmuth

Geyer Bros. Brewing Co.
415 Main St.
Frankenmuth

Stroh Brewing Co.
909 E. Elizabeth St.
Detroit

MINNESOTA
Cold Spring Brewing Co.
219 N. Red River St.
Cold Spring

G. Heileman Brewing Co., Inc.
882 W. 7 St.
St. Paul

Olympia Brewing Co.
720 Payne St.
St. Paul

August Schell Brewing Co.
South Payne St.
New Ulm

MISSOURI
Anheuser-Busch, Inc.
721 Pestalozzi St.
St. Louis

Falstaff Brewing Corp.
1920 Shenandoah Ave.
St. Louis

NEBRASKA
Falstaff Brewing Corp.
25 St. & Deer Park Blvd.
Omaha

NEW HAMPSHIRE
Anheuser-Busch, Inc.
1000 Daniel Webster Hwy.
Merrimack

NEW JERSEY
Anheuser-Busch, Inc.
200 U.S. Hwy. 1
Newark

Champale, Inc.
Lalor & Lamberton Sts.
Trenton

Eastern Brewing Corp.
329 N. Washington St.
Hammonton

Pabst Brewing Co.
391–399 Grove St.
Newark

Rheingold Breweries, Inc.
119 Hill St.
Orange

NEW YORK
Genesee Brewing Co., Inc.
14–33 Cataract St.
Rochester

Fred Koch Brewery
15–25 W. Courtney St.
Dunkirk

Miller Brewing Co.
Owens Rd.
South Volney

Jos. Schlitz Brewing Co.
2885 Belgium Rd.
Baldwinville

Schwartz Services
International, Ltd.
United States Brewers' Academy
230 Washington St.

West End Brewing Co.
of Utica N.Y.
811 Edward St.
Utica

NORTH CAROLINA
Jos. Schlitz Brewing Co.
4791 Schlitz Ave.
Winston-Salem

NORTH DAKOTA
North Dakota State University
Cereal Technology Bldg.
Fargo

OHIO
Anheuser-Busch, Inc.
700 E. Schrock Rd.
Columbus

Hudepohl Brewing Co.
5 & Gest Sts.
Cincinnati

C. Schmidt & Sons, Inc.
9400 Quincy Ave.
Cleveland

Schoenling Brewing Co.
1625 Central Parkway
Cincinnati

OREGON
Blitz-Weinhard Co.
1133 W. Burnside St.
Portland

PENNSYLVANIA
Erie Brewing Co.
2124–2212 State St.
Erie

Fuhrmann & Schmidt Brewing Co.
235–249 S. Harrison St.
Shamokin

Horlacher Brewing Co.
311 Gordon St.
Allentown

Jones Brewing Co.
2 St. & B. & O. R.R.
Smithton

Latrobe Brewing Co.
119 Ligonier St.
Latrobe

Lion, Inc.
5–6 Hart St.
Wilkes-Barre

Henry F. Ortlieb Brewing Co.
824 N. American St.
Philadelphia

Pittsburgh Brewing Co.
3340 Liberty Ave.
Pittsburgh

F. & M. Schaefer Brewing Co.
S.W. Cor of Rte. 22 & Hwy. 100
Allentown

C. Schmidt & Sons, Inc.
127 Edward St.
Philadelphia

Straub Brewery, Inc.
Rear 303 Sort St.
St. Mary's

D. G. Yuengling & Son, Inc.
5 & Mahantongo Sts.
Pottsville

RHODE ISLAND
Falstaff Brewing Corp.
Garfield Ave. & Cranston St.
Cranston

TENNESSEE
Jos. Schlitz Brewing Co.
515 Raines Rd.
Memphis

TEXAS
Anheuser-Busch, Inc.
775 Gelhorn St.
Houston

Falstaff Brewing Corp.
3301 Church St.
Galveston

Lone Star Brewing Co.
600 Lone Star Blvd.
San Antonio

Miller Brewing Co.
7001 S. Freeway
Fort Worth

Pearl Brewing Co.
312 Pearl Pkwy.
San Antonio

Jos. Schlitz Brewing Co.
1400 W. Cotton St.
Longview

Spoetzl Brewery, Inc.
603 E. Brewery St.
Shiner

VIRGINIA
Anheuser-Busch, Inc.
Williamsburg

Champale Products Corp.
710 Washington Ave.
Norfolk

WASHINGTON
Carling National Breweries, Inc.
2120–42 South C St.
Tacoma

General Brewing Co.
615 Columbia St.
Vancouver

Olympia Brewing Co.
P.O. Box 947, Tumwater
Olympia

Rainier Brewing Co.
3100 Airport Way
Seattle

WISCONSIN
Bio-Technical Resources, Inc.
[Experimental Brewery]
7 & Marshall Sts.
Manitowoc

Froedtert Malt Co.
[Experimental Brewery]
3830 W. Grant St.
W. Milwaukee

G. Heileman Brewing Co., Inc.
1000–1028 S. 3 St.
LaCrosse

Jos. Huber Brewing Co.
1200–1208 14 Ave.
Monroe

Kurth Malting Co.
[Experimental Brewery]
2100 S. 43 St.
Milwaukee

Ladish Malting Co.
[Experimental Brewery]
Jefferson Junction

Jacob Leinenkugel Brewing Co.
1–3 Jefferson Ave.
Chippewa Falls

Miller Brewing Co.
4000 W. State St.
Milwaukee

Pabst Brewing Co.
917 W. Juneau Ave.
Milwaukee

Pabst Brewing Co.
[Experimental Brewery]
1037 W. McKinley Ave.
Milwaukee

Jos. Schlitz Brewing Co.
235 W. Galena St.
Milwaukee

Stevens Point Beverage Co.
2617 Water St.
Stevens Point

U.S. Dept. of Agriculture
Crops Research Div., Nat'l Barley
& Malt Laboratory
[Experimental Brewery]
501 N. Walnut St.
Madison

Walter Brewing Co.
318 Elm St.
Eau Claire

Wisconsin Malting Corp.
[Experimental Brewery]
633 S. 20 St.
Manitowoc

Premises of the Jacob Schmidt Brewing Company, St. Paul, Minnesota
(1901)

GLOSSARY OF TERMS

acidic—having a taste of acid, a predominance of sourness.

acidification—to make or become sour or acid.

adjunct—a thing added to something else, but secondary in importance or not essential; in beer making there are malt adjuncts, such as corn and rice, which are used in place of barley to make a paler and less expensive brew.

aftertaste—a palate sensation that occurs after the beer has been swallowed.

ale—probably derived from the Norse *oel*, which originally referred to fermented malt beverages that were not flavored by hops. In the earliest times, all such beverages would have been ale by that definition. When the use of hops as a flavoring agent became prevalent, such hopped brews were identified as beer. At that time both ale and beer were top-fermented and in all ways identical except for the hops. Later, when bottom-fermentation came along, terms were revised. Today *beer* usually identifies lager specifically and the entire class of malt beverages in general, whereas the term *ale* applies only to top-fermented brews.

ambient—that which surrounds, as on all sides. The ambient temperature is the temperature of the room, or of the outside air.

aroma—fragrance, usually in a pleasant sense; applied to a beverage, it is the component of the odor that derives from the ingredients of the beverage, as opposed to the bouquet, which is the result of by-products from the fermentation process.

aromatic—of or having an aroma, usually in the sense of being particularly fragrant, sweet or spicy.

astringent—causing contraction or shrinking, as of tissue in the mouth; harsh, severe, stern.

austere—as applied to beer tastes, simple, lacking complexity. (The dictionary-preferred meaning of harsh and severe is not intended herein.)

balance—the feature of a beer concerned with the harmony of various flavors and sensations.

barley—a cereal grass with bearded spikes of flowers, and its seed or grain. Barley is the most suitable cereal grain for making malt beverages; it provides flavor, head, body, and color.

barley wine—a strongly flavored ale that dates back to the ancient Egyptians; today's barley wine is still strong in flavor and alcohol, assertive of both sweetness and bitterness in the nose and the mouth.

barrel—a large wooden cylindrical container with sides that bulge outward and flat ends. Usually made of wooden staves bound with metal bands. Also, a standard of measure for liquids; 31½ gallons in the U.S., 36 imperial gallons in Great Britain, and 42 gallons in the brewing trade.

beer—describes fermented malt beverages in general and bottom-fermented brews in particular. (See also ale.)

beery—that which is typical of beer, as an odor that is generally malty but having a noticeable level of hops.

bitter—the tangy or sharp taste in beer that results from hops; without the bitterness a beer has no zest, with too much bitterness it is hard and biting.

bock—a strong dark German beer. In America there are a number of so-called bock beers that derive their color and flavor artificially.

body—the mouth-filling property of a beer. Taken at its extreme, stout has a heavy or full body, pale low-calorie beer may be thin or watery.

bouquet—that portion of the odor caused by fermentation. (See also aroma.)

brackish—partly salty, but not necessarily unpleasant.

brasserie—the French word for brewery.

brewer—one who brews; the leading brewer at a brewery is called the brewmaster.

brewery—a brewing plant, a place where beer is made.

brewhouse—archaic term for brewery.

bright—a term used to describe appearance (its clarity and brilliance) and taste (its zest).

Burton—a location in England noted for the quality of its ales.

calorie—the unit of heat needed to raise one kilogram of water one degree Celsius; human-body intake and energy expenditure are measured in calories. A twelve-ounce portion of beer has some 150 calories.

caramelize—to turn into caramel, a burnt sugar.

carbon dioxide—CO_2, the ingredient in beer that gives it the bubbles; it comes to the beer either naturally through the fermentation process, through krausening, or through carbonic injection, the artificial charging of the beverage with CO_2 just before it is packaged.

cardboard—a taste or odor that is like wet cardboard. It is most frequently encountered in foreign beers, especially from the Orient.

cask—a barrel of any size. Brewers' casks come in seven sizes; butt (108 gallons), puncheon (72), hogshead (54), barrel, kilderkin (18), firkin (9), and pin (4½).

clarify—clear of particulate matter, either naturally with settling out or articially with fining agents.

clarity—the degree to which the beer is without particulate matter in solution, ranging from clear to cloudy or (heaven forbid) murky.

clean—fresh; makes your mouth feel refreshed and "clean."

cloying—too sweet or rich; a thick sweetness so intense as to be offensive.

creamy—foamy and bubbly; feel of liquid that is infused with small bubble carbonation. Needs to be accompanied with a good flavor to come off well.

dank—slightly moldly, as the smell in a damp basement.

dextrin—a soluble gummy substance obtained from starch.

dextrose—a crystalline sugar found in plants and animals; in beer it is produced from starch in the conversion of barley into malt.

Dortmunder—style of lager beer much the same as pilsener, developed in Dortmund, Germany.

draught (or draft)—beer drawn from a cask, or the act of drawing beer from a cask.

dry—not sweet.

effervescence—a bubbling up, foaming.

enzyme (amylolytic)—an organic substance that converts starch into soluble substances such as sugars.

enzyme (proteolytic)—an organic substance that converts proteins to soluble substances.

fermentation—the breakdown of complex molecules in organic compounds caused by the action of a ferment (such as yeast). In malt beverages, it is the decomposition of sugar into ethyl alcohol and carbon dioxide.

ferruginous—ironlike or like iron rust; in flavor it refers to a taste like spring water with a high iron content or water piped through rusty pipes.

fining—a process of hastening the clarification of a malt beverage (or wine); it usually involves the addition of fining agents such as isinglass, enzymes, gelatin (all coagulants), or bentonite or cellulose (mechanical).

finish—that part of the palate sensation that occurs just before and during swallowing.

flabby—soft and sweet; a derogatory term when speaking of beer.

flavor—that quality of a substance which gives it its characteristic taste taken either singly or in aggregate.

gallon—a liquid measure, four quarts.

green beer—young or immature beer, fresh from its first fermentation, before it has been aged or lagered.

hogshead—a large barrel with a capacity of 100–140 gallons; or a liquid measure of 63 gallons.

hops—the dried ripe cones of the female flowers of a climbing-vine member of the nettle family. The resin or extract from the cones is used for bittering and preserving beer.

India pale ale—a very strong ale of the type produced for British troops serving in India in the past century. It had to be produced very strong so that it could survive the long passage to India, which took over six months and involved equatorial crossings.

kiln—a drying oven (also oast).

krausening—a technique whereby young beer is added to fully aged beer before packaging to accomplish a "natural" infusion of carbon dioxide.

lactic acid—a clear syrupy acid created by the action of microorganisms on sucrose.

lager—the popular name given to today's bottom-fermented beer, which is chill-brewed and stored, or lagered for proper aging; it derives from the German *lagern*, meaning to store.

logo—short for logogram, a word referring to a trademark, symbol, or design that represents a product or company.

maltster—one who controls the malting process.

malt—barley that has been steeped in water to produce sprouting then kiln-dried.

malt extract—a sticky, sugar substance obtained from malt.

malting process—the process of producing malt from barley.

maltose—malt sugar, produced by the action of diastase of malt on starch.

mash—crushed or ground malt soaked in water for making wort.

mash tun—a large vessel wherein the wort is separated from the grist.

mead—an ancient drink of fermented honey and water.

metallic—of or pertaining to metal. A metallic flavor in a beer could be caused by either its container or a flaw in the brewing process. Sometimes an overage beer will take on metalliclike flavors, even in a bottle.

molecule—the smallest particle of a compound that can exist in a free state.

near-beer—a beerlike beverage brewed either to be nonalcoholic or to have a low alcoholic content (on the order of one-half of one percent).

nose—the total sensation in the nose; the total effect of the beer's odor; the combination of aroma and bouquet.

NR—nonreturnable.

oast—a kiln, especially one for drying hops.

over the hill—too old, gone by, bad tasting because it is overaged.

pablum—an old-time baby cereal consisting of finely ground oatmeal.

package—the container that holds the beer, either a bottle or can. Otherwise beer is on draft, or on tap. Packaged beer is usually pasteurized.

particulate matter—particles held in suspension in the liquid, such as protein matter, dead yeast cells, grain fragments.

pasteurize—to subject to a temperature of 142°–145°F. for thirty minutes to destroy disease-producing bacteria and to check fermentation.

photosynthesis—the formation of carbohydrates by the action of sunlight.

pilsener—a type of very pale lager beer, so named because the pinnacle of the style was first reached in Pilsen, Czechoslovakia. It is similar to the Dortmunder style of beer.

popular-priced—lower priced and therefore more popular with the consumer but supposedly less well made than premium beer.

porter—a dark brew; first made in England in the eighteenth century to fill the market for a mixture of ale, beer, and Twopenny, a popular drink of that time and place. Today it is not unlike stout except that it is lighter in body and may be more highly carbonated.

premium—a term used by brewers to indicate the top of their product line. (The term is much abused.)

pub—a business establishment in Great Britain whose principal wares are malt beverages.

quaff—to drink in large drafts.

rack—to fill a container with beer in a brewery.

saccharometer—a form of hydrometer for measuring the amount of sugar in a solution.

saturation—the degree of intensity of a color.

skunky—like the peculiar aroma of a skunk. A beer may smell and taste of skunk, a defect found usually in well-hopped beers and caused, it is believed, by photosynthesis.

spruce beer—a beer (alcoholic or nonalcoholic) made by steeping spruce boughs and fermenting the resulting sugared liquid.

stout—a rich dark brew made from roasted malt, often with the addition of carmelized sugar, and a reasonably high proportion of hops.

swampy—like a swamp, as in the odors of the rotting vegetation frequently encountered in such a damp area.

tangy—strong or penetrating.

tannin—tannic acid; an astringent.

tap—the lever that releases the beer from a tapped keg; to tap, or open, a keg of draft beer; a taproom, a place where draft beer is served.

tavern—a place where alcoholic beverages are sold for consumption on the premises.

tawny—brownish yellow.

texture—the physical "feel" of a beer in the mouth.

tied house—in England, a pub, inn, or restaurant under agreement to buy all its beer from a single brewer. Often owned by the brewer. There are brewery-owned public accommodations all over Europe.

tinny—a metallic taste in beer, as if from the "tin," or can; a term held over from the days when the cans were made of tin and not steel or aluminum.

trub—a protein precipitate which results when the wort is boiled.

vegetal—a vegetablelike nature in aroma or taste, as in raw broccoli or cabbage; frequently used in an unpleasant sense.

vinous—winy, winelike, fruity in a fermented sense.

Weiss—a type of beer still popular in Berlin. It is white in color, cloudy and foamy, with a very yeasty nose and taste. It is made from wheat, usually not pasteurized. Traditionally it is served in a large wide-bowled stem glass with a dash of raspberry syrup. *Weiss* is German for white.

wort—the solution of malt extract in water.

XXX—a guarantee of quality. Originally, *X* indicated the number of times that a liquor had been distilled, whereas XXX or XXXX showed it had been run through the maximum number of times that it was meaningful to do so, and therefore had reached its height of strength and purity. The term was adopted centuries ago to indicate beer quality. It is now greatly abused.

yeast—the ferment, or fermenting agent, which turns the wort into beer. In particular, in beer making the yeast is the strain *Saccharomyces cerevisiae*, or Brewer's yeast.

BIBLIOGRAPHY

Books

Abel, Bob. *The Book of Beer*. Chicago: Henry Regnery Co., 1976.

Anderson, Sonja and Will. *Beers, Breweries, and Breweriana*. Carmel, 1969.

Anderson, Will. *The Beer Book*. Princeton; Pyne Press, 1973.

Brewers Association of Canada. *About Beer and the Brewing Industry*. Ottawa, 1974.

Brewers Association of Canada. *Brewing in Canada*. Ottawa, 1965.

Carlsberg Brewing Co. *The Book of Carlsberg*. Copenhagen, 1976.

Dabbs, Robert L., and Harris, Davis S. *Worldwide Beer Can Collector's Guide*. Independence: World Wide Beer Can Collectors, 1974.

Kroll, Wayne L. *Wisconsin Breweries and Their Bottles*. Jefferson, 1972.

McWhirter, Norris and Ross. *Guinness Book of World Records*. New York: Sterling Publishing Co., 1969.

Martello, Jack. *Beer Can Collector's Bible*. New York: Ballantine Books, 1977.

One Hundred Years of Brewing. Chicago; H. S. Rich & Co., 1903.

Porter, John. *All About Beer*. New York: Doubleday & Co., 1974.

Vlantes, Stanley N., ed. *1977 Modern Brewery Age Blue Book*. East Norwalk: MBA Publishing Corp., 1977.

Weiner, Michael. *The Taster's Guide to Beer*. New York: Macmillan Co., 1977.

Wright, Larry, Ed. *The Beer Can*. Matteson: Great Lakes Living Press, 1976.

Encyclopedias

Encyclopedia Brittanica (1968), "Beer."

Journals and Magazines

"BD Visits the Cold Spring Brewing Company in Cold Spring, Minn." *Brewers Digest*, September 1972.

"BD Visits the Fred Koch Brewery in Dunkirk, N.Y." *Brewers Digest*, April 1966.

"BD Visits the Hudepohl Brewing Co. in Cincinnati, Ohio." *Brewers Digest*, July 1971.

"BD Visits the Spoetzl Brewery, Inc., in Shiner, Texas." *Brewers Digest*, October 1966.

Davies, Charles. "Pint Size." *Weekend Magazine*, 24 September 1977, pp. 4–7.

Fine, Steven M. "The King of Suds." (Article from unidentified Pittsburgh area magazine.) 1977.

"The Ortlieb Renaissance." *Brewers Digest*, May 1977.

"Pickett's Revisited." *Brewers Digest*, August 1977, pp. 24–39.

"Putting It All Together." *Canadian Beverage News*, May 1973, pp. 6–7.

"Schlitz Raids the Competition." *Business Week*, 21 November 1977, p. 54.

"A Struggle to Stay First in Brewing." *Business Week*, 24 March 1973.

Todd, Flip. "Prinz Brau, Alaska's New Brewery Is Banking on State's Future Growth." *Brewers Digest*, December 1976, pp. 12–18.

"Trouble Brewing." *Newsweek*, 23 July 1973.

Newspapers

"Decline of Breweries in Wyoming Valley Parallels Trends Reported in Other Sections of State, Nation." *Wilkes-Barre Times Leader*, 12 September 1977.

"New Ulm Industry Day." *New Ulm Daily Journal*, 9 September 1974.

Sedlmeyer, Angeline. "The History of the Brewing Industry in Shiner, Texas." *Shiner Gazette*, 29 July 1971.

Tomb, Geoffrey. "Something's Brewing in the Straub Family." *St. Mary's Post Gazette Daily Magazine*, 22 September 1977.

Reports

Eckhardt, Fred. *A Treatise of Lager Beers*. Portland: Hobby Winemakers, 1975.

U.S. Department of the Treasury. Bureau of Alcohol, Tobacco & Firearms. *Breweries Authorized to Operate*, July 1977.

INDEX

410

412

413